1995

Reclaiming the Heartland

For Angela
The best of life & love to you
Tess Wells

www.KCLighthouse.org
The LIKE ME Lighthouse
3909 Main
Kansas City, MO 64111

Reclaiming the Heartland

Lesbian and Gay Voices from the Midwest

Karen Lee Osborne and
William J. Spurlin, editors

University of Minnesota Press | Minneapolis | London

Eduardo Aparicio, "Colectivos Latinos Atrevidos/Provocative Latins Collective: Placards for the March on Washington as Displayed on the Streets of Chicago, April 1993," reprinted by permission of the photographer. Kathryn Kirk, "Three Dancers, New Philadelphia, Ohio, 1983," reprinted by permission of the photographer. Jess Wells, "Luke Giovanni's Canoe," from *Aftershocks*, published by Third Side Press, 1992, copyright 1992 by Jess Wells, reprinted by permission of the publisher. Maureen Seaton, "Miracles," "Poem Containing a Matrix Sentence," "The Sighting," and "Christmas in the Midwest," from *Fear of Subways*, published by Eighth Mountain Press, 1991, copyright 1991 by Maureen Seaton, reprinted by permission of the publisher. "A Flicker of Apocalypse" from *The Paris Review* 125 (Winter 1992), copyright 1992 by Maureen Seaton, reprinted by permission of the publisher. Ricardo Garza, "Lake Michigan Sunrise, 1995" and "Two Sailors, June 1991," reprinted by permission of the photographer. Claudia Allen, "from *Hannah Free*," from *She's Always Liked the Girls Best*, Third Side Press, 1992, reprinted by permission of the author. Michelle Paladino, "Mary Jo and Bert," reprinted by permission of the photographer. Lev Raphael, "Welcome to Beth Homo," copyright 1995 by Lev Raphael, reprinted by permission of the author. Genyphyr Novak, "Scott McPherson, Danny Sotomayor, and Scout," copyright by Genyphyr Novak, reprinted by permission of the photographer.

Published by the University of Minnesota Press
111 Third Avenue South, Suite 290
Minneapolis, MN 55401-2520
Printed in the United States of America on acid-free paper

Library of Congress Cataloging-in-Publication Data

Reclaiming the heartland : lesbian and gay voices from the Midwest /
Karen Lee Osborne and William J. Spurlin, editors.
    p. cm.
    ISBN 0-8166-2754-1 (hc)
    1. Gays' writings, American—Middle West. 2. Lesbians—Middle
West—Literary collections. 3. Gay men—Middle West—Literary
collections. 4. American literature—Middle West. I. Osborne,
Karen Lee, 1954- . II. Spurlin, William J., 1954- .
PS508.G39R43 1996
810.8'0920664'0977—dc20   95-46718

The University of Minnesota is an equal-opportunity educator and employer.

Contents

Part III: "Every Last Drop": Writing Desire

Part IV: "Faithful Past in Continuous Present": Text/Context

Part V: "Moving In/Moving Out": Writing the World

Acknowledgments

THE editors wish to thank the following for their kind assistance: Sheryl Fullerton, Todd Orjala, Louisa Castner, Mary Byers, Becky Manfredini, David A. Smith, JoAnn Ziebarth, Eduardo Aparicio, Midge Stocker, Jim Elledge, Joyce Goldenstern, Michael Riley, Arlene Greene, Paula Karrasch, Deborah S. Wilson, Matthew Naglich, Owen Keehnen, Jordan Miller, and David Kodeski. We also thank Columbia College of Chicago for a Faculty Development Grant and Illinois State University.

Eduardo Aparicio, "Colectivos Latinos Atrevidos/Provacative Latins Collective: Placards for the March on Washington as Displayed on the Streets of Chicago, April 1993"

Introduction: *What?!* Queers in the Midwest?

William J. Spurlin

WHEN we examine the gay and mainstream media, the recent surge of books in the growing field of lesbian and gay studies, and advertisements for lesbian and gay cultural and political events, it often seems as if the places to truly self-identify as lesbian or gay are in New York or San Francisco. These cities, as well as others along the eastern and western seaboards, appear to be the only locations where one can discover, develop, and experience a more or less "authentic" queer identity and fully participate in the various cultural, social, and political networks inhabited by other queers. But is this really the case? To what extent is queer culture limited to urban coastal areas? A few years ago, the *New York Times* reported that issues of gay identity and activism have been slowly moving over the past two decades from the East and West coasts to the heartland (March 5, 1993, A14), but neither our literature nor our scholarship has adequately reflected or chronicled this significant geographic shift. Indeed, for many lesbians and gay men living and writing in Michigan, Ohio, Wisconsin, Minnesota, Missouri, Illinois, Nebraska, and Kansas, the Midwest—the heartland—is a significant vantage point from which to create as authors, poets, artists, intellectuals, and cultural workers.

Reclaiming the Heartland: Lesbian and Gay Voices from the Midwest is a multigenre, multicultural anthology of short fiction, poetry, drama, memoir, essays, and photographic work by gay women and men who live or who have spent a significant portion of their lives in the Midwest. This collection challenges popular assumptions that the seaboard cities are the only centers of queer culture and the primary locations from which lesbians and gay men can create queer culture. There are many lesbian and gay male identities and cultural spaces, and no one location can speak for them all. Having lived, taught, written, and traveled in the Midwest myself, I have found that many lesbians and gay men there and in other parts of the country often express dissatisfaction with gay communities in large urban areas on the coasts because many gay people in coastal cities seem to have a rather narrow image of what constitutes a queer identity and simultaneously exclude or marginalize those who do not fit their notion of queer.

Similar to other work in lesbian and gay studies, our book questions an essential lesbian or gay identity, reduced to sexual difference alone and defined a priori by discrete markers, and calls attention to the social and cultural construction of queer identity. Queer identity, like other identities, can take multiple, contingent, and fluid forms in a variety of contexts and may be intertwined with other axes of social positioning such as race, gender, and social class. Queer theorists, such as Eve Sedgwick, Diana Fuss, David Halperin, and others influenced by Michel Foucault, have helped us to understand sexual identities not as fixed or stable, but as socially situated, eliciting Otherness, and breaking down the hetero/homo opposition by which we have traditionally categorized sexual identity. Diana Fuss, for example, most succinctly argues the case in pointing out that "borders are notoriously unstable, and sexual identities rarely secure." "Heterosexuality," she continues, "can never fully ignore the close psychical proximity of its terrifying (homo)sexual other, any more than homosexuality can entirely escape the equally insistent social pressures of (hetero)sexual conformity" (3). But what about the formation of new hierarchies (and therefore new margins) in our readings and interpretations of lesbian and gay identities and communities that privilege urban coastal cities as sites of queer power, cultural capital, and solidarity over other locations? Lesbian and gay studies needs to begin to address the difficulty of identifying and isolating a set of "common" attributes and experiences that supposedly unite gay people. How do we define that "common" ground? Who has a voice in defining it?

Besides complementing present work in contemporary lesbian and gay studies, then, this collection further destabilizes representations of lesbian and gay male identity by calling into question the coast/midcontinent opposition that often divides American queers. Michael Warner has seriously questioned the notion of a lesbian/gay community altogether, as we are differently sexualized and politicized and also because our history has much more to do with noncommunity and dispersal than with localization (xxv). This collection supports Warner's concern about the problematics of narrowly ascribing gay culture to concentrated geographic areas. The pieces in the volume, written from a variety of perspectives and positions to reflect the cultural diversity of the Midwest, and written by lesbians and gay men from rural, suburban, and urban locations in the heartland, invite us to especially consider how locations other than coastal cities play a role in our (re)reading of lesbian and gay identities and culture, and how cultural representations of the Midwest, or more accurately, the culture of the Midwest as we stereotypically *imagine* it, may be affected or revised by the intervention of queer cultural practices. With this in mind, we have resisted collecting material that only addresses the Midwest as place, since this would propagate another geographic bias and not accomplish very much; we have similarly resisted essentializing a distinctive midwestern queer identity, sensibility, or literature. In other words, the book represents queer midwestern writing as *broadly* as possible, as local and as dispersed, and shows how queers in and from the Midwest contribute to queer culture and to queer ways of looking at and understanding the world.

What do we think of when we imagine the Midwest? What are some of the cultural myths about the Midwest that prohibit us from imagining it as a possible site of queer cultural production? From a historical perspective, much American literature of the first half of the nineteenth century, perhaps influenced to some extent by Emerson's and Thoreau's reflections on nature as well as by a concerted effort by many writers of the time to embody in fiction a quintessential American experience, romanticized small town and farm life. Much literature of this period celebrated the grandeur and beauty of settings where people could live in harmony with nature and avoid the moral temptations of large cities. Later in that century and early in the next, writers such as Edward Eggleston, Frank Norris, Sinclair Lewis, and Sherwood Anderson critiqued this agrarian myth, showing in their novels that there is more to the Midwest than Eden-like innocence and the simple pleasures of small town life. As Ray Lewis White and other critics of midwestern literature point out, such works as Eggleston's *The Hoosier Schoolmaster*, Mark Twain's *The Adventures of Huckleberry Finn*, some of Hamlin Garland's stories in *Main-Travelled Roads*, Edgar Lee Masters's *Spoon River Anthology*, Anderson's *Winesburg, Ohio*, and Lewis's *Main Street* debunked the innocent, pastoral image of midwestern small towns. White argues that these works

helped shape a new image of such towns as being "replete with loneliness, repression, restriction, and only occasional rebellion and liberation" (25).

However, the agrarian myth and the subsequent refigured image
of the Midwest as repressive have not only helped to influence current constructions of the Midwest in general, which do not seem to
make it an attractive place for queers, but also have been reinforced
by the axes of contemporary queer power on the East and West coasts.
For instance, Edmund White (who spent part of his childhood in Cin-
cinnati, Ohio), in a chapter on the Midwest in his book *States of Desire:
Travels in Gay America*, casually observes that gay men and women in
Kansas City and other parts of the Midwest "untouched by gay liberation" seem to equate gay identity and gay life with either being in gay
bars or being in bed. White goes on to say that after emerging from
either of these enclosed, private spaces, one lives one's public life in
the world of heterosexuality, adhering to the beliefs of the dominant
culture; he offers that "the notion that affectional preference, sexual
appetite, shared oppression might color all of one's experience"
eludes gay people in the Midwest (156). White does acknowledge
that the heartland is what one makes of it, that the "stability" of
the Midwest can be felt as "irredeemable despair," a cultural trope
perhaps inherited from late-nineteenth- and early-twentieth-century
American fiction, or as "wholesomeness," in that many lesbians and
gay men, especially couples, are able to adapt to "the work-centered,
down-to-earth, conservative Midwest with ease and satisfaction"
(193). But the problem here is that queers are merely included, that
is to say, minoritized, in the Midwest with dominant cultural constructions of the Midwest, including queer oppression, left intact. As
Warner reminds us, it is not enough to merely include lesbians and
gay men in a theory or view of the world that would otherwise remain
unaltered (xv-xvi). Linnea Johnson, in her essay in this collection, reflects on how critics have "off-read" Willa Cather's life by their elision
of the prominence of Edith Lewis, thereby missing the landscape of
which Cather wrote. A complementary question one needs to ask is
not only how queers form part of the already constructed landscape
of the Midwest, but how we may reread and revise that landscape as a
result of queer cultural intervention. Many of the pieces collected in
this volume visibly contradict the rather dismal picture that Edmund
White portrays of queers in the Midwest; indeed, what is most inter-

esting are the pockets of resistance to queer oppression that White found in his travels through the heartland, not just resistance to the status quo, but resistance to the cultural image of queers in the Midwest as lonely people, conforming to dominant social practices and internalizing homophobia. This is best evidenced in White's conversation with Evan, an activist in Kansas City, who speaks of entrapment and arrest for cruising ("'soliciting'" was the charge) in a gay bar and who was sentenced to see a psychiatrist:

"I got off lightly," Evan said, "but my lover didn't. He had rheumatic fever. He also drank too much; he had never been able to accept his homosexuality. When he heard I had been arrested, he went to bed and drank himself to death. He was just forty-one. His relatives descended and stripped our house bare. When I removed my own things, they accused me of stealing them. They still call me at work to harass me. I have no legal rights. Though we'd been together for years, we weren't married. It was an illegal relationship. That's when I became an activist." (161)

Of course, resistance can work in a variety of ways besides overt political activism, and this volume is testament to the fact that resistance, in this case cultural resistance, is not limited to what White refers to as a rara avis or a few isolated incidents in the Midwest, as it is much more widespread than we may have otherwise believed. In addition to the artistic accomplishment and aesthetic appeal of the work collected in this volume, many of the poems, short stories, essays, and photographs, whether or not their authors *intended* them to be political, resist heteronormativity in their struggle to speak to and name the world queerly. The book as a whole works to deconstruct the notion that lesbian and gay experience is essentially or distinctly urban and coastal as well as the idea that lesbian and gay writers and artists seek to escape the rural, oppressive, unsophisticated milieu of the Midwest in favor of acceptance and self-understanding in East or West coast cities.

On the other hand, the prominence of cities such as New York, San Francisco, and Los Angeles in queer literary and cultural achievements is certainly justified, though it is not the case that there is something *inherently* urban, cosmopolitan, and coastal about queer experience. This becomes more evident when we look at the history of the gay movement in the United States. Lillian Faderman, Jonathan Ned Katz, Allan Bérubé, and others have noted, for example, how World War II, in ironic contrast to the antihomosexual stance of the military and its discharges of "undesirable" lesbian and gay personnel after the war, contributed not only to the creation and development of lesbian and gay communities in the seaboard cities, but to the eventual emergence of a lesbian and gay political movement as we know it today. Allan Bérubé, in *Coming Out under Fire*, notes that mobilization for the war helped to loosen the constraints that locked many gay people into silence, isolation, and self-contempt and points out that the significance of homosexuality was intensified by the military as it built a bureaucratic apparatus to identify and manage homosexual personnel. Because it was disrupted and exposed by the war, gay life in the postwar years grew as gay veterans identified with each other's struggles and formed communities as members of a homosexual minority (256-57). But, for the most part, these communities formed in large coastal cities. Lillian Faderman further elaborates that the war brought huge numbers of women together in these cities to participate in the civilian workforce where they were also able to appreciate other females as serious, self-sufficient human beings away from restrictive family relations, and where relatively large lesbian communities could be created where only an inchoate lesbian consciousness had been forming (121). The military further contributed to the development of gay culture when it became even less lenient in its policies toward homosexuals once the war was over; Faderman speaks of how thousands of gay personnel were loaded onto "queer ships" and sent to the nearest U.S. port—New York, Los Angeles, San Francisco, Boston, and others. Because many of those discharged for being queer believed they could not go home or were too embarrassed to do so, many stayed where they disembarked, and their numbers helped to form large homosexual enclaves in port cities along both coasts (126).

While certainly the large concentration of lesbians in metropolitan areas on the coasts during the war and of discharged lesbians and gay men after the war led to the development of queer communities in these areas, it is important to bear in mind that the reasons for the urban bicoastal prominence of queer communities are *social* and *historical*. Queer identity and queer culture, because they are not monolithic and homogeneous but instead are subject to history and to social context (and therefore variable and contingent), are not inherently bound to urban coastal areas. This becomes more apparent when we examine the specificity of lesbian cultural practices in the 1970s, many of which flourished across the heartland. Lesbian-feminist communities sprang up in many parts of the Midwest, in cosmopolitan cities like Chicago, Minneapolis, and Detroit, as well as in smaller college towns such as Bloomington, Indiana; Ann Arbor, Michigan; Madison, Wisconsin; and Iowa City, Iowa. Women's music festivals attracted huge crowds with self-affirming lyrics of lesbian politics, love, and unity, and the first National Women's Music Festival was held in Champaign, Illinois, in 1974 (Faderman 220, 222). Women's presses provided periodicals that spoke to lesbian-feminist issues and some, such as *Lesbian Connection*, which began in 1974 in East Lansing, Michigan, kept down expenses so poorer women could buy them at reduced cost or obtain them for free (Faderman 224). Looking at the Midwest through the lens of lesbian-feminist cultural practices helps to further dismantle the stereotype of the Midwest as a place for social conformity with little or no resistance. Faderman notes that in the eighties, cultural events such as the Michigan Womyn's Music Festival and the Midwest Women's Festival became sites of intense political differences and disagreements between lesbians who were cultural feminists and tended to see pornography, public sex, and sadomasochism as connected to violence toward and exploitation of women, thereby validating the system of patriarchy, and more sexually radical lesbians, who saw these practices as ways for lesbians to resist sexual politics that repressed women and to explore sexual feelings and practices that had been marked as taboo for them (250-51).

Queer identity and queer cultural practices do thrive in the Midwest. Through our book's "a-coastal focus" and our shift toward the heartland and its diversity, it becomes clear that the privileging of coastal cities as exclusive sites of queer identity and queer culture is questionable. While lesbian and gay communities often play a role in helping to define, articulate, and sustain queer identity in the cities on the coasts, in the Midwest, where the concentration of lesbians and gay men is smaller, the construction of queer identity—the social positioning of oneself as "queer"—is much more contested. It becomes a more rigorous struggle between assimilation to larger heterosexual worlds and the simultaneous resistance to invisibility through asserting difference. The work represented in this volume illustrates, in varying degrees, this continuing struggle. In some pieces, the struggle to assimilate plays a more prominent role, as in Gary Pool's story "Victims of Circumstance," about a gay male couple who own and operate a French restaurant in Springfield, Missouri, and who want to jointly adopt an African-American son, or in the poem "Christmas in the Midwest" by Maureen Seaton, in which a woman brings home her lesbian lover hoping for acceptance and validation from her parents. Similarly, Renata, a professionally successful and rather sophisticated lesbian still very much in the closet at work and with her family, struggles with her desire for the younger, more spontaneous and sexually open Kimberly in Carol Anshaw's story "Mimosa," and over an exquisitely prepared dinner a group of urban gay male friends in D. Travers Scott's lively story "Digestion" debate such issues as monogamy in gay relationships and gender conformity.

Some readers may assume that such issues of social and sexual conformity and assimilation are the definitive markers for lesbian and gay midwestern identity and writing, but as soon as one attempts to fix these categories, new areas of indeterminacy arise, further destabilizing our paradigms for representing sexual difference and region. Other contributors write poignantly and unapologetically of the *difference* of queer desire, addressing the need to name and represent our sexual lives despite hetero culture's insistence that we remain silent. Joseph Like, in his poem "Boxers," homoerotically rereads the relation between two men engaged in boxing. Diane Williams's "Honey Sister" speaks to gender and sexual politics among a group of urban African-American lesbians and their dominant sister Daddy Rae. Don Mager's poem "Canto Faggoto" energetically describes the diversity of gay men and their bodies in various parts of Michigan. Antler's poem "Hot Summernight Cloudburst Rendezvous" celebrates the (homo)sexual coming of age of adolescent boys, and Karen Lee Osborne's experimental story intertwines two narratives of survival, one physical and literal, the other emotional, between two women who were former lovers.

We cannot assert, then, that there is a strictly defined lesbian and gay midwestern literature, identity, or sensibility; to do so would essentialize both the Midwest and queer midwestern writing as well as maintain the heartland/coastal split. In much of the writing collected here, one finds recurring images of snow, flatlands, cornfields, cows, farms, and prairie that form part of the midwestern landscape; yet the region geographically and socially is obviously not reducible to these agrarian images. As Linnea Johnson reminds us in her essay, land-

scape, weather, and the like are "narrative carriers of myth and continuity and art"; they serve as backdrops or as metaphors, as vehicles
for deeper meanings. Another problem is that, unlike New England
and the South as sites for regional literature, the Midwest is an expansive area, indeed the largest region of the United States, and to attempt to reduce it to distinguishable criteria runs the risk of eliding
differences within it, which runs contrary to our purposes. In order to
create a context wherein ideas about queer midwestern literature can
emerge, and in order to begin a conversation on the politics of geographic location and lesbian and gay identity, we have assembled a
rich variety of work by a culturally diverse group of lesbians and gay
men from various parts of the Midwest whose work contributes to the
complexity of queer identities, desires, and experiences. The book
ranges from reflections on growing up in the Midwest and a specific
focus on the Midwest as place (Parts I and II), to the broader issues of
queer desire and the various contexts at work in the construction of
queer writing and culture (Parts III and IV), and concludes with midwestern perspectives on and in other locations (Part V). Each section
begins with a photograph that depicts the focus of that section. The
organizing framework we have provided is only one set of lenses
through which to read the work collected in this book; because queer
writing often consciously and unconsciously works to resist disciplin-
ary boundaries, the observant reader may notice that the categories
we have created are helpful but not absolute. Many of the pieces may
also fit in other sections or may be read through multiple, intersect-
ing trajectories. In other words, our organizational framework is not
intended to fix, and therefore limit, the meanings of the texts but is
suggestive and reflects our own specific, yet contingent, acts of reading as editors.

Because there are numerous selections, space does not permit me
to comment on each piece, but I shall briefly highlight some of the
selections in each section to provide an account of how the book is
organized. The volume begins with reflections of growing up in the
Midwest. Thematically, several of the texts in Part I address struggles
between self and Other experienced in various phases of midwestern
childhood. In the first story, for instance, Jess Wells's character, Tracy
Giovanni, in "Luke Giovanni's Canoe," beautifully recalls her father's private but intense battle to protect the wildlife near their
home in Michigan, her coming to terms with his deteriorating mental

health, as well as her own personal conflict between the private world she shares growing up with her father and the wider social world she must also inhabit. Similarly, Virginia Smiley writes about a young girl's fascination with and not yet fully realized desire for a woman who saves her from danger on a Wisconsin farm, a woman who leaves a lasting impression because of her striking difference from other women the child has known. The protagonist of Renée Lynn Hansen's "When You Were Young and Had a Rescue Complex" reflects on the childhood memory of a rather remote father who committed suicide by driving his car into a tree on a neighbor's farm; because the story is told in the second person, the gender of the narrator remains ambiguous as the emphasis seems to be on that character's search for permanence and meaning in a world that appears increasingly uncertain. The self/Other split begins to break down in David Kodeski's early platonic identification with a somewhat campy and unconventional new aunt (through his uncle's remarriage) who wears a dress of "mint green chiffon" with gold sequins sewn on her handbag at his "First Communion Celebration"; she is a woman who seems "Other" to him at the time, but she is one whom he admires for her "rough-and-tumble beauty," which he will "one day learn to wear." Sometimes one discovers something Other about the self, as is the case with Gregg Shapiro's "Swimming Lessons," in which a young boy experiences the first stirrings of homosexual desire, and in "For Liam When He Grows Up," William Reichard's poetic reflection on having a nephew named after him who may grow up to experience him as Other, despite the bond that was intended to be created between them. Robert Rodi, in the final piece in this section, writes a tribute to an older gay neighbor, Mister Kenny, whom he knew while growing up in suburban northern Illinois. On a superficial level Mister Kenny may seem Other from the point of view of Rodi and his friends as children, but what seems more Other to Rodi in the present as he recalls this neighbor from the perspective of the gay man he has himself become, is the homophobic anxiety in our culture associated with children in the company of gay people.

The pieces in Part II focus in varying degrees on the Midwest as place. Some poets, such as Joseph Like in "Main Street" and Jim Elledge in "A Solstice in Southern Illinois," reflect on the midwestern landscape, whether imaginatively, as an "inverted ocean," or philosophically, pondering the connections between family roots and one's independent life while heading "home" for the Christmas holidays on a train from Chicago to southern Illinois. In other poems, the physicality of the landscape is combined with gay longing and desire, as in Antler's "On My Way to Lake Michigan Sunrise on the Milwaukee Lakefront Breakwater," which celebrates spring and the sunrise on Lake Michigan as well as the slumbering, not yet fully conscious sexuality of young boys sleeping, and in Terri L. Jewell's "Bad Ass," which richly portrays the movement, resistance, and sexual possibilities of the black lesbian body through metaphors of landscape. In still other pieces, the specificity of midwestern landscape takes a less prominent position, forming a backdrop to other meanings. One example is coming out to one's sister amid unusual news of a brutal murder committed by a boy in Woodstock, Illinois, in Maureen Seaton's poem "The Sighting." Another is the letter Rachel writes to her lover, Hannah, who has gone to New Mexico as part of her military service during World War II. In this scene from Claudia Allen's play *Hannah Free*, Rachel describes how much she loves and misses Hannah but how she cannot leave the midwestern town where she lives. The Midwest as place also forms a backdrop to Pamela Olano's play *In and Out of Harm's Way*, written in the style of a Greek tragedy using both queer theory and the written reflections of lesbian and gay graduate students about being gay in academic contexts. The play represents both the personal drama and the risks graduate students face in claiming a lesbian or gay male identity as they launch their academic careers at a major midwestern university and powerfully confronts the myth of tolerance of gay people in the supposedly enlightened world of academia.

Not all of the material collected in this volume, however, specifically addresses the heartland as place; beyond signifying a geographic space, the Midwest is also a perspective, a way of positioning oneself in the world. While the selections in the first two parts more or less foreground the specificity of midwestern location, queer writing in the Midwest is not only confined to that geographic space, disembodied from other social spaces, but also connects to other queers and to other contexts and locations outside of the Midwest. The writers in the following three parts show their connections to, rather than their distinction from, other queers, other contexts, and other locations without necessarily losing something of the Midwest. Mary Jo Bang's poem "Semiotics," in Part III: " 'Every Last Drop': Writing Desire," beautifully combines the interpretation of lesbian desire with the interpretation of language and symbols. The body of the Other she desires is only surface, shadow, and light until it is undressed. Bang is not making any transcendent claims to understand the object of her desire or desire itself; what she is able to comprehend is relative to the reading of the signs at that specific moment of stripping away superficialities that evoke "nakedness / and meaning—*mine* for the naming" (emphasis added). William Reichard's poem "Bonsai" similarly attempts an understanding of gay desire through its focus on the image of careful, painstaking pruning to negotiate the often tangled and difficult process of love. Don Mager ascribes an erotic sensuality to the men who sell fruits and vegetables in the Chene-Ferry Market in Detroit, and Terri L. Jewell makes use of natural images such as soil, planting, and fertility to describe the orgasmic eroticism between two women in her poem "Agrology." Other pieces in this section take a more sobering tone; Steve and Barry, in Lev Raphael's story "Welcome to Beth Homo," try to gain perspective on their intense sexual relationship, kept mostly private, by attempting to reconcile the rather difficult subject positions of being openly gay and more openly Jewish as students at Ohio State University, despite anti-Semitism and homophobia on campus. Jeannette Green starkly contrasts a woman's life-affirming, spontaneous, and playful desire for a lover in 1937 with a later, more horrifying, Holocaust-like existence in 1942, stripped of basic needs. The two very different worlds of desire and despair are eerily linked by exuding bodily fluids, near-nakedness, and a pair of wire-rim glasses. Charles Derry's stream-of-consciousness story struggles to make sense of the uncertainty and ambiguity of a negative test for HIV infection, and Gerard Wozek's poem "Brother Balm" celebrates gay community, spirituality, and the erotic healing of a gay man who returns from the city with AIDS and is embraced by his gay "brothers."

The pieces in Part IV call attention to the interplay between text and context, that is, between the various contexts that shape the work being written and read as opposed to the work as a self-contained artifact. These contexts include, of course, midwestern location, as well as authorial intention and production, myth, ethnicity, history, and biography. Owen Keehnen inverviewed the late Scott McPherson, one of the most successful playwrights to come out of the Midwest, shortly before his death from complications resulting from AIDS in 1992. In

the interview, McPherson comments on his own process of composing and creating characters in his play *Marvin's Room*; he mentions
how many of the characters in that play can be traced to people from
his own life, especially family members, who then took on lives of
their own as they developed in the fictional situation. He discusses
how the death earlier that year of his lover, activist and political cartoonist Danny Sotomayor, affected his work. McPherson's lack of pre-
tentiousness and his indifference to the trappings of literary success
that come across in the interview reveal, at least in part, his midwestern connections. Edward Thomas-Herrera gives a feminist rereading
of Clytemnestra in his poem "Clytemnestra's lament," wherein she
mourns the impending loss of her independence and a return to
wifely duty and exploitation as her husband, Agamemnon, is about to
return home from the Trojan War after ten years, suggesting that her
motive for his eventual murder is tied to her wish to be emancipated
"from matrimony patriarchy and servitude." Kitty Tsui makes use of
her native Chinese language to frame feelings of grief and sadness
and to cope with the pain of abandonment and separation in her
poem "open heart." Linnea Johnson's exciting prose reconstruction
of the life and work of Willa Cather, influenced by her visit to the
Cather-Lewis cottage on the island of Grand Manan, New Brunswick,
concludes this section. Johnson's essay is not about Cather's texts per
se, but about Cather's fascination with detail in reading landscapes
and whose narratives helped Johnson read the Nebraskan region
when studying Cather at the University of Nebraska. Unfortunately, in
spite of Cather's respect for landscape and detail, many of Cather's
critics "off-read" the landscape and details of her life by erasing the
specificity of her relationship with Edith Lewis, missing "what and
whom she loved." Johnson urges us to remember that Lewis formed
a crucial context for Cather's life and work; Johnson writes that "the
landscape Cather wrote *in* is as important as the landscape she wrote
about. Where she could and did write, with and for and because of
whom, informs what she wrote."

Finally, the selections in Part V represent a diaspora of midwestern
perspectives on and in other locations, an outward (re)writing of the
world, the motion of which is effectively captured by Jim Elledge's
poem "Frog Prince, Cape Cod," a paean to movement, transition,
fresh visions, new possibilities. In some of the selections, other locations figure quite prominently, whether in small winding paths in San

Antonio where two lovers meet in a poem by Allison J. Nichol, or in the narrow, cobblestone alleys on the hills of the Alfama in Lisbon that come to life for the fish market in another poem by Elledge. Some poems are about psychological or imaginative movement, connecting another location with something or someone in the Midwest. Robert Klein Engler, in "Low Hangs the Moon," reads the transitional Florida skies and landscape to comprehend the serial killings of young men by John Gacy in Illinois. Kitty Tsui, while on a plane heading for San Francisco from the heartland, considers the link between overcoming her fears and anxieties, especially of earthquakes, and her lingering memories of a woman she has left behind, in her poem "coming into light." And sometimes, as in the case with other pieces in this anthology, location itself is not foregrounded; what receives more attention is the attempt to understand the meaning of specific events that occur in one's passage through space or time. In Nikki Baker's "Missing Pieces," the narrator gazes back at her tumultuous relationship with her mother at a stop in Gallup, New Mexico, while on a cross-country car trip from Chicago to San Francisco. The story calls attention not only to the geographic location she and her mother inhabited at the time, but also to the further memories the trip evokes, and to the ways in which significant events and episodes are narratively reconstructed, or edited out altogether, depending on the selective point of view of the person recounting them, particularly in the case of an African-American mother's refusal to believe her daughter is a lesbian. Likewise, William Reichard, in "Time Lapse," yearns to view the world dioramically, wrenching unpleasant and unexplainable events out of context so as to hold them still and try to make sense of them. Novelist Carole Maso has written a reflective essay on her one-year experience of teaching creative writing at a midwestern university from the perspective of having lived most of her life on the East coast. In this final piece of our book, the lens operating in this section reverses, and observer and observed change positions as someone from another location peers inward at the heartland. Maso seems to have momentarily captured a Midwest that refuses to remain fixed or stable—indeed, an important theme of our book. She writes of the striking contrasts and contradictions of the austere midwestern landscape and its fertile earth, of clean-cut serial killers, and of her students—"children of the Midwest"—cinder-blocked, landlocked, "wholesome," yet "like the landscape, filled with longing and possibility."

This collection shows that the Midwest is not antithetical to lesbian and gay identities and cultural practices; in fact, the work collected in this volume strongly suggests that the Midwest *enables* the production of queer culture. To assume otherwise, to disparage queer location and cultural production in the Midwest dangerously serves and perpetuates homophobic ideologies that assert that there is no place for lesbians and gay men in "Middle America." Many of the writers in this volume are prominent nationally, and the fine quality of writing by both established and emerging writers stands firmly on its own merits and contributes to ongoing understandings of queer culture in addition to making a larger cultural contribution. Although this book does not claim to be the final or definitive work in lesbian and gay midwestern literature, we hope it will help to initiate and sustain a much needed discussion among writers, critics, artists, scholars, readers, and students of literature about more inclusive ways of being queer and producing queer culture from the different locations from which our voices can be heard.

References

Bérubé, Allan. *Coming Out under Fire: The History of Gay Men and Women in World War Two.* New York: Penguin, 1990.

Faderman, Lillian. *Odd Girls and Twilight Lovers: A History of Lesbian Life in Twentieth-Century America.* New York: Penguin, 1991.

Fuss, Diana, ed. *Inside/Out: Lesbian Theories, Gay Theories.* New York: Routledge, 1991.

Katz, Jonathan Ned. *Gay American History: Lesbians and Gay Men in the U.S.A.: A Documentary History.* New York: Penguin, 1992.

Warner, Michael, ed. *Fear of a Queer Planet: Queer Politics and Social Theory.* Minneapolis: University of Minnesota Press, 1993.

White, Edmund. *States of Desire: Travels in Gay America,* rev. ed. New York: Penguin, 1991.

White, Ray Lewis. *Winesburg, Ohio: An Exploration.* Boston: Twayne, 1990.

Part I

"When You Were Young": Growing Up in the Midwest

Kathryn Kirk, "Three Dancers, New Philadelphia, Ohio, 1983"

Luke Giovanni's Canoe

Jess Wells

HER mother had died in childbirth, and Tracy Giovanni had grown up alone with her father. They lived on a lake in Michigan where the upper class came in the summer to launch their boats and buy fishing tackle they never used. Their house was on an inlet, not sprawling across the sandy shore, open to the breeze like the modern, wood-and-glass homes of the doctors, but pushed up against a small shingled cottage along the marshy strip, where the cattails and brush stopped the breeze before it reached the screened porch off the kitchen and the little window of her bedroom. Her father insisted it was the best place for a year-round home, protected from the winter wind, circled by birds that perched on the puffy ends of the cattails, singing in the morning. It was a nice house, built in the 1950s and carefully decorated by Tracy's mother before she died, with drapes that matched the carpets, solid furniture, rooms that had designated purposes and unique color schemes, not the helter-skelter mishmash of the summer renters next door.

They had coffee on the porch every day, Luke Giovanni, a lanky man with a narrow chest and expansive hands, receding brown hair and a jutting chin, and his daughter, Tracy, flat-chested, all legs, lash-less bright green eyes, with blond hair that didn't seem to grow but to spin out of her head like cotton candy. Luke would intone the Latin names of the red-winged blackbirds and the blue martins. Tracy would clutch a big cup of warm milk with a dash of coffee and lift her moustached lips to say, "Blue jay, male."

Her father owned Middle Lake Boat Sales off the highway but would have nothing to do with the powerboats he sold. His passion was canoeing, silently moving across the water before the sun had burned the mist off the lake, creeping up on the egrets and black-birds, while the water dribbled off his paddle with a sound that didn't disturb a single wing.

Tracy was also a good canoeist, and it was a source of pride and

3

companionship between them, until the summer she was ten. She had been sitting placidly watching a young nest of blackbirds being fed by their mother when she was startled by the sound of a revving powerboat. The teenaged driver pounded the dashboard and cursed. Tracy hid her canoe deeper in the reeds with a simple, noiseless turn of her paddle and watched the kids pull aluminum cans tied with fishing wire from their motor. The cans were tangled hopelessly in the blades, battering the boat each time they tried to break away. They shouted directions at each other, produced a knife, cut themselves free, and with an enormous surge of power that frightened all the birds into the air and stirred the silty bottom, they cut across the lake, throwing the twisted cans behind them.

Tracy paddled through the reeds to the cans and pulled them into her canoe. The boys shouldn't have been in this shallow water: they were disturbing the birds, she thought. They were lucky the wire hadn't destroyed their motor altogether. All the cans had their labels carefully removed, and she hadn't seen any debris in the water. This could not have been simple rubbish. Who would tie cans together just to throw them away? As she held the dripping puzzle in her hands, the last can on the string caught her eye: it was a very old canister of ice-skate wax, a can easily twenty years old, with dark red printing and bold letters on the metal, the same brand her father had always used and, dipping the last crusty bits from the bottom, had ceremoniously walked to the trash two days ago. She looked across the lake at her cottage. What was her father doing? Sabotaging the summer residents? Why would he do this? She covered the cans with a parka in the bottom of the canoe. If anyone found them he'd be ruined, she thought, furtively looking around and suddenly filled with a fear not just of the doctors and their wives, but of her father. For the next two weeks, every day after Luke went to work, Tracy launched the canoe and pulled scores of booby traps from the nesting grounds of birds.

"What are these?" she said softly when she returned one evening, pulling several lines of cans out of a sack. Her father turned his back on her and walked onto the porch.

"They're picking on the birds," he said quietly.

"You can't ruin their boats, Dad," she said incredulously. "I mean, it's crazy."

"Starling."

"What?"

Her father sat in his chair on the porch and didn't turn around. Tracy stood behind him, holding the cans.

"Daddy, what are you going to—"

"Goldfinch, martin," he said plaintively.

Tracy let the sack of cans drop to the floor in front of her and looked from the bag to the string of cans in her hand to the back of her father's chair.

"Red-winged blackbird."

"But tell me why, Dad."

"Barn owl, white-crested hawk."

Tracy stood very still, the cans still hanging from her hand. She wanted to turn to someone else for the answer, but there was no one here.

"OK. We'll take care of it, Dad," she said, with a tone she had never heard in her voice. "It'll be OK."

Every evening of her childhood after that, her father went out in the canoe and laid more traps. Tracy got up in the morning and pulled them out. She volunteered to do the grocery shopping and stopped buying canned food. Luke stopped asking her about her day. In the evenings, he would sit in his chair reciting the nesting habits of the local birds, sometimes halting mid-sentence to take her hand and spend the rest of the evening in silence.

At the end of summer, when the wind started battering the willow trees not just in the evenings but in the afternoon as well, her father would announce with great jubilance: "The egrets and we will be happy to know that the season is over!" Luke would lay off his staff, shutter the boat depot, register for unemployment, put away his canoe, and chop wood for the fireplace. Tracy would go back to school.

As the snow fell, her father would bring out his binoculars and watch the lake turn black and freeze, holding a finger up in the morning over coffee to silence her. "The ice is cracking. Two feet thick now," he would say with a smile, then rise to bring his skates out of the closet. The lake was deserted, the bars and clubs shuttered, the rental units empty most of the time, the expensive homes sitting vacant. The birds that remained stayed silently huddled in the twisted bushes. The landscape was a black lake draped in white like the couches and chandeliers in the homes of the rich.

Tracy's father would glide into this motionless landscape on a pair of old black skates, looking, she thought, like a giant crow, his arms tight at his side, hands clutched behind his back. Tracy would pick up her school books and watch him leave, never sure how many hours he would stay out or where he'd go. He now knew the names of the birds of South America.

The Giovannis' nearest year-round neighbor was Maggie, secretary at the Lakeside Chamber of Commerce. The next spring, Tracy watched Maggie load an overnight case and her purse into her car when Luke strode across the lawns and clambered into the passenger seat. Maggie shrugged her shoulders, palms up, as if confused but resigned, and drove off with Tracy's father.

Four hours later, Maggie screeched to a halt in the driveway and burst into the house, dragging Luke by the arm.

"Your daddy's a lunatic, do you know that? Crazy as a goddamn loon," Maggie said.

"You OK, Dad?"

"He makes us go into this antique store, I don't know why, and I don't think he does either. He finds this lamp, a dancing hippo. Pretty soon, he's skating around the place, laughing like a maniac."

Tracy smiled.

"This is no laughing matter, my dear. I had to drag him outside, he was laughing so loud. People stepped into the street to avoid us. Like he was Manson in a cutlery shop or something. I'm tellin' you, the man is tetched."

"Hippo's figure eight," Luke announced, skating around the room and holding his arm up like the hippo lamp.

"What in the name of God is goin' on here?" Maggie asked, looking at Tracy, who had been standing with a screwdriver in one hand, the door of a small cabinet in the other. A jumbled pile of mail cascaded onto the floor at her feet, envelopes of bills and past-due notices covering the ends of her shoes. Maggie had turned and stormed through the house. She opened all the kitchen cupboards and found them empty, inspected the dirty refrigerator, scowled over the state of the oven. She opened all the crusted metal canisters. Maggie checked the sheets on the bed and pushed her way into the laundry room, where the dirty clothes were piled so high they kept the door from being opened.

"Lord God, child, who's been takin' care of you?" When Tracy didn't answer, Maggie rubbed her face with her hands and walked around the kitchen.

"Dad," Tracy said softly, "go onto the porch and watch the birds. I saw an egret this morning."

"Egret," Luke said, dropping his arm and striding to where his binoculars hung from a peg, hurrying onto the porch.

"We can manage," Tracy said defiantly.

"Oh, you can manage. Who's been doing the cooking?"

"We eat peanut butter. And baloney. I used to buy boxes of stuff I saw on TV but—"

"Oh you do?"

"And I copy what other kids have in their lunch bags."

Maggie turned away, bit her lip.

"I can take care of him," Tracy said.

"This is not about who's takin' care of *him*," Maggie said angrily. "This is about who is takin' care of you. Your grandma alive?"

"No."

Maggie put her hands on her hips. "You got an aunt, or a cousin? How about an uncle?"

"I don't know them," she said. "Maggie, teach me to run the washer-dryer. Everything's got spots when it comes out."

"You're an eleven-year-old child."

Tracy threw her shoulders back in her wrinkled white blouse, her plaid school uniform and white socks that bagged around her ankles.

"We're learning about the food groups in school."

"The food groups," Maggie said. She leaned on the counter. "Well, God knows being a ward of the state isn't a pretty way to grow up either. I'm not suggesting that. Seen too many girls turn to hookers and potheads after juvie hall," she said under her breath. Then, to Tracy, "He ever hit you, or get mad?"

"No!"

"Is there a gun in this house?"

"No. Just teach me a couple things, Maggie. I can do the rest."

Maggie folded her arms and sighed. "I daresay a bright little thing like you prob'ly could," she said with resignation. "But we're writing letters to your relatives." She pointed at the pile of envelopes on the floor.

Then Maggie rolled up her sleeves and followed Tracy to the laundry room, pulling mounds of clothes from behind the door.

"First thing you gotta do is separate the whites from the colors."

Maggie taught her to preheat the oven and iron her school

blouses, took her to the grocery store every week, and taught her to plan meals. She bought a step stool to put in front of the washing machine and to reach the kitchen cabinets.

"These are your best friends," Maggie said, holding the instructions to the washing machine in one hand, the recipe on the back of a box in the other. Together, they hung instruction booklets from short white strings on the knobs or handles of all the appliances. My best friends, Tracy thought, looking at the small white papers that fluttered from all corners of the house.

THE summer of Maggie's discovery, relatives arrived in a steady stream. They sat on the edge of the sofa, wringing their hands, cajoling Luke to enroll her in a boarding school. He just laughed and leaned toward Tracy, nodding his head toward Uncle Sid.

"He's a horny owl," he whispered, and Tracy tried not to smile.

Relatives timidly offered to send her themselves, but she wouldn't go, not to a school, not to their homes, even for a summer, she said. They looked at her with cautious eyes. Mental illness was hereditary, wasn't it? they seemed to ask. Foster homes were out of the question: middle-class children did not go to foster homes, and if they did, the child was never middle class again. No, the family would have to make the best of it by themselves. Besides, their concern and their half-hearted attempts to make a difference were met by the closed face of a wild-haired girl standing resolutely behind her father's chair, one hand protectively on his shoulder.

The relatives began to send money. Distant cousins arrived to inspect the cupboards and refrigerator, cautiously opening the doors, as if a box of insanity might jump off the shelf and spill on them. Then, a few days after their departure, they sent a check. Numbers became things to rely on. The dividends from her mother's life insurance arrived in small manila envelopes marked "from the account of Lucille Giovanni." Tracy held each to her cheek as if it were a kiss.

When her father's lawyers sold the boat business, the check had more numbers on it than Tracy had ever seen. As the pile of mail grew on the hat-rack table and her father sat deeper in his recitations, Tracy learned to forge his signature and pay the bills. She sat on a footstool in front of him and checked his teeth, then scheduled his dental appointments. She took him shopping for new clothes, ushering him around with a magazine picture in her hand.

In the evening, Luke would pull out a map of the lake and begin his winter's plotting. "There's a gap in the ice here," he would say solemnly, warning his daughter away from that area. Every day the circles changed, carefully drawn in pencil and then erased. Tracy regarded him with a suspicious eye. If he had spent the summer sabotaging boats, what was he doing in the winter? When the two or three ice-fishing shacks sent up a thin plume of smoke on a Saturday morning, Tracy took out her own skates to check for markings of another secret campaign.

Each day that winter, she watched her father sliding across the ice with a feeling that he was slipping further away, pushing across a lake that expanded every morning, taking him deeper into a world where no one heard the rhythmic scratch of his blades on the ice. When was he going to lose track of the fissures and fall in, lost in a place that was forbidding, uncharted, governed by rules he couldn't see, just like the world he inhabited above the ice?

SEVERAL years later, Tracy was home from college on spring break. Luke had just returned from the hospital, and the doctor said he had been stabilized by a new medication. "If he stays on his pills, we may have this thing licked," the doctor told her. Tracy was surprised by the lucidity of her conversations with Luke. He had taken the canoe from its rack on the side of the house, and she had fought her first reaction to take it away, like a sharp knife from a child. He was bright-eyed and clear. Luke had maps, he had water and trail mix, and he suddenly looked like a father again, someone who knew that the gear had to be strapped just in front of the bow seat, someone who could actually navigate water. He gripped the gunwale of the boat for her like a man who could be counted on to steady the craft for her step. She sat in the stern seat and let him paddle, though she insisted they stay close to the shore. She sat jubilantly listening to him talk about current events and instruct her in the proper way to tack against the wind.

Later that summer when she got the call from the sheriff, she knew the scenario before he described it. Her father had drowned, the sheriff said, but she knew he had finally just sailed away. The meals had continued to arrive and the house to be cleaned, but he had slipped through the net she had built. She saw him paddling in circles, sitting backward in the boat, endlessly sliding on the lake that became a river, turned into creeks, broke open into estuaries, water that constantly traveled and took her father with it, pointlessly, end-lessly, out of control and chartless, a man in a boat not capable of see-ing where he was going or why he should come ashore, a man sitting cross-legged in a canoe reciting its parts: "stern thwart, bow, sheer line, freeboard, keel, stern thwart, bow," as the sun baked his head until it balded and tore, and the water made his feet black and cracked. He had finally become completely lost, rocking back and forth, in a canoe tumbling down a river, the only sign of life visible from the shore her father's hands gripping the gunwale.

Tracy replayed in her mind the sight of her father sailing away and knew that she was the one who had pushed him off the shore. She had collected the bills, packed his checkbook, cut up the credit card, but had taken the bus back to college. What was the medication? She hadn't asked. She hadn't set up a system for him to take his pills. She had wanted to live a life like other people, and she had made him vulnerable as a result. She had watched him take the canoe down from its rack, knowing she had nothing left to give. There was no way to put things in order again. Her hands were his as he died, helplessly clutching a paddle in water he didn't know.

Swimming Lessons

Gregg Shapiro

NEITHER of my parents could swim. That's why, they insisted, it was so important for me to learn how to swim. "Swimming lessons," they said, the same way they said "Sunday school" or "clean up your room." I agreed, swayed by their generosity. Their willingness to make me the best person I could be. Another set of lessons, another notch in my belt of accomplishments. Tap-dancing lessons at the Art Linkletter Dance Studio, acting lessons with Mrs. DeWitt (the former Shakespearean actress), violin lessons with Mr. W. at school. I even played Little League baseball and youth basketball (one season of each), just so my parents and I could say I did it. Each one, an example of overachievement and excess. I could do anything, just not do it well.

Water sports snuck up on me late in life. By fourth grade, most of my contemporaries were already accomplished swimmers, bearers of Red Cross lifesaving certificates and patches. Whenever I went to the pool with my family (even though they couldn't swim, my parents found the public pool an excellent place to get sun and socialize), I remained at the shallow end, never getting into water I couldn't stand up or walk in.

After dinner, one winter evening, my parents were watching *Hawaii Five-O*, eating popcorn, and looking at a brochure from the Leaning Tower YMCA. I wondered if they were considering that pottery class my friend Joey was enrolled in that met on Tuesdays and Thursdays.

The way Joey talked about it, it sounded really cool. There were boxes of gray clay in cellophane that everyone took a handful of and put on their pottery wheel. Drawers full of special tools and jars of cloudy paints. Even an unusual oven, called a kiln, that reached extra-high temperatures, to bake each student's creation.

There was something in their eyes, as they huddled close together on the off-white couch, their legs entwined, the bowl of popcorn suspended between them, that told me they were investigating something a little less creative and a little more serious than throwing clay.

"Two weeks from Saturday," my father said, "you are going to begin swimming lessons." Usually they asked about the prospective lessons, giving me the chance to mull it over, or pretend to, and after giving the subject careful consideration, to make time in my schedule of after-school and weekend activities. They must have sensed my uneasiness in water and went ahead without my participation in the decision-making process and signed me up for swimming lessons.

As it turned out, my advanced drama lessons were coming to an end in a few weeks, and, while I was hoping for voice lessons with Judith Lee at the Voice of Reason Vocal Conservatory, I was not surprised at my parents' action. And not really disappointed, either. Because, at some point last summer, I realized two things. One was that I was missing out on a lot of fun. We took our first trip that summer to Nippersink, a resort in Wisconsin that we would visit each summer for the next ten years. Nippersink boasted one of the finest Olympic-sized swimming pools in all of southern Wisconsin, and while my parents were sunning and all the children my age were diving, racing, and retrieving weighted rings off the bottom of the pool, I was befriending Carmen, the effervescent entertainment hostess.

I became her assistant, without pay (the recognition was enough). Putting the needle on the record when she gave group dance lessons, helping her supervise the decoration of the teen activity room (she valued my youthful opinion—she was pushing sixty), and offering my attention to her wardrobe, which mostly consisted of low-cut one-piece bathing suits and kimonos.

The other thing I realized was that I loved to look at men. Not just men: teenagers and boys my age. While they were all turning their heads at whiplash speed every time a scantily clad female walked by, I couldn't keep my eyes off of them. Suddenly, the way a voice begins to crack or dark curly hairs begin to appear between a belly button and a penis, I knew something was beginning that I couldn't stop.

By avoiding the pool and the locker room, I was missing out on the chance to really see up close what I could look at only from a distance. How else could I see Steve Bernstein or Ricky Podowski, two of my favorite older kids, without shirts? I didn't go to the softball or volleyball games that seemed to be so popular with most of the boys (and girls) at Nippersink. I imagined that the minute they hit the playing field and felt the sun beating down on them, they took off their T-shirts and polo shirts and threw them in a pile near where the girls sat.

At the pool, there were no shirts, only solid and striped Speedos or baggy trunks. There were wide shoulders and brown nipples and tight skin. One night during our weeklong stay, I dreamed that I fell into the pool, that I struggled to stay above water in the deep end. One by one, the swimmers I admired from the balcony of the patio with one eye, while I watched Carmen lead a group of great-grand-parents through the Hokey Pokey with the other, dove into the pool to rescue me, getting underneath me, lifting my limp, almost lifeless body up over their heads to carry me to the safety of the deck, where they took turns trying to revive me by administering the kiss of life. When I awoke, I was sitting up in the center of my bed, my summer pajamas on the floor with the pillow and top sheet. All the lights were on in our suite, and my parents were looking at me with concern from their king-sized bed across the room.

On the Friday before the Saturday that my swimming lessons at the Y were to begin, my mother took me to S & M Sporting Goods downtown to buy a bathing suit. While we were there, I picked out nose clips, ear plugs, and goggles. I hated buying a bathing suit be-cause you couldn't try it on and you couldn't return it if it didn't fit. You had to hold it up against yourself and guess. I chose a pair of light blue trunks that I wouldn't feel too self-conscious wearing.

I wore the swim trunks under my corduroys on Saturday. The other accessories were in an old gym bag my father found in the back of his closet that seemed to be saved for an occasion like this one. My stomach felt queasy, and it hurt to breathe. I was sure I would drown during my first lesson, that no one would know how to save me, that my mother would go to the bathroom, stepping away for just a minute, and come back to find me dead, floating facedown in the water.

I was looking out the window, not paying attention to the passing scenery, when I saw the Leaning Tower go by and felt the car make that right turn into the driveway of the Y. I considered pleading with my mother, asking her to change her mind just this once, promising to do better at the next lesson, no matter what it was. I knew she would say no. "No," she'd say. "Besides, you've already worn the bathing suit, and we can't return it now."

The smell of chlorine that permeated the lobby of the Y never bothered me before. Now, it caused my eyes to water and squirmy stars to appear in the air. I staggered, dizzy and terrified, but my mother kept walking, with a purpose and a mission, to the registration desk. I wondered if I could make myself faint, maybe hit my head on a piece of furniture, do something, anything, to avoid getting into the pool.

I could see the pool through the gigantic picture window in the lobby. There were sofas and chairs arranged in front of the window so that parents could watch the lessons, beaming proudly at their waterborne offspring. I saw my mother put the latest James Michener novel in her bag before we left the house. She obviously had no desire to watch me flounder in the water. "Just give it your best effort," she said as she handed me the key-pin to my locker, the same thing she always said before a new set of lessons began. Then she pointed to a door that said Men's Locker Room and gave the order, "March."

For the first few steps I stumbled, then dragged my feet, then walked pigeon-toed. My mother cleared her throat, unimpressed with the display I had hoped would convince her of her and my father's grave and hasty mistake. So I marched, straight-backed and determined, into uncharted territory, with my gym bag and a bad attitude.

The light in the locker room was brighter, harsher, as if to make whatever lay on the other side of the door seem that much better. I walked past two rows of lockers, past the locker that my key-pin, #907, would unlock, to the two exits on the other end. One door had a plaque that said Track/Courts. The other said Pool, and below that in smaller letters, Caution: Wet Surface. I stood firmly rooted between the two doors, wondering if one of them had a secret emergency exit for situations like this one. A ladder perhaps, up the wall that led to a trapdoor in the ceiling and out onto the roof. I stepped forward, both arms outstretched toward both doors, when someone yelled, "Hey, you," and I dropped them to my sides like a soldier at attention.

Another voice, almost identical, asked, "What do you think you're doing?" I turned around to answer, curious to see who was asking the questions. For a moment I thought I was seeing double: two skinny boys with gray sweatshirts and cuffed blue jeans, with gym bags over their shoulders. I closed one eye and looked. There were still two of them, blond hair almost white under the humming fluorescent tubes in the ceiling. They took a few steps toward me and I stepped back. "Are you coming or going?" the one on the right asked. "Leaving or staying?" the one on the left asked.

"I haven't decided," I said. "Who wants to know?" That didn't sound as tough and self-assured as I wanted it to, and I instantly regretted saying it.

The twins looked at each other, seeing themselves, and shrugged. The one on the left said, "We were only asking because we know that Mr. Keith doesn't like anyone in the pool area with shoes on, and he'd probably start yelling and make you swim twenty laps or something."

"Twenty laps," I said. "Is that all?" The one on the right walked over to a locker and opened it with his key-pin. He took his bag off his shoulder and put it on the bench behind him. He said something in a soft voice to the other one, and I realized that they knew I was bluffing. They looked to be about my age, maybe a year older. They both sat down on the bench and began to undress. They took off their black Keds, left shoe first, then the right. They peeled off their white socks in the same order. I walked toward them, looking for my locker number at the same time. I wanted to say something to break the silence but didn't know what to say.

I found my locker about ten away from the twins. I put my gym bag down on a different bench and unzipped it. By this time, they had already taken their sweatshirts off, and they were both wearing bleached white T-shirts. And then they did something I couldn't believe. The one on the right pulled the T-shirt over the head of the one on the left and handed it to him. He hung it upon a hook in the locker and turned to the one on the right and did the same for him. He saw me watching and winked at me. I quickly looked away and began to undress, throwing, not hanging, my clothes in the locker.

When I looked at them again, they were adjusting their jockstraps, then stepping into their bathing suits. I closed my locker and took my towel with me, trying to attach the key-pin to my trunks as I walked. Through the door marked Pool were the showers, hissing and steaming like prehistoric water snakes. I hung my towel on a hook and stood under the beating spray for a few seconds. As soon as I felt sufficiently damp, I got my towel and walked through a second door marked Pool.

At the shallow end of the pool, closest to the picture window, mothers were lowering infants in diapers and rubber pants into the water. They splashed, sank, and rose like bubbles, giggling and slapping the water. The mothers wore bathing caps, some with flowers on them, their hair dry and invisible.

There was a group of kids, younger and older than I was, leaning against the wall under a hand-printed sign that said Minnows/ Beginners. I looked over at the picture window and saw my mother standing close to the glass, pointing in the direction of the wall and sign. "Over there," I mouthed, pointing, and walked slowly, cautious of the slippery tiles around the pool.

There was a clock on the opposite wall. 11:59, it said. The lesson was supposed to begin at noon, and I decided to give the teacher until 12:01 to show up. After that, I would meet my mother in the lobby and request that she demand a refund. At 11:59 and 57 seconds, the door from the men's locker room opened and Paul, the instructor, walked through it.

He had thick brown hair, parted on the side, that seemed to stay in place without Brylcreem, even after the showers. He wore a green racing suit, the same color as Robin's on *Batman*, but Paul filled out the front better. His skin was the color of clay pots and looked as if it would be warm to the touch. The part of his stomach above his belly button (which was an outie) reminded me of sand at the dunes after the wind blew it, little peaks and valleys, ridges. Where his bathing suit ended at the top of his thighs was a spill of brown hair that ran down to below his anklebone and ended at his feet. The only other hair that color, besides on top of his head, was under his arms, which he raised above his head as he stretched.

"OK, swimmers," he said. "Everybody into the pool." Everybody but me got into the water, one way or another. Some sat on the edge of the pool and slid in. Others walked to where the ladders were and climbed down a step at a time. A few of the braver ones jumped in, and it made me wonder if they knew more than they let on. Paul walked over to the wall where a clipboard lay among the life preservers, rubber toys, and kickboards.

Out of the corner of my eye I could see the twins near the deep end of the pool by the diving boards. Apparently, they were more advanced swimmers, learning how to dive or whatever it was that swimmers at their level did. I thought I saw one of them look over in my direction, but I couldn't be sure. Paul had begun to call roll from the list of names on the clipboard. He called mine, the last name on the sheet of paper, and smiled at me. "All right," he said. "Everybody pick a swim-mate. You," he said, looking into my eyes with eyes bluer than water, "will be mine."

First Communion Celebration

David Kodeski

Uncle John's new wife Beverly
Tips her head back
Opens her red-painted lips
And tosses out a laugh
Full of throat
She's got lipstick on her teeth
Large white and uneven
She's laughing at a joke
That in my prepuberty
Preheartache years
Is lost in their heavy
Double entendre

In my preadolescent way
I love her
In a way Uncle John cannot love her
With the purity
Of love
Reserved for maiden schoolteachers
Who squeak white chalk
7's 2's 9's
And complicated plus-and-minus
Billy-gave-Susie
Nickels-for-a-peek problems

When she laughs
I love Beverly more
For her mint green chiffon
That is more than
My mother's dress budget
That is less than
My mother's dress size

She possesses a rough-and-tumble beauty
I will one day learn to wear
It is a beauty
Steeped deep in highballs
Filterless cigarettes
And deep deep mugs of hot black
Steaming morning coffees

It is a beauty earned
By several marriages
By country-and-western dilemmas
Tear-filled screaming matches
That end with loud slamming doors
The eternal hope for the unattainable
Settling for less
Wanting more

At this festive occasion
We whirl on the dance floor
To standard Polish-American
        1-2-3
        1-2-3
        polkas
And she is leading me
Across the polished wooden floor
She presses me
Into the space
Below her breasts
The chiffon crackles
In my ear
The sequins
On her handbag
Full of secrets
Gold and glimmering
Scratch into my memories

1-2-3
1-2-3
And I am delivered

Dizzy with joy
Delirious with love

We dance
Spiraling upward
Lighter than air
I hold her tightly

And all those months
Of rigorous religious education
Spin round and round and round
1-2-3 1-2-3 Father Son Holy Ghost
    Father Son Holy Ghost
I know now the nun's long lessons
This is what Heaven must be like

Saved from the Bull

Virginia Smiley

I

LIKE tunnel vision, there was light in the center, straight ahead, but on either side the blackness seemed to close in on her. She wanted to break through. "Red Rover, Red Rover, let Jennie come over," her friends had chanted last year at school. They joined hands and defied her to break the connection, and she wanted to, to prove her strength. She wanted to fail and feel the strong, warm arms of her friends give and then envelop her without breaking the connection. Now she pushed herself and ran through the darkening barn and heard the hoot of the barn owl and the hiss of a mother cat caught licking the head of one of her young. Then she was free again, outside where the sun and moon lit the sky and the light was muted, absorbed by the tall grass that came up around her like water in a pool. The grass tickled her armpits and grazed her earlobes as she swam through the green water at high tide, and she began pushing the grass apart, no longer in a field in Wisconsin, but now on safari in deepest Africa. Would a lion appear, an ape swing down from the tree? She heard a swoosh in the grass and knew Dash, the collie, was caught in an adventure of her own.

Then she heard a heavy foot strike the dirt and echo through her small frame. The sound caught in her elbows, her Adam's apple. She opened her mouth to breathe it out as a bell sounded just ahead of her.

As she spread apart the next section of grass, she came upon the brown-and-white face of a cow whose large, dry, black nostrils twitched. The brown face and soft eyes were separated by a large white shock of fur shaped like Florida. It looked soft and clean, like new kitten fur, like the polar bear she left sitting on her bed at home. She wanted to touch the nose, touch Florida and see if it felt as soft as it looked.

The cow stepped closer, and she took it as a sign. She reached her hand up and ran her fingers down from between the warm brown eyes to the blackened snout that moved slowly from side to side with what seemed like contentment. The fur was softer than any of her stuffed animals, and it electrified her to feel life coursing through the biggest animal she'd ever touched. The cow was standing, blinking, taking her petting as the collie had only moments before.

"You're a pretty cow," she said, reaching up now to scratch the place where the ears connected to the head. She felt tiny, hard bumps beneath the skin.

"I bet they don't pet you very often."

And with that, she felt her balance go, her view of the cow's nose turn sideways. She got a horizontal instead of a vertical view. She felt herself being pulled backwards rapidly. The grass folded shut on her new friend like curtains at the end of a school play.

"Shouldn't be out here with the bull," a voice said from above her. She felt a strong arm beneath a flannel shirt sleeve wrapped around her middle. Then she felt a hand clutching her under her arm release and turn her upright again.

"I didn't think I was doing anything wrong," the girl said, looking up into the woman's sky-blue eyes. "I'm sorry."

"Don't be sorry. Just be glad you're still alive," she said without smiling. "Supper's ready."

II

By the time they were half through with dinner, the rescue story had become a good joke that brought the brother, sister, mother, and their two guests closer together. As the adults talked among themselves, the young girl heard phrases like "second mortgage," "had to sell that off," and "not sure what next year will bring." She didn't know what to make of her experience in the barnyard. She believed Ellen when she said bulls can be killers—she'd seen bullfight movies on TV on Sunday afternoons—but she had felt some connection, had felt something like trust pass between her and the animal. She pictured the bull's warm brown eyes as she petted him and decided Ellen had been wrong.

III

Darkness came quickly around the five sitting at the round oak table in the kitchen, and after the blueberry pie and ice cream had been served, Jennie felt a wave of tiredness pass from one person to the next. She'd already noticed there was no TV in the living room and decided it'd be OK to just go up to bed.

"Leave the dishes. We'll do 'em in the morning," Ray said to his mother.

Jennie and her father climbed the narrow wooden stairs behind Mrs. Green on their way to bed. In their room, they whispered.

"Get undressed and put your pajamas on," her father said.

"Where?"

"Here. Now."

"In front of you?"

"Since when are we so modest?" he asked, laughing, until he saw her blush.

"Stand behind the door if you're shy," he said. Then, "Oh, Little Miss Modesty," more to himself than to her.

She took her seersucker shorty pajamas and slipped them over the doorknob and stared at the cracks in the white paint as she peeled her T-shirt and shorts from her body. The big brown eyes came to her again.

"You don't think that cow would really have hurt me, do you, dad?"

"It could have killed you in a flash," her father whispered, and she heard the bed creak under his weight and the comforter fold over his body.

She woke up the next day feeling lucky to be alive. She owed Ellen her life, and she knew that as clearly as she'd known yesterday that it was all right to pet the cow.

IV

Something startled Ellen the evening before when feeding the pigs. She caught sight of the girl from the corner of her eye and turned to watch as the young one from Illinois, the child of her brother's friend, leapt from the car barely stopped in the driveway. Leaving the door to swing in the breeze, the child shot to the grass in the front of the farmhouse, then threw herself on her belly in front of Dash, who barked, announcing the two city folks coming for a visit.

Ellen finished feeding the eight pigs before she wiped her hands on her Levi's and walked toward Lou and his daughter Jennie. Ray had come out of the back barn to greet his friend, and all four of them stood around Ray and Ellen's mother who sat and rocked slowly on the porch, watching the sun set over their cornfield across the road as if there were no one on their farm.

"You're just in time for dinner," Ellen said, putting her boot on the first step to the porch and leaning her weight back on her narrow hips.

"Hi, I'm Jennie," the girl said, reaching her hand out to the woman.

"Well, I figured as much," Ellen said, grasping the soft, solid hand in her own, darkened and callused after years of work on the land. "This your first time on a farm?"

"Yes. And I simply love it already," Jennie said.

"Why don't you go explore, and we'll have supper ready in a half hour or so."

"There's some new kittens in the barn over there," Ray said, pointing to the large building behind the house.

"Or you can go watch the pigs eat," Ellen said. "I just finished feeding them as you were pulling up."

The child sprang past Ellen, and they all watched her supple young body race back toward the barn. When Dash caught up with her, she effortlessly reached down into the dog's thick coat to give her a scratch on the neck as they ran along together.

V

"Oh, to have that kind of energy," Lou said, sitting on a chair beside Ray's mother.

"Maybe we'll get some help with the chores around here."

"Well, she's not much good in the kitchen, according to her mother, but she might be good with the animals."

"I've seen girls like her before," Mrs. Green said, breaking her self-imposed silence.

"She'd love a dog, but the apartment we live in . . ." Lou shook his head, letting his words trail off into the cool evening breeze. He took a deep breath. "God, it's nice to be out of the city for a while."

"We're glad you've come," Ray said. "Too bad Ramona couldn't make the trip."

"It's probably just as well," Lou said, following Mrs. Green's gaze toward the cornfield. "We need a break from each other."

"Well, you relax here with Ma while Ellen and I finish with the chickens and cows."

"Your room's all set upstairs," Ellen said over her shoulder. "Whenever you want to unload, just take your suitcases up and make yourself at home."

Lou watched as Ellen touched her brother's arm, said something, then separated from Ray to follow Jennie toward the other barn.

VI

Jennie hadn't been around many grown women who didn't serve a purpose in her life—teachers, relatives, an occasional friendly shop clerk, mothers of friends—but she could tell Ellen was different. She wasn't used to kids, and she dealt with it by treating Jennie as an adult, by dismissing the girl as she did everyone else.

Jennie knew Ellen was different because she lived in two worlds. The girl could never tell exactly who did what in the kitchen, but it seemed Ellen spent part of her time setting up for, preparing, and putting away the meals that seemed to appear magically and the rest of her time doing man's work helping Ray keep the farm going.

She had eyes the color of the sky—slick blue eyes like glass or sheet metal. And even though she stared right at Jennie, it was as if her gaze didn't hold, couldn't connect. There was that same smoothness to her chiseled, handsome face and the tanned, muscled, lean arms that protruded from the chambray shirt with the sleeves cut off. Jennie never saw her in anything but Levi's and dusty brown-leather cowboy boots, but she imagined Ellen's legs matched her muscular, lean arms. Her quiet reminded Jennie of pictures of Eskimos and Indians—people who'd seen so much, there was nothing left to say. Jennie wanted the woman to like her, but had to settle for acknowledgment.

Jennie became coy around her. Each morning she'd set out to find Ellen and watch her work the farm; then, when she'd spot the woman, she'd hang back, watching from someplace where she couldn't be seen. Sometimes Jennie would pretend to be doing something else while she took peeks at her new friend feeding the chickens or loading ears of corn into the screened storage bins between the two barns. Jennie pretended to be invisible, but Dash was always at her side, so Ellen must have been able to see if she cared to.

VII

Jennie's father talked about Ray when they were alone together in their room at night. The only other times he had spoken of his friend was when Ray wrote him letters from the farm in Pulaski, Wisconsin. They were the only personal letters Jennie ever saw her father get. She could tell he liked getting them, but she never knew if he answered back.

"Ray used to be the best ballplayer on our team," her father said, shaking his head one night. "We all thought he was going to the majors, and look where he ended up." Jennie could hear the disappointment in his voice, but life here didn't seem bad. There was something in his words she didn't understand. "You just never know where life is going to take you, kiddo." Then he turned on his side and fell asleep.

That night, Jennie couldn't sleep and crept down the thin wooden stairs until she saw the half-moon of light spread over the living room floor. She sat on a step near the top of the stairs and looked at Ellen sitting at the desk.

Watching Ellen, the young girl was confused by the feelings inside her. She wanted to be like the woman—cool, confident, and competent. She wanted Ellen to be her mother—to take care of her and teach her everything she needed to know about living in the world, but most of all, she wanted Ellen to like her—to be interested in her. Staring at the woman bent over the huge ledger book, Jennie wondered what she could do to make that happen.

"What?" Ellen jerked as she heard a stair squeak.

"It's me." Jennie slipped down the remaining stairs on her butt until she landed on her feet at the bottom.

"You scared me." Ellen squinted at the child in her pink-and-white-striped cotton robe. "Anything I can get for you?"

"Couldn't sleep." Jennie walked toward the desk. She watched as Ellen continued entering numbers in the green leather-bound book.

"You do a lot of work around here," Jennie said.

"Somebody has to," Ellen said without looking up. "Darn it." She pulled a bottle of correction fluid from the top desk drawer and smeared it over the column of figures. "I do the books in pen because I don't usually make mistakes." She blew over the streak of white paint on the page.

"I better let you get back to work," Jennie said. "If there's ever anything I can do to help you . . . " Her voice trailed off as she went back upstairs.

Ellen watched until the child was out of sight, then stood to look out at the front yard and apple orchard lit by the high beams off the barn. Seeing Jennie and her father reminded her of the few years she had spent in the city, of her daily commutes in and out of the Loop on the train that rode half the trip above ground before sliding gradually into the long narrow tunnel beneath the city. She had only been a clerk at Field's, but that life seemed exciting to her now as she stood staring at the still barnyard and orchard. She recalled her three friends, Holly, Carol, and Lois, women her own age filled with dreams and hopes and always ready for adventure.

But that was before her dad died and she and Ray came home to help her mother run the farm. Because they never talked about what they'd left behind, Ellen rarely thought of those days; but something about the young girl made her remember her friends and long for them in a way she hadn't thought was still possible.

She pictured them on their way to the Goodman Theatre after work, bustling through the revolving doors, the breeze off the lake catching their hats and tugging them off their heads. In the stillness of the farm night, she heard Holly's high-pitched laughter, and it took more strength than she had to pull herself away from the memory to finish the bookkeeping and get into bed.

That night, the women's voices came back, too. Their smell, the softness of the skin on their faces, and an unbearable sadness and longing came over Ellen like a fever meant to run its course. She knew all she could do was lie still and hope it would pass.

VIII

What was it about the girl? Ellen's mind raced over the easy answers as she hooked each cow up to the machines for milking. It was still dark in the barn, and the cows looked as tired as she felt. *She reminds me of myself; she's young and I'm getting old.* Ellen knew it was something like that, but not exactly either of those two notions. All she knew was that bit by bit, the more the girl stared at her, the more she started hating her life. She had to drag herself out of bed in the morning—her will a trapeze above a nearly paralyzed body. Each day she'd awaken, look up, then reach and reach until she'd pull herself up out of bed and into the darkness.

Ellen knew the young girl followed her and stared at her. *Doesn't know what she's looking at, what she's so interested in,* Ellen thought, smiling to herself. She felt flattered by the girl's attention, then angry with herself for feeling that way.

IX

One morning Jennie caught up with Ellen as she walked across the barnyard to the silo. The sun was just coming up, turning the dark sky pink.

"Up kinda early for a city kid," Ellen commented, biting the inside of her cheek to keep from smiling.

"I like getting up early." Jennie smiled when she caught Ellen glancing at her.

"Think you're strong enough to do some real work around here?"

"I'm ready for anything."

"You'll have to leave Dash behind," Ellen said just matter-of-factly enough to make it sound like a dare.

"OK."

Ellen led the girl to the tallest silo and explained how to climb the ladder and knock the hay down with the pitchfork she handed to her. Jennie could barely lift the heavy steel fork from the thick wooden handle, but she wouldn't let on there was a problem. She put the pitchfork between herself and the ladder and began to climb. Ellen stood on the ground, holding the ladder and watching the child climb one step at a time.

"It gets pretty hot up towards the top," she called out.

"So?" The girl shot back without looking.

The girl's eagerness suddenly frightened Ellen. In the center of the hot, humid silo, she felt a chill and climbed the ladder until she could reach the girl's ankle.

"That's far enough," she said. "It's too hot—you'll pass out, and I'll have to carry you over my shoulder to get you out of here."

"Would not," the girl said, wiggling her ankle within the woman's grasp, but she did as she was told.

Ellen took the pitchfork from the girl and pulled the hay down herself, leaving Jennie on the ground to organize it in neat piles. As Ellen worked, she measured her endurance against the child's and felt young again, stronger than she'd ever felt. The muscles in her arms pushed tight against her skin. The nerve endings in her fingertips pulsed with the increase in her heartbeats. As she worked, she looked forward to Lou and Jennie leaving so she could get back to her daily routine.

X

Later that year, Lou got a letter from Pulaski again. This time Jennie was even more excited to hear what was inside. She watched her father's eyes dart back and forth across the page.

"What's he say?"

"They lost the farm," her father said without looking up.

It was as though he told her someone died.

"How?"

"Bad bookkeeping mistake. Ray and his mom got a place in town, but Ellen's living here in Chicago."

"How come she hasn't called us?"

Jennie's father shrugged. "Ray's a hired hand now on a farm near the place they used to own." Her father looked away, sad and distracted. "There's something wrong with a country when a farmer can't afford to keep his land." He stood up from the kitchen table and put his hand on his daughter's shoulder.

"And we think we've got trouble, huh, kiddo?"

THE girl was too young to understand everything her father said and didn't say. Off and on for a while, she wondered why Ellen didn't call or stop by. When she was lonesome in the backseat of the car while her folks were busy arguing, she'd look out the window and hope to see the woman walking down the street. Then, for years, she didn't think about Ellen at all until one night, her new friends took her to a dark neighborhood bar where Ray and Lou wouldn't be allowed in. As her eyes adjusted to the darkness, she saw a handsome woman leaning against a paneled wall looking at her. Even in the dim light, she saw they were the same sky-blue eyes.

Miracles

Maureen Seaton

I am a miracle. Not
the only miracle. A fox

living in the dark perfume
of the reservoir

counts. You,
from your father's bed—

pure, intact, that
aqua light. Is it

greedy to gather berries
from the cliff-face,

gulp them, your other hand
free to clasp air? I

sensed a hollow where
his small flame lingered

among ash. Now color
pours from my hands.

When I touch you,
the heat startles. You say:

Here are the miracles:
the fox, the berries,

the child, grown lovely
and gorged with light.

Poem Containing a Matrix Sentence

Maureen Seaton

"After my mother beat my ass, I'd sleep
like a baby for days," she says, round
in my arms like this smooth egg nestled
in its envelope of wood. She sculpts
ceaselessly through white heat of August while
insects welt her incandescent skin, through nights
of raccoon and gold moon above the woodpile.
The woman I love is obsessed
with perfection, beginnings of life held
in suspended animation—like a babe
before disintegration of the matrix
and childlike hope begins. "The woman
is obsessed" is the matrix sentence, "I
love" the core of perfect life within.

For Liam When He Grows Up

William Reichard

She told me she named him William,
Liam for short, for the Gaelic in him,
and now I should know,
at least in title, I would live.
She would see to my legacy,
and I let it pass, though I did not care
to see a child called after me
after most of the brandings
I have worn.

Some days I sing lullabies to those unborn,
all of my sons and daughters,
and I wait for the things
I do not want: those children,
that kind of family, a wife.

Some days I wonder if my mind
will change and I let the thought through
as I search for that particular desire,
the longing for a child,
in a chest that does not
accommodate the need.

And some days (most days)
I just sit; content to seek
what my love will bear,
what his love will create with mine,
and there is never a child here,
not from our twin hands.

She carries Liam in her arms
and that sweet flesh,

the flaxen hair and water eyes
speak for her.
Now, she has found a new voice,
and it will carry and comfort her
through another seventy years.
By then, I will be dead.

I give her my proxy to bear all my children:
William and Billy and Willy and Bill
faggot and cocksucker, homo and queer.
I will her my legacy of names and hates,
and she passes on the small memorials:

in the searing laughter of a growing child,
in cards sent at Christmas to
"Dear Uncle Bill, funny uncle,
I hope you are well."

When You Were Young and Had a Rescue Complex

Renée Lynn Hansen

It is true, as your mother has often said, that the house was never finished. The subdivision that was supposed to go in over the field of corn never materialized. The fields stayed until Berry Fields took over your subdivision, eventually building a shopping mall there.

But at the time you believed the cornfields would be there forever, running forever into the horizon. Suburbs sprang up around you while your house sat in the middle of the cornfield.

The bedrooms to your house hadn't been built yet, and so you grew up in the dining room. Your parents slept in the living room on the mattresses that were laid on the floor at night and put up against the wall during the day. You remember sleeping in the dining room on a green cot while your brother slept on a brown one. You kept clothes in the toyboxes with the toys. None of this bothered you too much, though it is true, at times, that you were vaguely aware that your family needed to be rescued from its rescuer, that is, your father, and you would watch TV for the contests that you could enter and win and the prize would be a house.

Beyond your four-room unfinished house, there was nothing but cornfields. Your father called the cornfields "the oceans," and this struck you as being true. Your father was excellent at uttering truths. He was terrible at day-to-day living, at responsibilities. For instance, he never remembered to stop off at the market when he said he would. He never remembered what grade you were in, nor did he know your middle name, or your exact age, when the questions came up.

But it was true that the cornfields, when they were waist high and silvery in the moonlight, looked like the oceans. In August, the cornfields came in from all sides and lapped at the edges of the windowsills. One field ended at the stable, another at the forest preserve; and the square of corn along the western horizon began a mile away, at Army Trail Road, and ended at your house. You liked to play in the corn when you were young. You wonder if you were morbid, playing in the corn and looking up at the sky and thinking that when you were dead that's exactly where you would be. On the other hand, you had fantastic daydreams there about how you would be famous; you would fall in love with someone beautiful and go to beautiful parties where you would make a beautiful couple, and you would travel together, go to Rome for the weekend winetastings and then come back to your beautiful mansion in Chicago.

Scattered in the cornfields were the piles of lumber for the rest of your house, which your father meant to build soon. You liked to listen to him talk about it. There would be a swimming pool, and a high waterfall made of boulders, all built inside something he called "The Crystal Palace." The Crystal Palace would be the glass-enclosed midsection of the house. It would contain palm trees, rocks, waterfalls, and a garden under glass. Built around the Crystal Palace, in a sort of Pentagon shape, would be the three bedrooms, the den, and the master bedroom suite. All rooms would lead to and from the Crystal Palace. "You see, you kids, we can come out of our bedrooms each morning, with the sleep in our eyes, and walk into the Crystal Palace and continue our dreams right there as we stand awake!" He would say this over dinner, which became quiet because your mother never responded. He would take a pen and a piece of paper out of his pants pocket and sketch it for you several times. He would get so worked up over his drawing that he would set his fork down, then go outside and start working on it. He would move around some rocks, setting them into a particular spot. The rock pile did resemble the waterfall—you noticed that one day, shortly before his death, as you stood next to the rock pile, looking at it.

You get nostalgic often. You don't know what triggers nostalgia— your strong desire to remember sentiments—but you are nostalgic. You remember the impact of events more than the events themselves. You remember that after your father died your mother became more beautiful. She had her thick hair cut into a pageboy. She began to wear cashmere sweaters. You remember that after your move to the city, your brother, Thomas, became more calculating. When he was ten, he somehow learned the art of wiring. He gutted every radio, TV, and telephone in his efforts to learn. From age ten through twelve he made his living as an electrician. The nuns at the Catholic grammar school down the street paid him $250 to rewire classrooms K through five. He put all his money in the bank, and when he was fourteen he bought a black Ford Mustang, which he garaged for a year until he could learn how to drive it. By this time you had moved to downtown Chicago. After your father's suicide, your beautiful mother got a good job at the same bank your father had worked at. She moved her family to a glass high-rise in the city, where you all worked on forgetting.

And now, finally, this summer it seems that all you can do is remember. You take walks and try to remember; you sit on your beach a few steps outside your beach house and try to remember; you eat breakfast and stare out the window of the white beach house and try to remember. You are trying to remember if you ever saw or knew of anything that was complete, or if you ever came across something that would complete you and you somehow missed it.

You remember digging in the dirt, and sitting around the stables, and watching the Molls plant their crop, and you remember the carnival that went up once near the stables, and that was the summer your father committed suicide, the summer of the carnival next to the stables. Really, you cannot know for absolute certain whether he did commit suicide because he was alone at the time. He was alone at the wheel and it was near sunset and the sun could have been in his eyes when he drove his car into the tree. But you are old, too old to sit around and come up with a percentage, the chance that it was not suicide. It was suicide. When you look back on it, you can see it clearly, as clearly as you can discern and expound upon the great themes of any art movement.

And so your father committed suicide one summer. He was coming home from work one late summer evening and he drove his car into a tree and it happened to be a tree on the Molls' farm. The Molls were huge, interesting men. Each one of them was tall, with gaunt cheeks and sunken faces. They rode tall green tractors that were nearly as high as a house. You almost never got to see a Moll except early in the morning when they walked from their front porch out into the fields to the tractors. It was a solemn march, a father with three sons at his side, all of them squinting into the sun as they walked toward their tractors. You remember that once when you were on the Molls' farm road, you were in the car with your mother and you saw an older woman with long, soft, gray hair, and she looked kindly at you as you passed in the car. You craned your neck out the back. You asked your mother who that might be. "Mrs. Moll, I think," she said. "Why do you ask?" You didn't know what to answer. You were left speechless by Mrs. Moll's silvery beauty. You wanted to rescue Mrs. Moll. You began asking questions. Well, how long had the Molls been there? Did they own all the land? Did their fathers own all the land? Or might Mrs. Moll own the land? Who was Mrs. Moll married to? Had anyone heard if she wanted to get off the farm or not? Not once did anyone have an answer for you. At some point you concluded that the Molls were like stones—they had been there since the land began—but that Mrs. Moll was different and that one day you would have a chance to speak to her and tell her what you thought. She would understand you completely, and you, her. It was not long after your rescue complex formed over Mrs. Moll that your father's car crashed in the Molls' cornfield. The car crashed, in fact, against the only tree that stood in the Molls' cornfield.

It was the Molls who came by and brought the news of his death.

You were playing on the cement patio in front of your house, which your father had just poured and smoothed the week before, when the three men came walking slowly through the corn. They walked so slowly and evenly that it seemed they were floating, and when they came across the patio they seemed like ghosts. They made a slow stop together and the elder Moll knocked on the screen door. Your mother came to the door. At first she stood silently on the other side, but then she opened it. She stood erect. Her face seemed frozen. They spoke in low murmurs. "Sorry, sorry, sorry," they seemed to be saying. They turned away and your mother clutched at the door for strength. You remember the Molls, tall, with their shoulders hunched, disappearing back into the fields. Off in the distance you could see the solid form of Mrs. Moll, her silvery hair blowing in all directions. She was waiting for them; she had sent them. You seemed to know this. Then you turned back toward your mother, who was now standing behind you. Her fingers brushed your neck. She said, "Come with me." You went back around to the side of the house where the rocks were piled for the Crystal Palace waterfall, and you sat on the rocks and she told you. "Your father is dead," she said. And she explained how he died, how Mr. Moll had tried to save him. And you did not cry, because even at that age you thought you were advanced. Too advanced to cry. You were not surprised, not too surprised. "At least he got what he wanted; he is free, and we are free . . ." You had cynical thoughts along those lines. And because at that age you were deep in your rescue complex, you thought you would be strong for your mother.

Mister Kenny

A Memoir

Robert Rodi

THE current reputation of sixties suburbia as a paradise of homogeneity for middle-class nuclear families is a bit off the mark. I lived in one such suburb, Sherwood Village, a development outside Chicago where all the houses were new and all the trees were saplings. And while the cookie-cutter division of blocks and lots was indeed designed to accommodate as many Mom-Pop-Junior-Sis incursions as possible, anomalies persisted. In Sherwood Village there were two short, blocky apartment buildings where dwelt some older widows and widowers, a few retirees, and some younger families of dubious quality. And Mister Kenny.

He was old—how old I can't say, because to us kids anyone older than eighteen seemed ancient. But Mister Kenny told us he'd been in the war, so we knew he was pretty near prehistoric. (We didn't ask *which* war because they were all far enough off to be equally irrelevant.) We got to know him because he was the only one who tended the flower beds that ran around the perimeter of the two apartment buildings. He'd come out wearing a smock, a wide-brimmed hat, and enormous canvas gloves, carrying a plastic basket filled with gardening tools. Then he'd set himself down by a different section of the beds each day and proceed to spend hours fussing over the blooms. We kids, in our wild roving and ranging, were inevitably attracted to something so patently odd. (A man, gardening? In a *lady's hat?*) We surrounded him, asked him what he was doing, why he was doing it, what would happen if he didn't do it, why he didn't have an office to go to, and all the other questions that seemed so urgent to our feverish half-formed minds. He answered as well as he could, working methodically, rooting out weeds, turning the soil, trimming the encroaching bushes. Polite man. It was only a matter of time before he invited us into his apartment. (He served us Popsicles, which, looking back, I can only assume he bought specifically for us.) In the early sixties, in midwestern suburbia there was nothing unwholesome or alarming about children being invited into strange houses without their parents' knowledge. Far from it; part of the supposed glory of such communities was precisely that they were a safe haven for families of a certain caliber and that all doors would therefore be open to any and all of the neighborhood kids. Even so, my parents—Mom, in particular—seemed a little uncomfortable at the prospect of our spending so much time ensconced in Mister Kenny's lair. "You should be outside, playing," she'd say, unwilling to forbid us outright. "The weather's so beautiful." But we were fascinated by Mister Kenny's apartment because it was one of the few homes to which we had access that wasn't ruled by children. It was a strictly adult domain, and despite its tidiness and order Mister Kenny allowed us to root through it, to pull out photographs and knickknacks and say what's this and who's that and where did this come from. We were especially intrigued by any photographs from the Olden Days, as we called them. Mister Kenny had a lot of those, albums full. Many dated from the war. I recall shots of him, thin and pale and smiling and twentyish in bell-bottoms, on the bow of a ship, so I suppose he must have been in the navy, but to us kids any branch of the service—navy, air force, marines—fell under the blanket heading of "army." The snapshots from Mister Kenny's later, civilian life were mainly of him sitting in dark rooms squinting at the flash with other thin, pale men in skinny ties and white socks, which we found utterly hilarious. It was a special treat to find a photograph of a woman because she would invariably be wearing something even funnier, but pictures of women were few in Mister Kenny's albums. Mister Kenny had a record collection, too, which consisted mainly of boxed sets of operas. He would occasionally try to play us an aria from one of these, telling us to listen, children, just listen to the melody, but as soon as he set the needle on the vinyl and the trill of the soprano filled the room, we would clutch our necks and make choking sounds, and Mister Kenny would have to give it up. We much preferred his small but intoxicating collection of novelty records. He had "Hinky-Dinky Parlay-Vous" and "Mairzy Doats & Dozy Doats" and our special favorite, "High Hopes," which we called the "Whoops Song" (because of "Whoops-there-goes-another-rubber-tree-plant"). When we found out that Mister Kenny had lived in Chicago, we asked him if he'd known Al Capone, who we knew from *The Untouchables*. He laughed and said he'd been a mere boy when Capone died, but he *had* met Ava Gardner. *Who?* A very great movie star. And Joe Kennedy. *Who?* President Kennedy's father. Oh. We were singularly unimpressed. What value was there in having met anyone's father? Shortly thereafter my sister Cindy became disturbed by what she perceived as Mister Kenny's loneliness, and we decided he ought to be married. It seemed too odd that there was not (and as far as we'd been able to tell, never had been) a Mrs. Kenny. We scoured the neighborhood for possible candidates, finally settling on Mrs. Choake, the old widow half a block away who wore her nylons rolled around her ankles and who always cracked us up by the way she trilled "yoo-hoo" like a character in a cartoon. We thought she was a good catch because, even though none of us had ever said a word to her, she hadn't gotten angry the previous winter when a snowball thrown by Toby Jelnick had gone awry and hit her in the head. Instead, she'd bent down, cobbled together a snowball of her own, and thrown it right back at Toby. When it fell short by about four yards, she'd just shrugged, laughed, and gone on her way. With a cool attitude like that, she'd be perfect for Mister Kenny, we thought. So we went and found him gardening. "Does Mrs. Choake ever come talk to you while you're gardening?" we asked him coyly. "Not if I see her coming first," he said. We weren't exactly sure what he'd meant by that, but it was enough to put us off our plan. One day Mister Kenny foolishly let it slip that he still had his old uniform, and we were unrelenting in our pleas to see it. He was forced to submit. We followed him to a closet from which he pulled a cedar chest, and when he crouched down and opened it, releasing that wonderful lift-your-spirits scent, we gathered around it and began gently (for us) folding back the cotton sheets and uncovering the treasures from his past life. Medallions. Binoculars. He even had a canteen, a real canteen. Absolutely thrilling. It was a wonderful afternoon, intimate and exciting and filled with awe and laughter, but I remember, too, that little Gordy Raddatz (Shorty Gordy, we called him) squeezed by me and settled into Mister Kenny's lap to watch the proceedings. Mister Kenny let him sit there for a few moments but appeared enormously uncomfortable—I remember to this day the contortions of his face—and eventually slid free of little Gordy and stood upright for the remainder of our visit.

A summer or two passed, and when I had reached or was about to reach double digits, an incident occurred in which teenage boys pelted Mister Kenny's Cadillac Fleetwood with stones and wrote

"QUEER" on the windshield with tempura paint. None of us actually witnessed this horrific event but got it secondhand from one of the scary kids who lived in Mister Kenny's building. I knew the word "queer" from having read *Alice in Wonderland*, but I couldn't make it relate to Mister Kenny in any real way and was too afraid to ask for an explanation from the scary kid or (especially) from Mom. Confused and more than a little afraid, we stayed away from Mister Kenny after that. I believe it was soon after that my mother finally forbade us to visit Mister Kenny at all, but we'd already stopped on our own, so we didn't ask for a reason. It was too good an opportunity to raise our stock by seeming to obey her without question. We still waved to Mister Kenny when he was out gardening, but only from afar. Then my family pulled up stakes and moved to Oak Brook, a much tonier suburb farther west. We lived in a brand-new development not far from a polo field. Two or three summers later a big fair was held on the polo grounds, and all the kids in the neighborhood looked forward to going. But before the weekend arrived, my mother and father led me into their study and told me I was forbidden to go because they'd heard reports that one of the fair workers had been exposing himself to young boys. "You're old enough to know about such things," they said somewhat nervously. I had a sudden flash of insight that this decree, so like the one that forbade me to visit Mister Kenny's place years before, was founded on a similar fear. But I didn't dwell on it; at fourteen, I was far more intrigued by the idea of somehow getting to the polo fields to see what that fair worker had to show. (Alas, I never made it.) I didn't actively think about Mister Kenny after that, but he remained part of the private language I shared with my brothers and sisters; whenever we would espy a fastidious, prissy older man we would lean close to each other and whisper, "Mister Kenny." Over time such references began to take on a disdainful and even derogatory tone. I had long since learned what "queer" meant, and even though I was wrangling with homosexual longings of my own, I had no intention of allowing them to turn me into Mister Kenny— ineffectual, timid, a joke.

In 1992 my grandmother died and I returned to the old neighborhood. After paying a last visit to Grandma's house, I got in my car and began my drive home. But as I approached the old, squat apartment buildings I found myself thinking about Mister Kenny again, more clearly and with more affection than ever before. I realized he wasn't a joke, that his prissiness and fastidiousness were in fact a refuge for him after a life—an exhausting life—of defiance and anarchy and even criminality. I'd been through a long, hard coming-out process myself and had even become something of a gay spokesman by virtue of my gay-themed novels; I'd been in newspapers and on national television discussing gay this, gay that, and gay the other thing. And here, I realized, was this untapped resource from my youth. A man who must have lived a life of secret signals and hidden liaisons and furtive service affairs, yet who managed to travel in the circles that intersected Ava Gardner's and Joe Kennedy's. A man who had been queer during a time when the country could think of no greater offense, and who had survived, if only barely, to hand out Popsicles to children. A man who had loved men and, as a result, in later life had gently forced a child off his lap because, like Caesar's wife, he'd had to be above suspicion. Not quite knowing what I intended, I pulled into the parking lot of the apartment building and left my car. I checked the legend next to the building's doorbells; it was then that I realized that I'd never known Mister Kenny's last name, and last names were all that were listed here. I crept to the side of the building and climbed the exterior staircase to the second story, where I remembered Mister Kenny's having lived. I glanced at the window of the apartment I thought had been his, but there was a ceramic statue of the Virgin Mary in the window next to a plastic sticker of Jean Claude Van Damme, and I thought *not Mister Kenny* and scampered down the stairs and back to my car. And then I drove home. He was probably dead, I thought. And what would I have said to him, anyway, had I found him? I thought about it. At length. And there was really only one answer.

I would have said, "I know you were a sexual outlaw."

I would have said, "I'm one, too."

I would have said, "Tell me *everything*."

And then I would have listened.

Hell. I might even have sat on his lap.

Part II

"Lake Michigan Sunrise":
The Midwest as Place

Ricardo Garza, "Lake Michigan Sunrise, 1995"

On My Way to Lake Michigan Sunrise on the Milwaukee Lakefront Breakwater

Antler

In spring a smell comes from the Earth,
    my nostrils widen,
And I find myself staying up all night walking,
Remembering how many nights I've stayed up all night
    walking,
Thinking of all the boys asleep
      in beds in the dark houses
      in the sleeping neighborhoods
      surrounding me,
Picturing all the sleeping boys as I pass,
    their postures, expressions, movements,
Wondering which houses walked by
      hold what possibilities
      of warm and carefree young friends,
So close from this sidewalk, behind what doors,
      up what stairs, into which rooms,
      on what beds,
Sleeping boys with erections
      and the postures, expressions, movements
      of sleeping boys with erections
         they never know they have—
I stop, stand motionless for a minute,
    struck by the thought,
Looking up at the stars
    to honor them.
The whole city sleeps,
Not even a solitary car,
The first birds sing in the twilight.
All the erections boys have in their sleep
    and never know they have

I know they have, I feel.
One man in the blue-dark smell of spring
    walking toward sunrise Lake Michigan,
Honoring the boys in the dark sleeping
    with erections they'll never know they had.

A Solstice in Southern Illinois

Jim Elledge

Christmas creaks near,
and the train wheels
rumble, flinging up
snow: first a dusting, then
a smear until farmhouses
and groves, all that lifts above
ground from town to
town, blur, fade to shadows
flickering across a veil.

This morning at Union
Station, folks departed,
arrived. Terminal. Where
we begin, where we end,
the time between—no
distinction, only
flickerings and a lolling
dip and rise of high-tension
lines in two directions
along a track.

Half my life's been spent
elsewhere, one city, the next—
home a load hoisted
onto my back, never lifted
off. The lucky ones stand and stretch
years away, even if up to their
knees in snow, the only trace
of them left behind,
deep footprints headed out.

So much to learn, the hard
way: back is forward—
and back: the same
carols by different voices,
old ornaments on a new
evergreen, remembered faces more
deeply wrinkled,
and snow to shoe-top,
another flurry expected.

Three generations
down to dinner: they,
my sister and I,
and her child, wriggling
through a balmy ocean, here but
not—like the phantoms
in whose shells
we hear eternity.

Salt into Wounds

Jim Elledge

Maybe lyrics of some oldie I forgot
long ago slipped over my Walkman's ear
phones and catapulted you
over the centuries back into my life,

or maybe the way sunlight sliced
through what few clouds clogged the east
lit you crouched in some corner of my
silly mind as I walked to the office

where others' lives and fantasies
arrive in packets daily, queue at the door
each morning, pat me on the back,
say, "¿*Qué pasa*, babe? Take a load
off. How's the missus, the kiddies?"
and laugh as "Dude" I address each and lean
back in my chair, into sunlight.

One image in a posh clothing store
display window's all it took, a mannequin
white as flesh below tan lines
struck by morning's rays,
arm outstretched, handcuffs
dangling from the cradle of thumb and fingers,
one candle-thin ceiling beam reflecting
off the bracelets'
moody rims.

Frightening, how the years here to
you collapsed, evaporated like contrails
strung one county line to the next,

streaming across a prairie's summer sky.
Strange, when memories register as moments
in a decade. Silly, how broken
down into nanoseconds, one perfect
morning's pain stretches into a century's.

Main Street

Joseph Like

The bow of the blued street
leaves cars beached
next to the shores
of white sidewalks.
How far the ocean is from here,
it's anybody's guess.

Pale awnings scallop out
over the last downtown grocer.
Still the shade pools under them
like a schooled body of fish.
The tail of one flounders
in this August heat.

All the farmers gather
at Cozy's Corner Cafe and dream
of water. Of their wives' hair
floating out from cuneiform of curls,
of coiled buns and platinum
beehives. Of seaweed tangled

in their arms until they wake
to bleached buildings wavering
in the sinking humidity. Tall
dark windows flowing with sunset.

The pink shell of lights,
strung above the street,
glistens, whispers,
calls them back to this sky,
this inverted ocean.

Canto Faggoto

for Jim Perrizo

Don Mager

The faggots of Michigan
they sing in the bushes
their banners are flesh
their voices fly solos
the faggots of Michigan

come in all shapes
they drive fast cars
black, golden, and auburn
or sullen hushed screams
ride water and stone

In Saginaw's delta
Hispanic, Jamaican
the sun draws slow steam
it works them up
Saginaw's faggots
Bay City's faggots

they work the flat fields
in tank tops and cutoffs
from the dike-held lowland
into lathers of thirst
dance hard at the bar
drive noisy cars

In Monroe and Wixom
horsetail hair
they stand in their stations
tight in their T-shirts
overtime hours
the autoplant faggots
the autoplant faggots

they strain against noise
tied up in bandannas
assemble big cars
smoke marijuana
six-day workweeks
cruise while they work
wear the hell out of jeans

In Grand Blanc and Holly
old family land
hard walnut tables
their lovers beside them
after chores after supper
but in Grand Blanc and Holly

they plow out their fields
with grandmothers' quilts
granger-built barns
they raise happy kids
they porch-strum their songs
they get beat by teen gangs

In Marquette and the Sault
wind sirens the fir trees
they walk out in snowshoes

their dreams are of winter
sky masses with cloud
they fish through thick ice

their Chippewa faces
in stove-heated fish shacks
fur skins smell oily
the faggots of Michigan
in Marquette and the Sault

And down in Detroit
teach science in schools
they bike on Belle Isle
alone on streetcorners
their pains are panicked
the faggots of Michigan
have lynx eyes, are cunning

translate ancient time
    their passion grows hot
tongues swirl with sun
    ride water and stone
    love's a slow burn

black faggots drive buses
    go home to wise lovers
    harbinger dances
their glance steels the sun
their laughter holds fire
stunned with desire
they'll impregnate your soul

Honey Sister

Diane Williams

It began as a flurry: a blouse, a sweater, a pair of jeans floating past the windows of the Victory Apartments. Then the blizzard came: a suitcase full of half-packed lingerie and dirty laundry plummeted from the fourth floor—the penthouse floor we called it—and we hurried to our windows to watch. Despite the November chill, tightly closed windows opened slowly so that we would not miss the rush of voices that followed.

"Get out! And I mean now!" Daddy Rae's voice washed over us first, large, growling.

Honey's voice followed, whining in that baby-doll way we had known and envied.

"Oh, Daddy, let me explain."

"Explain what? You brought that woman here . . . that woman . . . here . . . in my sheets . . ."

That woman. And we wondered which of us had dared to walk the tightrope to Honey's bed, to Rae's domain, which of us had felt the silkiness of those sheets. *That woman.*

"You ain't got nothing to explain except why you're still standing here in my face."

All the air fled our lungs at once. We never thought that Rae Ann Clover would ever grow weary of Honey, the girl who had become Rae's sugah dumplin', her butter roll, her sweet and sticky—no matter what Honey did—and Honey always did something. But Rae had tired of her little Amazon toy, and we who should have applauded her release from servitude could only feel sorry for ourselves because when Rae whispered in Honey's ears, we heard Honey's love sighs, too. When she kissed Honey's mouth, we tasted Honey's lips, too.

Now what could we do except remember the first time and the few times in between then and now when we saw Honey with Rae's knowing.

ON the night of Honey's grand entrance into our waking dreams, we did what we usually did on weekend nights. We sprawled for hours in the booths by the jukebox, sipped sodas at the cool Formica-topped counter, filled our bellies with greasy cheeseburgers, and dished each other's dirt. This was our ritual before heading to Chicago's North Side and the white girls' bars.

Then *she* walked into Rae Ann Clover's Big Boy Grill—no, she didn't *walk*. She *glided* in under the rumble of the Lake Street El and sliced through the crowd as though we were not there—like a shark through water—and we could only part for her or bleed from our wounds.

She aimed for Daddy Rae, who was confident in her maleness—fortyish, big-boned, silk-suited—and none of us spoke to that gliding woman or to each other. We merely admired her as she stood shimmering just out of Rae's reach, a woman-child seen in a steamy distance or under seawater. She straddled one of the black padded stools at the counter, gripped it with grown-up thighs, and we tried not to stare as she unfolded against the Formica, stretching in her beat-up bomber jacket. When she looked over her shoulder at us as we coated our lips in Burning Atlanta red, she smiled sphinxlike, and something gave between our thighs.

"Can I help you, miss?"

Rae shifted a toothpick from one corner of her mouth to the other and leaned into the space between Miss Bomber Jacket and herself.

"I hope so, Ms. Clover, ma'am." Miss Bomber Jacket's voice was cotton candy, our carnival craving. "I was hoping you'd remember me."

"Remember you? I don't think I'd forget somebody like you, Miss . . . um . . . what's your name, darling?"

That chilled us. Rae could call her "darling" already, and we could not.

"Wait, let me guess. Oh, and don't call me Miss anything, Honey. I'm just Rae to the folks around here. Now, where do I know you from?"

"Greenwood."

"Greenwood? Mississippi?" Honey answered each query with that smile and a nod. Doors opened and closed in Rae's brain. She smiled in return. "Last summer. The family reunion. You're Old Simon's little girl."

"I'm not really a little girl now, am I?"

We measured her with our stares, shook our heads.

"No, you're not. How could I forget you?"

"You told me to look you up whenever I came to Chicago, and here I am."

"And here you are."

And here you are, we echoed to ourselves.

"I came by bus."

"You came all that way by bus?"

. . . all that way . . .

"I just got a room at the Victory Apartments."

Mention of the apartment building made Rae look at us and remember that she and Miss Bomber Jacket were not alone.

"That's nice, darling. It's good to see you. And you do look older."

"I just turned twenty-one in December."

She unzipped her jacket and revealed a cotton shirt. Goddess have mercy on our wicked souls, but those of us who could, held our breath and counted. The first one, two, three buttons were unfastened, and the creamy tops of her breasts hovered above the stripes of the shirt. Rae's gaze was as heavy as her hands could be, and we could feel her opening the other buttons in her daydreams and reaching in.

"Well, now, Honey, what are we going to do with you now that you're here?"

Honey shrugged, and Rae removed her toothpick and flicked it into an empty glass on the counter.

"Hey, boy, come get these dirty dishes."

At Rae's command the new counter man, Nick, came around the corner, bobbing on his heels as though he were trapped on a rerun of *The Ed Sullivan Show*. He picked up the ketchup-spotted plate and the glass and paused to smile at the Girl in the Bomber Jacket. He was only seventeen and entitled to drool. What excuse could we present to Our Sister?

"Why don't you come around after closing—say nine—and we'll talk about stuff and thangs. All right?"

"Sure."

We sucked our teeth and adjusted our skirts as Honey disappeared through the screen door. We could tell that she had practiced this flirt, but we wondered on whom. She seemed too young and full of Southern sweetness for this tawdriness, no matter how delicious it was . . . and it was delicious.

We knew what would happen when she of the jacket and the faded jeans and the thick black hair appeared at the Grill after closing that night. It had happened to each of us in turn: the fat of us, the thin of us, the peachiest of us, the darkest of us. We had gone through this rite of the Back Room because we had been too young to fully understand it and because it had been expected of us: submission. Submission to Daddy Rae. Submission to men. Submission to anyone who would take advantage of our hunger to become real women. We knew that exactly at nine Rae would open the door when Honey rapped ever so lightly on the frame, not sure of anything except her need for self-preservation. Rae would look out to see if anyone was watching, and if no one were there to set tongues clucking, Rae would be disappointed, but she would still usher Honey into her empty palace and lead her to the throne, a sofa in the back room, and offer her soft promises and hard sex. Honey's careless nipples would harden at the touch, and Rae would soak herself in Honey's brownness, her scents, and compliment her on her womanhood, her lipstick, her long fingernails, the back-scratching kind. Honey would be no dyke, no undefinable woman. She would be ever accessible in that spike-heel sort of way.

And as the night stretched into morning, we would shower, scrubbing our breasts, our bellies, our thighs, our backs as though we could make Honey pure again with our soap and our water. As though we could forgive ourselves for wanting to be where Daddy Rae had been.

The smell of gen-u-ine leather became our opium that spring, and we regretted the passage of cool weather and the coming of T-shirts that made Honey look far too vulnerable. We needed her to remain tough in our imaginations, to fend off soft reality.

Honey attached herself to our consciousness. She rose with us in the morning, rode the El train with us to work, and went to bed with us, all without ever leaving that studio apartment on the West Side.

We wondered what Honey did when Rae was not escorting her in Daddy's 1976 classic Cadillac or pretending to pay attention to customers in the Grill. Then someone on the fourth floor who stayed home except when the checks came told us that she had seen Honey's room fill up with books, boxes of them, hardcover and paper-back, Hemingway and Baldwin, Walker and Lorde. We blushed, un-able to imagine our torn-jeans, barefoot girl reading. We began to read, too, after our days of waitressing and clerking and secretarying. We even memorized lines of Emily Dickinson, hoping to impress.

We invited Honey to dinner. She came to our apartments jacket-less and lonesome. We did not know whom she pined for, but some-one always clouded her face, shadowed her eyes.

We always performed a ritual for her, love rituals we thought we would save for someone else. We set the table with real silverware and plates not made out of paper. We bought real flowers for a center-piece. We bought a roast at the Jewel, fresh snap beans, ice potatoes, and peaches for a cobbler, too. We chilled wine and poured goblets—not jam jars—full for her. She drank, ate, laughed, complimented, and spread herself like a queen on our clean, made-up beds. She talked about slicing open watermelons back home, eating chunks, and letting the sugary juice run down her chin. We bought her water-melon and let her drift into our sleep like a phantasm. We wanted to cradle her, but we did not. Instead we poured more wine and let her curl into our dreams.

A few weeks after her first visit and before the Big Bang, we sat on the hotel steps, savoring an October breeze and crunching leaves un-der our feet. We saw her coming, teetering from the direction of Red's Corner Tap, and we shook our heads, amazed at her early-evening state of drunkenness. She flopped down beside us and whistled a tune we could not decipher.

"It's still hot." When she spoke, it startled us. The sugar was gone.

Yes, we said softly. It is. Are you OK?

"Sure I'm OK. Can't you tell?"

She stank of beer and sweat and cigarettes. Her T-shirt and jeans looked slept in. No, we could not tell.

Are you OK? We repeated our question as though we were talking to a child.

"No . . . I . . . no. I just want to go home."

Words tumbled out; we knew she meant the home of her cold watermelons.

"I miss Rita."

Who's Rita?

"My friend back home. I thought I could make it without her or . . . well . . . or anything, but I miss her all the time now."

Honey's words hung heavily in the air.

"I loved her, you know?"

Yes, we knew.

"She was my . . . my . . ."

Sister.

"Yes, my sister."

And Honey was our sister. And we laughed. Not because anything was particularly funny, but because we understood so fully what she meant.

Honey washed away that night with sleep, and she never mentioned Rita's name again, but the letters began after that, the envelopes stuffed with Greenwood, Mississippi, ones in response to Honey Sister's perfumed notes from Chicago. The more down-home Honey got, the further away from Rae—and us—she became. Nothing—not the cheeseburgers, the boxes of candy, the movies on Saturday night, not even the rent—could keep Honey from slipping away from us. She slipped away from us and into someone else's arms. *That woman's* arms.

We took up a collection to buy Honey a bus ticket back home and went up to give it to her after we heard Daddy Rae's footsteps leaving. Honey was calm, sitting on her bed, wearing nothing but the bomber jacket and a pair of red-striped panties.

"No, please don't," Honey said. "I've been saving this money Daddy Rae gave me. I'm going to go to San Francisco. And I'm taking my friend with me."

She smiled again this sphinxlike smile. And something familiar gave in our bellies.

Digestion

D. Travers Scott

"Putting on a skirt is the second most liberating experience for a man," Ted said proudly. Alan started to ask what the most liberating thing was, but figured it out and bit his tongue. Ted had not been the first to do *that* to him, but he was definitely the first to coax him into a skirt.

"See? Little peasant skirt like this? It's great for housework or just lounging." Ted sat on a folding chair in his closet doorway across from Alan, holding up a thin, ankle-length skirt, maroon and orange batik. Alan pushed his hips closer to Ted's face. Ted knotted the skirt around Alan's waist. Alan grabbed the molding of the bathroom doorway to support himself, leaning out into the hallway. He remembered seeing Ted in this same skirt for the first time: answering his door big, meaty, and barefoot, a bottle of Soft Scrub in hand and sweat pearls on his bare chest, shoulders, and bristly buzzed hair.

"There!" Ted smiled at his handiwork, running his hand across Alan's backside as he stood up.

Alan grinned. He tried to swish a little but his knees were locked.

It was liberating, though, jiggling the weight of his chest, gut, and groin.

"Whiteheads." Gary squeezed out a colony of fragrant curling cylinders, waving the garlic press across the table in Alan's and Ted's faces. Alan noticed the fluorescent ceiling rings, a halo around Gary's thinning dishwater-blond hair. The Patron Saint of Seasonings, Alan thought, framing Gary against the faux-wood paneling of his and Dennis's garden apartment kitchen.

"Gary!" sputtered Dennis, trying to throw his lover a disapproving frown without turning away from his bacon fat and scorched sugar. "That's a nice way to ruin our guests' appetites." He rattled his smoking iron skillet against the gas range. "They haven't even started the bread yet."

"Don't you worry, honey," Dwayne said from the head of the table, twisting a corkscrew in deeper with quick, tight yanks.

"Hey, pus toast's my fave," cooed Ted. He propped his elbows up on the avocado vinyl tabletop, cradling chin in palms dreamily. Alan leaned his chair back on its hind legs and rested against the refrigerator, smiling when his boyfriend looked back at him.

Gary sat down at the corner beside Dwayne, sliding over his glass. "Is this the same cheap stuff you were swimming in Friday night?"

"Oh, no," Dwayne said gravely, eyeing Gary over crooked wire-rimmed spectacles as he poured. "Friday I was sucking down a charming burgundy in a chic cardboard box minikeg."

"Not all you were sucking down," Gary said, taking his glass.

"Dish!" Ted said, scooting closer.

"Oh, child, please." Dwayne tossed his dreadlocks in disdain. He waved for Alan to hold out his glass.

"Was this at Val's party?" Alan said.

"Yes, but I don't know what this one's talking about." Dwayne shook his head.

"That guy following you around all night," Gary said, a touch impatiently. "Didn't you two fuck around?" Alan concentrated on the red wetness nearing his rim, warily recalling childhood spills.

"Ew, honey! Ick. No thank you."

"Dwayne only does snow," Ted explained, shoving his glass under the bottle.

"You don't sleep with other black guys?" Gary asked.

"I already have dreadlocks; I don't need to sleep with anyone else's."

Dennis turned, dabbing the sweat below his gray temples with a cat-shaped oven mitt. "You really should have this conversation with our friend Paul. Don't you think Paul would find this amusing, Gary?"

"Paul's this doctor we know in Houston. Runs the whole damn African-American AIDS project there. He's got real fixed ideas about race and sexuality."

"Yeah, yeah, yeah." Dwayne popped in the cork. "I'm subconsciously racist and self-hating because I only date white guys. I've had that lecture before. Been there, done that, hated it."

Ted shrugged, palms outstretched. "One man's fetish is another man's objectification."

"Oh, talk for days, Miss Chocoholic." Dwayne glanced at Alan and reached over to pat his hand. "Or should I say ex-chocoholic."

"Look out, boys!" Dennis swooped down between them, drizzling hot dressing onto the salad at the table's center.

Alan recoiled his hand. "I do feel kind of pale after meeting his exes," he said and grinned lopsidedly.

"Right, now I'm racist?" Ted jabbed a crusty heel of bread at Dwayne. "I don't recall you ever complaining at the time."

"This is all so novel," Dennis said, removing his oven mitt. "I thought dinge queens and such went out with my generation."

"Dennis!" Gary said, "Don't call our guest a dinge queen! Leave those old school perversions at the Gay Studies Department."

"Do you have a preference, Alan?" Dennis asked politely.

"Oh, no. Of course not. No preference," he lied.

"I'll say," said Dwayne. He and Alan exchanged grins. Alan wondered if Dwayne knew he was the only black guy he'd ever slept with.

"You're not the only one," Ted said proudly and prodded Alan in the shoulder. "Al did pretty well himself Friday, I hear."

Alan stared at Ted, taken aback by his confession made public.

"So that's why you weren't at Val's," Gary said.

Alan threw together a grin he hoped could be read as either pride or modest embarrassment. He wasn't sure what was expected.

"Did you have a recent tryst?" Dennis asked Alan expectantly.

"Oh, you're calling it," Dwayne chided Ted. "You got busy yourself after the Gran Fury lecture." Alan's fingers twitched in the middle of tearing bread.

"Guess you're right," Ted said carefully, looking out of the corner of his eye at Alan.

Alan concentrated on Dennis's face, not acknowledging Ted.

Ted went on. "I guess we're even now, so I can tell you about—"

Alan cut him off loudly. "I had this nostalgic fling with an old beau of mine. He and his new girlfriend were fighting." He spoke determinedly, commanding the table and silencing Ted.

"Getting some straight dick!" said Gary.

"Home-wrecker," said Dwayne with a deadpan gasp of mock shock.

"My lover, the he-whore," Ted added.

Gary raised an eyebrow. "So it's 'lovers' now?" he asked.

Alan and Ted exchanged glances, mouths partially open.

"Oh, Ted?" Alan said lightly, hoping to make a joke. "What would you say we are currently? 'Significant others'?" Alan twisted the words with sarcasm, but eyed Ted closely.

"Oh," Ted said nonchalantly, "I'd say you're my . . . steady hole."

Alan fought a smile, tickled by Ted's vulgarity. He turned to Gary, nodding soberly. "Steady hole. That's what I'd say, too."

Dennis threw open the oven door. "But you obviously sleep with others?" He bent and poked the roasting red bell peppers.

"Yeah," Ted promptly said.

"Wonderful." Dennis waved his fingers at his lover. "Gary, get the broccoli from the fridge."

Dwayne held up his right hand. "I can vouch for that."

"Gang Bang of Four?" Ted asked.

Dwayne smiled. "First time I ever met Alan was at this all-night party I had after the National Healthcare demo here last spring. He and Ted and I, and this ACT UP boy from Detroit, all became . . . better acquainted . . . on my living room futon." He sliced a veiny red sliver of pepper. "These look delicious. Are they stuffed?"

"Lamb, capers, mushrooms . . ." Dennis frowned. "Something else . . ."

"That's how Alan and I met," Ted said proudly.

Everyone at the table looked at them. Alan smiled benignly. Through radish-stuffed cheeks, he said, "It was a new experience for me."

"So you are an open relationship," Gary concluded.

"We're both committed to each other," Ted said, "but we don't own each other. We do care about each other a lot, but we still have our own lives."

"We take each situation as it happens," Alan began carefully. "The only ground rule or requirement we've established is to be honest about what happens and how we feel." He drank wine, wondering if he sounded too stern. The table seemed quiet and his mouth was stinging. He suddenly realized he was the youngest man there.

"Men and monogamy just don't mix," Dwayne said. "Can you name one successfully monogamous relationship? Certainly not Den and Gary."

"Damn right," barked Gary.

"No," Dennis said defensively, "but we have never claimed to be. We both agreed early on that sexual monogamy was a ridiculous heterosexist notion based on archaic patriarchal attitudes of owning women. Being gay men, we were free from such misogyny and had the opportunity, power, and potential to create alternate relationship paradigms."

Alan wondered if this was how Dennis had proposed to Gary. A bite of lamb coated his throat with gamy grease.

"Fucking around wasn't a health risk then, either," Gary added.

"And where do you draw the line, anyway?" Dwayne asked. "Dave Wilkinson's husband nearly choked me to death with his tongue last month at the City Hall kiss-in."

"But that's an altogether different issue," Dennis said. "That was for politics."

"I always keep an eye on Ted at those things," Alan said, listening for Ted to laugh. "Some of those activist boys are just too cute."

"I've got to agree with Dwayne," Ted said. "I think—for queers at least—marriage is an unnatural concept or, for that matter, any sort of long-term relationship."

Alan tongued a piece of fat out onto his napkin. He waited for someone to challenge Ted. No one did.

"But can't monogamy be a healthy experiment?" he asked. "Of course, no relationship is immune to infidelity forever, but can't an indefinite period of attempted monogamy be a vital *stage* in a relationship? Can't you learn valuable lessons about yourselves, intimacy, jealousy, stuff like that?" Alan blushed angrily at having used the word "stuff." "As long as the couple is honest in their communication of needs and how they change, can't a monogamous *phase*— whether at the beginning, middle, or end of a relationship—be a legitimate growth experience?" Alan exhaled and looked over to the stove to see if there were more courses.

"Sure," Dwayne said.

Everyone double-checked his silverware.

Dennis got up to get more wine.

"Ted, honey, you going to bring this one to Dogwood Lakes this year?" asked Dwayne.

"That summer drag camp you all go to?" Gary asked.

"The Radical Faeries, yeah." Ted set down his silverware. "But it's so much more; it's a whole movement of exploring gay male identity—"

"And fabulousness," added Dwayne.

"And spirituality." Ted spoke excitedly, his food forgotten. "It's a mixture of pagan nature religions, sexual liberation, identity rediscovery and redefinition. We're trying to reembrace our faggot histories as shamen, people with unique gifts to see between worlds."

Dwayne leaned in on his elbows. "Where else can you sit in an isolated forest, listening to the loons echoing off the lake—"

Ted did the obligatory Kate Hepburn: "The loons, Norman, the loons!"

"While tying ribbons in some macrobiotic boy's pubic hair?"

"Or paint your toenails by a roaring bonfire?"

"Or pierce your nipples during high tea?"

"Or get a tattoo in a log cabin?"

"Or spontaneously burst into the Mary Tyler Moore theme song while watching the Northern Lights?"

Dennis looked at Dwayne and Ted intently. "So it's something of a campy subversion of the Robert Bly experience?"

Dwayne sat back in his chair. "Oh, please. The Faeries predate that old goat by ten years. Harry Hay called the first gathering in . . . what was it? '80 or '81."

Alan shifted his weight in his chair and tried not to scowl. He'd heard these stories and manifestos all year.

"There is drumming and dancing and serious ritual work," offered Ted.

"Like burying yourself in dead leaves for three hours?"

"I was processing some issues that day."

Dwayne pointed at Dennis. "Don't tell me these Iron John macho boys with their adolescent initiation never-never-land crap have a goddamn solar-powered disco surrounded by thirty-foot trees with strobe lights and Vikki Sue Robinson blasting up to the full moon."

"Do you have special names?" Dennis asked, replacing the empty plates with clean bowls.

"Lamé," beamed Dwayne.

"Prairie Anus," said Ted sheepishly.

Alan stopped making circles in his gravy so that Dennis could take his plate.

Gary stretched back. "What was that about macrobiotic boys?"

"Vegetarians have such unpleasant body odors," noted Dennis.

"Thanks, Den."

Dwayne fanned himself with his hand. "Let me tell you, child . . ."

Dennis set down four cartons of sorbet in the center of the table. "Alan, did you know all this would be going on there?"

Alan reached for raspberries and cream swirl. "Oh, yeah, I'd heard all about it." He set the carton beside his bowl. "I mean, I talked to Ted about it beforehand."

Dennis looked at him quizzically.

Alan picked up a large spoon. "We had just started to date regularly then." He caught everyone's eye, even his own, twisted upside down in the spoon. "I mean, I told Ted I didn't mind if he slept with these other guys there. I mean, I expected it."

He stabbed the spoon into the dessert.

Dennis laughed. "No, I mean how could you stand missing out on all those boys yourself?"

Alan blinked.

Ted lunged forward and grabbed the Italian lemonade. "Oh, Dwayne is exaggerating. I only slept with a couple of guys there. It was no big deal."

Alan licked his spoon. "Of course you didn't tell me about them till three days after you got back."

Ted dished out the sugary ice. "Well, it was just Buck. You already knew him—"

"And Orpheus and Sky Bear and the HIV-positive redhead from Tennessee."

Dennis sat down. Ted and Alan ate. "Well," Gary said with cream on his lower lip, "the forest and all the frolicking sound great, but you don't have to go to the boonies for sex. You can just walk three blocks to Reverchon Park for that."

Dennis touched Gary's shoulder. "The park's closed at night, dear. Has been for about three years."

"Well, you know what I mean."

"Anyway," Dennis said, "at our advanced years—"

"Speak for yourself, Den."

"Sex isn't such an all-consuming issue anymore. Over ten years we've found plenty of other things to worry about."

Dwayne sat up straight. "I just go to the baths. Thank goodness we live in a city that still has them. I carry condoms and spermicidal lube in my fanny pack."

Ted reached to the center of the table, inspecting the remains in the cartons. "You want any more, Al?" he said.

"No thanks," Alan said. "I love this stuff but I'll make myself sick."

Ted looked at him. "You're probably right." He looked at the sweet sweating piles. "You probably don't want to listen to me bitch about my stomach cramps all night again, either." He scooped out a fingerful, licked it off, and popped the lid back on the carton.

ALAN listened to Ted in the bathroom, feeling his own guts descend. Hanging upside-down from Ted's lofted bed, he felt safely dizzy and disoriented. He closed his eyes and watched the optic fireworks. He heard Ted spit out toothpaste; the door of the medicine cabinet jangled shut. Ted pissed, flushed, and the light switch clocked off. The soft padding of Ted's bare feet crept toward him, sticking to and peeling off the hardwood floors. They stopped beside him. Alan anticipated the sensation of Ted touching his stretched-taut abdomen.

Ted kissed each of his nipples. "Dennis's lamb give you a coronary?"

Alan breathed deep, smelling his lover. "Fat-stuffed peppers . . ." He curled upward until their faces were parallel. "I just got tense sitting all night. Feels good to stretch my back out."

Ted ran his hands along Alan's sides. Alan leaned back, Ted's arms circling and supporting him.

"Did you not have a good time?" Ted asked.

"Oh. No, they're nice," murmured Alan.

"Gary and Dennis are so sweet."

"I just like being just with you sometimes."

"I'm glad you could stay over."

Alan closed his eyes. He could smell his lover's soapy face, dank breath, smoky hair, and acrid sweat, all so very close to his own.

The Sighting

Maureen Seaton

Two people are murdered in Woodstock,
Illinois, a murder of gin and vengeance.
Their child—altar boy, A-student, murderer—
escapes to the Wisconsin Dells where
he's sighted on the water slide, now
entering the Cave of Mounds, now running
through the labyrinthine House on the Rock.
Back home, the neighborhood is bereaved,
terrified.
        My sister, two blocks away
with her new baby, says: How do you stab
two people at the same time? And calls a friend
from bible study whose husband serves
as detective in Woodstock. What constitutes
a sighting? she asks. The woman is helpful,
confident. Her voice, evangelical,
helps Melissa through the night without
Dan who's delivering speedboats in Jersey.
I choose this day to tell her I'm gay.

Christmas in the Midwest

Maureen Seaton

I brought a lover home
in midwest snow.
My parents said:
You sleep here, he there,
so we made love here
and there when the garage door slammed
and the house beat like a clock
around us. I dreamed

I was arrested
in a VW bug with the stick shift
hard against my leg
by the Cary police force shining
high beams on my breasts. Why
does sex ignite authority?

My parents received word
of my defection to women
peaceably. They pretended not
to be surprised—
"the way the world is . . .
the way men are . . ."—
and said they'd treat her
kindly at Christmas
as they would any female friend.

They made no mention
of "here and there." We slept
like children in a double bed
beneath handmade quilts,
trying heroically to stay afloat
without their disapproval, the headlights
of a straight society to validate us.

A Flicker of Apocalypse

Maureen Seaton

If the man who called you nigger in Dominick's parking lot
had only dialed 1-800-882-Mary earlier today,
he may have been a better Boy Scout. I bet
his wife would be patting him right now, saying: Meatloaf?
It seems there's been heavy-duty Jesus activity
on the East Coast lately and His mother is behind it.
I see Him bodysurfing in the Atlantic, sharing parables
of large North Shore families and small sea urchins
with teenagers and sandy toddlers. I wonder where
He's hiding—prefab in Wantagh? Coach house in Old Westbury?
We'd been supermarket shopping as usual, a little
decaf, a few oranges, and this Christian man of uncertain
origin spits at the parking lot and says the word.
It sounds like "igga" or "neeah," but you get the point,
and you look at him with one of your kiss-of-death looks,
your obeah-in-the-blood-there's-a-knife-in-my-pocket glower,
and his wife begins to pull on his sleeve like a little girl,
whimpering. And clouds marshal in from the South Side.
And I swear the lights click on at this exact moment.
Every pigeon stands still. Every Toyota. Only the streamers
and banners over Dominick's parking lot rustle in the wind.
I send you my message by archangel—Honey, between us
we could choke this skinny man before the courtesy patrol
arrives to collect his cart. So religion falls shorter.
In reality, his wife dragged him away to a tasteless roast.
And we stood shaking in the light of the all-night supermarket
until the archangel released Chicago and carried us home.

Victims of Circumstance

Gary Pool

"LET's at least check into the possibilities," Jason was saying. "I mean, you never know anything until you try. Right?"
I was skeptical. "If we go through with this," I said, "it's going to
bring us totally out. Everyone will know we're gay, so if you have any
reservations about taking a long walk in the hot sun of public scrutiny,
you had best leave them behind."

"Come on, Craig. We've never tried to hide the fact that we're
gay," Jason countered. "Everyone knows that two men, both in their
middle thirties, don't live together for nearly seven years just because
they're roommates."

"It's seven and *a half* years, and I wouldn't take too much for
granted. This isn't New York or San Francisco, you know. It's important to lots of straight people, especially on the fringe of the Bible
Belt, that that which is unsaid remain unsaid."

"But why?" Jason asked. "I don't get it."

"Well, part of the reason may be that they like you. They know
you."

"What?!"

"They feel they couldn't be friendly with a fag, Jason, so they just
ignore all the signs. That way the social order is maintained. Everybody is kept in a nice, neat, straight little line. Hell, most people
around here would probably answer no if you asked them if they had
ever even *met* a gay person."

"I can't believe it!" he declared. "It's too hypocritical."

"Jason, sweetheart, we've got a Baptist preacher not far from here
who is one of the biggest campaigners in the country against a
woman's right to choose to have an abortion. But the fetal tissue
used to save the life of his own child was a different matter. That
was OK. He is still out there picketing abortion clinics. Talk about
hypocrisy!"

73

"But our friends aren't that way," he objected, slate-gray eyes betraying growing dismay. His right hand swept a disobedient swatch of straight, blond hair from his forehead with a gesture that I had always found irresistible.

"You can't judge this world on the basis of our friends. They aren't the ones who are going to be deciding whether we can adopt a child or not. If we're really serious about this, it might be better if we moved to another part of the country."

"But I don't want to move to another part of the country," he objected. "I like it here. I want to live in Springfield. Our business is here. We've spent the last four years building up that restaurant, and it's the best French restaurant in ten counties."

"It's the *only* French restaurant in ten counties," I interjected, trying to be funny. Jason wasn't laughing.

"We're a part of this community, damn it," he declared, a dark frown overtaking that all-American face of his.

"Well, then maybe it wouldn't have to be a whole other part of the country," I conciliated. "There's always Louisville, or St. Louis, or maybe Kansas City."

"I don't want to move to Louisville, or St. Louis, or Kansas City. We left Chicago because we agreed that we wanted to get away from the big city. We have a right to live where we want, don't we? We're good citizens. We run a profitable business. We support the United Way. We pay taxes, big taxes. Look, we've paid enough property taxes on this house alone to send a half dozen other people's kids to school. I would like to send a kid of our own to school."

Jason had what might be termed the American dream childhood: a house filled with love, lots of siblings to play and grow up with, and enough money to support the whole operation comfortably. He was raised in suburban Chicago, while I was an only child from a small town in south-central Indiana. We share a fairly traditional system of values, which helped to secure our commitment from the very beginning. Jason's upper-middle-class, Episcopalian rearing provided him with a kind of earnestly idealistic view of life and its possibilities. Being the only gay kid, or so I thought at the time, in a small-town high school of fewer than five hundred students, and the son of an alcoholic father who used to beat me like a drum whenever he got drunk, left me with a more—shall we say—pragmatic outlook.

Jason stood in the bay window staring out at the maple trees along both sides of Jefferson Street leading up to the courthouse square. His hands were jammed deep into the pockets of his jeans, and his big shoulders were raised in a kind of frozen shrug. Embracing him from behind, I placed the side of my face against his broad, strong back.

"Maybe we should give ourselves a little more time to think this one over," I murmured.

"Yeah," he sighed, relaxing his shoulders. "Maybe we should."

We did not discuss the subject of adopting a child again for more than a month, though it was never far from my mind, especially when I was alone. Sacrifices would have to be made. Jason and I would have less time for each other. How would the child react to having two gay men for parents? What about the prejudice of other children at school? What about the other parents? Eventually, we did have several lengthy discussions, and we realized that our mutual desire to expand our family to include a child far outweighed all our misgivings.

"We could go on forever with just the two of us," Jason said one Sunday morning in June. "Craig, you know I would never do anything to jeopardize what we have. I think having a kid around would enrich our relationship even more, and if we didn't do it we would always feel that we had missed out on something really important. Don't you think?"

"Well, yes. I guess so. I'm a little scared, that's all. This is a big responsibility, bigger than leaving Chicago, bigger than starting the restaurant. Maybe it's bigger than we are."

"We can handle it, Craig. You'll see," he said, grinning like a schoolboy. In every word I could hear that infectious excitement of his drawing me toward him, making me forget all my trepidation. "So what do you want, a boy or a girl?"

"Oh my God! Do we have to decide that, too!?"

Mrs. McCleerey was the very soul of cordiality. Friendly and disarming, she was one of those people who gives the impression, at least, of being totally nonaggressive, nonjudgmental, and interested in everything. She was undoubtedly considered perfect, by whoever it was who had hired her, for the job she now held.

"So, you wish to adopt jointly," said Mrs. McCleerey as she scribbled something on her yellow legal pad. "How very interesting.

Of course we do not discourage single parents in this state, but it is a little unusual, you understand, for two single men to wish to adopt a child jointly.''

"We are a gay couple, Mrs. McCleerey," I said, without dropping a beat. "That is the reason we wish to adopt jointly."

"Oh, I see," she said, eyes widening a bit. "How *very* interesting." She scribbled away furiously on her pad. "Well, there is certainly no law in our state to prevent gay people from adopting. I think perhaps you might have a better chance if one or the other of you should adopt the child as a single parent."

Here it comes, I thought, the moment of truth. "That is not the way we wish to do it," Jason said, beating me to the punch. "We are a committed couple, life partners. The child cannot belong to one of us and not the other. We are a family." I was so proud I could have kissed him right then and there, but I restrained myself manfully.

"I think that's just wonderful," Mrs. McCleerey declared, with overly obvious sincerity, dropping her pencil onto the legal pad as she leaned forward across her desk and presented us with her most earnest expression. "You two are just about the most interesting people I think I have ever met. Well, we will just have to see what we can do to help you fellows, then. Now where was I? Oh yes. We have our standard agreement that we require you to sign, which sets forth the terms and the fees and all that sort of thing. I'll have that drawn up right away. Then we need financial statements from you both and references for our background check. Now then, do you have any preference as to the child's sex?''

"No," Jason and I said simultaneously.

"Oh. Well, how really very interesting, indeed. I'd have certainly put my money on a boy for you two. That's for sure," she chirped, as the pencil raced across the yellow paper.

"We discussed it," Jason informed her, "and we decided that if we were the child's biological parents it wouldn't matter, so why should it matter to us as gay parents?''

"Oh, I think that is just so special," cooed the unctuous Mrs. McCleerey, wagging her tastefully coifed head from side to side. "Now, let me caution you a little about age. The younger the child, the longer the waiting list. Also, Caucasian babies are very highly prized so—''

"Mrs. McCleerey," I said, the slightest note of annoyance creeping into my voice, "we would like to have a child. It would be nice if that child were somewhere between the age of one and puberty. The sex, race, or color does not matter to us."

"You are such an interesting man, Mr. Preston. Oh, and you, too, Mr. Collier," she added, turning her gaze upon Jason. "I'll just have these forms drawn up, and I'll be right back."

After the door closed, Jason rolled his eyes and announced, "If she says that one more thing is 'interesting,' I will have to strangle her on the spot."

"Oh, that would be just so very special of you," I mimicked. A moment later Mrs. McCleerey, heels telegraphing on the tiles, reentered the room.

"Now then," she said, settling herself back into the chair behind her desk. "If you will just sign right there, Mr. Collier, and you on the line below, Mr. Preston, we will be all set. Good. That's it. Thank you both so much. I'll need your financial statements and lists of references as soon as possible. Since your preferences are so nonspecific, we will be able to put you on several lists." She stood up and extended her right hand to me across the desk. "It has been so interesting meeting both of you fellows," she said, offering her hand, in turn, to Jason.

THREE weeks after our meeting with Mrs. McCleerey she telephoned to inform us that her review of our finances and our "backgrounds" had revealed us to be among the best-qualified adoptive parents she had ever worked with.

"Oh, and I've heard such marvelous things about your restaurant," she gushed, "especially from your friends over at the college. What's it called again?"

"L'Île-de-France," I replied.

"That's right! Oh, I've never been any good with foreign languages. Well, I guess you don't have to be able to pronounce it for it to taste good," she joked.

"That's right, Mrs. McCleerey," I said, trying my best to laugh convincingly. "Well, thanks for calling. Hope to hear from you soon. Good-bye." I'm sure she means well, I considered for a moment after hanging up the phone. She's just slightly crackers.

Then the waiting set in. After three weeks Jason called the agency but could find out nothing. Another two weeks passed without word.

More phone calls were placed. Two months passed, then three. Finally, on the second of October, Mrs. McCleerey called us. She had a nine-year-old boy named Andrew she would like us to meet.

"There are a few things you should know about the boy before you even decide if you should meet each other," she told Jason over the telephone while I listened from the extension in the kitchen. "There is no point in setting you or Andrew up for a big disappointment." She explained that Andrew's mother had put him up for adoption as soon as he was born. "She was not married to the father, and then he deserted her during the pregnancy. She was only eighteen at the time of birth, and a high-school dropout, and did not possess the wherewithal to support both herself and the child. Her family refused to take them in, and the welfare authorities all but forced her to relinquish custody of the child to the state."

"Why wasn't he adopted as a baby?" I asked.

"Most probably because he's mulatto," she replied, with a deep sigh. "Mulatto children are frequently the hardest to place. White families don't want them and black families don't want them. Of course, we seldom see any mixed-race children around this part of the country. Just your usual garden-variety black or white," she laughed, amused by her own little joke.

"What happens if he isn't adopted?" Jason asked, no mirth in his voice.

"He will probably go back into foster care. He's been in care several times before."

"What happened in foster care?" I asked.

"Let's see here, once he was returned after eight months because the foster parents found Andrew incompatible with their own children."

"Incompatible?" I said, puzzled. "How incompatible? In what way?"

"Oh, that just means they didn't get along."

"Who didn't get along? Andrew or the other kids?"

"Well, the file indicates that Andrew did not get along well with the other children. Of course, you have to understand that in a situation where there is friction between the foster child and children who are already in the home, it is usually the foster child who will receive the blame. After all, the foster child can be returned to the agency; the family's biological children cannot." She gave another nervous laugh.

"What about the other foster care situations?" asked Jason.

"Let me check the file," she said, and we could hear her shuffling papers about. "In the most recent case, Andrew ran away after five months. Hmm . . . there was some evidence of physical abuse."

"Abuse? What kind of abuse?" I wanted to know.

"It appears he was beaten," she replied.

"Was this substantiated?!" I pressed her, shocked and feeling the muscles tense up in the back of my neck.

"Yes."

"So, the kid's foster father was beating him up."

"No," she said. "The foster mother."

There followed a kind of stunned silence. "Is there anything else we should know?" Jason managed at last.

"Let me see here. Did above average on his intelligence test," she said, rather matter-of-factly. "Does poorly in school, though. Seems to lack sufficient motivation. Hmm . . . some emotional problems. Quiet and withdrawn at times. Is afraid of the dark. Cannot stand to be left alone." Then, "No, you're probably not interested in this little guy after all. Too many problems, and nine years is getting a bit old for adoption. We'll just have to keep looking, I guess, until the—"

"How about if Craig and I talk this over for a while and get back to you?" Jason interrupted. "We wouldn't want to be too hasty, now would we?"

"Certainly not, Mr. Collier. Most certainly not. You just take all the time you need. You know where to find me when you have reached your decision. Good-bye, gentlemen."

Later at home Jason sat, resting his elbows on his desk, thumbs supporting his chin and his folded hands over his mouth. I took a seat on the leather sofa against the wall opposite the desk. We sat there watching each other, looking for some sign, some indication of how we felt, until I could hold out no longer.

Jason knew how I felt about battered children, having been one myself, and that's where I began. "There are so many battered children. This could be an opportunity for us personally to help at least one. Besides, we might have to wait months before another chance to adopt comes along. It seems foolish to let this opportunity pass us by."

"Good. Then we agree," declared Jason. "And don't look so surprised," he added. "You know what a sucker I am for a good sob story. What could I do?" He shrugged, giving me his best Jack Benny imitation. It felt very good to laugh.

AT our first meeting Andrew was quiet and shy. He looked small and lonely seated in one corner of a huge, overstuffed, vinyl-covered sofa, his feet not quite touching the waiting-room floor. He was four feet, three inches tall, and his hair was cut in a kind of mini afro, reminding me of the kinder and gentler days of the mid-1970s. His skin was pure *café con leche* and he gazed out at us, a little apprehensively, through large dark eyes. Andrew seemed determined to expend as few words as possible in answering all questions put to him. We did manage to find out, however, that he liked video games, basketball, junk food, and Michael Jackson, though not necessarily in that order.

The second time we met Andrew was on a warm, sun-drenched, golden autumn day. We drove to the small park near the center of town. The assistant chef at L'Île-de-France had kindly prepared a delicious box lunch for us. We spread an old army blanket out on the ground and had a picnic.

"Well, what do you think?" Jason asked, as he sat down beside me on a park bench. We were watching Andrew climb on a large jungle gym with several other children.

"He doesn't trust us yet. That's going to take some time. I like him. He's bright and inquisitive. I think things will be fine, if he will only let us in."

"One thing seems certain," Jason observed.

"What's that?"

"This business about his being incompatible with the other kids was a lot of bunk. Just look at him."

Later that evening, as I was driving us back to the adoption agency, with Andrew sleeping in the back seat, Jason and I, for some reason that now escapes me totally, got into a rather animatedly silly discussion about former U.S. presidents.

"Nah, nah, Jason, you've got it all wrong," I said with mock scorn. "Grover Cleveland was a Democrat. You're thinking of Taft. William Howard Taft was a Republican."

"I'm thinking of the big fat one with a face like a walrus," said Jason, puffing out his cheeks. "Wasn't that Grover Cleveland?"

"They were both big fat guys with the face of a walrus," I replied, looking away from the road and over at Jason. "Only Taft had these little, tiny, beady red eyes like a white rat."

"Yeah, well, you can keep your little, beady red eyes on the road, if you don't mind."

"Or maybe it was Millard Fillmore who looked like a white rat," I mused.

"Oh, well, they were all rats of one kind or another, with a few notable exceptions."

Suddenly, in the midst of this thought-provoking argument, came a peal of youthful giggling from the back seat.

"What was that?" Jason whispered.

"Beats me. Sounded like it came from back there," I murmured, nodding my head over my shoulder in the direction of the rear window.

"There it is again! Think I should have a look?" Jason said, continuing to whisper.

"Yeah, but be careful," I cautioned dramatically.

"You guys are funny," Andrew said, through a cascade of laughter, as Jason peered at him playfully over the seat. "You guys are really funny."

Two weeks later Andrew was with us for his first overnight, so we decided to drive to St. Louis. The zoo, the Gateway Arch, and Union Station were among the highlights of our trip.

"We're going to have to make a decision soon," I said, after Andy had been put to bed in the adjoining hotel room, with a lamp left burning. Jason was lying in bed reading. "We're getting to the point now that if we don't adopt him, Andrew could be headed for another big letdown."

"As far as I'm concerned he's the greatest little kid in the world, and that includes all my multitudinous nephews and nieces," Jason replied, laying his book, open side down, on his chest. "I say, let's tell McCleerey."

"You know I talked with him a little about gay people today," I said as I got into bed.

"You did!" he whispered, rolling over toward me and resting the side of his head on the palm of his left hand. "When did this come up?"

"It was when we were at the Gateway Arch and you were standing in that long line to buy the tickets to go up to the top. He brought it up."

"*He* brought it up?! He's only just turned nine years old!"

"Listen, Jason, these kids are way ahead of where we were at the age of nine. They learn a hell of a lot more from television, for one thing. There's even a gay character on *Roseanne*. Also, kids aren't like adults. They don't hide things. They say what's on their minds. We were sitting there on this concrete bench, munching away on our Cracker Jacks, and he says, nonchalant as you please, 'Are you two guys gay?' "

"Jesus! Why didn't you tell me?"

"There hasn't been any time up until now."

"And what did you say?!"

"I said *yes*. Then I told him we had been together for a long, long time, almost as long as he's been alive, and that we loved each other very much."

"Yeah, yeah. Go on. Go on," Jason said, sounding a little embarrassed.

"Then he said, 'You mean like husband and wife?' And I said it was kind of like that, only with a few differences, the obvious one being that we are both men. I told him that sometimes the deepest kind of love a man can feel is for another man. Sometimes that love is so strong that these two guys want to be with each other all the time, to the point of spending the rest of their lives together, and that was how you and I were. I asked him if this bothered him."

"Yeah, so what did he say?"

"He munched his Cracker Jacks thoughtfully for a moment, and then he said, 'If you guys love each other, why shouldn't I be cool about it, man? I mean, it sure beats bein' alone, if you ask me. Anyway, you two have been all right by me. That's all I know.' "

"I'll be damned," Jason smiled. "Well, that pretty much wraps it up."

"Not quite," I continued. "He's a little worried about AIDS. I reassured him about it by saying that you and I were not at risk because of the kind of life we live."

"Did he accept that?"

"He had some questions, but he seemed to. I'm not one hundred percent sure, though. He may think that AIDS is a disease connected with *all* gay men, as the media often seems to portray it, rather than understanding that HIV is an infectious agent dependent upon all sorts of things in order to be transmitted, regardless of whether people happen to be gay or straight."

"In other words, does he think that gay men get AIDS because they're gay?"

"Right," I replied. "So, before we go calling McCleerey and telling her to draw up the papers, I think the three of us should sit down together and talk about a few things. Suppose Andy should reject us, for example? You and I may agree that we want Andrew for our son, but the question still remains as to whether he wants us for his parents."

"Do you realize that when you and I were nine years old, Lyndon Johnson was in the White House?" Jason said, in a kind of stunned, mesmerized murmur.

"And on that pleasant note, perhaps it's time for us old codgers to get some sleep," I sighed, reaching for the lamp above the bed.

Unable to fall asleep, I lay staring up into the semidarkness trying to remember what it was like to be nine years old. I had been very efficient at blotting out most childhood memories. My life's history seemed to begin on the day I finally left my father's house for college. I never spent the night under his roof again. I could not weep at his funeral five years ago. In order to grieve, one must have a sense of loss. I did not. I was glad when my mother sold the house and moved into an apartment near her sister in Indianapolis. My mother and I remain on friendly terms, but since I told her that I was gay, a year after my father's death, we have more or less kept each other at arm's length. I travel to Indy two or three times a year to see her, though she has visited us in Springfield only once. She has a cordial relationship with Jason but never inquires after him during our weekly phone conversations. She would prefer that things with me were different but very rarely talks about it. I hadn't revealed to her anything concerning our plans to adopt a child.

Jason was everything I had ever thought I could want or need. Our life together had worked so well largely because we had both wanted it to work. I listened to his even breathing as he lay sleeping peacefully beside me. I snuggled closer and kissed him gently, and gratefully, on the cheek. After a while I got out of bed, moving gingerly so as not to wake him. Through the partially open door to the next room I observed Andy as he slept, the dim, shaded light from the lamp falling softly across his angelic face. I had to smile, having earlier that same day experienced the boundless energy and youthful

mischievousness of the boy who now lay so serenely beneath the
blankets. I glanced over at Jason, then back at Andy. How right it
seemed, our being together like this. How natural it felt. There was
something pure and utterly fulfilling about it that I couldn't quite define. "We can make this work, too," I whispered to my sleeping family. "I know it."

It was a crisp, early-November Friday. The sun shone gloriously
through the reds, golds, and pale greens of the trees and dappled the
carpet of fallen leaves on the sidewalks along Jefferson Street. Our
hearing before Family Court Judge E. Maxwell Hunter was set for ten
o'clock that morning. We wore our most conservative three-piece
suits, white shirts, solid-color ties, and wing-tip shoes.

"Now I know the real reason why we left Chicago and the fast-
track world of big business and high finance," Jason declared.

"Oh? Why?"

"So we wouldn't have to wear this ridiculous corporate drag every
day."

Mrs. McCleerey and Andrew were waiting for us in the corridor,
just outside the Family Court. Andrew put on one of his big grins
when he saw us approaching and took Jason's and my hands as we
walked into the courtroom. There was no one else in the room, except for a rather odd-looking man wearing an old-fashioned fedora
and a rumpled, double-breasted suit, who sat in the very last row of
the spectators' section jotting something in a little notebook. He
looked like a character from a comic strip, and he smiled weirdly at us
as we entered.

Judge Hunter was a man, perhaps in his middle sixties, with silver
gray hair combed straight back from his high forehead. He had a
long, thin face, and a pair of wire-rimmed glasses rested on his very
straight, slender nose. A stenographer appeared at a little table between where we sat and the Judge's dais. He was wearing judicial
robes. How strangely formal, I thought. One would think Judge
Hunter was about to conduct a murder trial, rather than a simple
adoption proceeding.

"This is a hearing on a petition of adoption of Andrew David
Metz, a minor in the custody of the state, by Craig L. Preston and
Jason W. Collier, petitioners for joint custody," Judge Hunter droned,
as he shuffled through the file before him. "Which one of you is Mr.

Collier?" the judge demanded, scrutinizing us over the top of his glasses.

"I am, Your Honor," Jason responded, raising his hand.

"And I presume that you are Mr. Preston," Hunter said, casting his stern gaze in my direction.

"Yes, sir," I nodded.

"You gentlemen come to this hearing very highly recommended," the judge continued, examining various pages from the file one by one. "I must say, however, that a petition for joint custody by two men, or two women for that matter, is most unusual. In fact, I've never heard of such a thing before in my fifteen years as a family court judge in this district. Even single-parent adoptions are somewhat uncommon. Tell me," he demanded, suddenly removing his glasses and looking squarely at Jason. "Why do you wish to adopt this boy jointly, Mr. Collier?"

"As we explained to Mrs. McCleerey, Your Honor, Craig and I live together as a couple," Jason began, calmly. "We're life partners. We've been living together for more than eight years and are committed to remaining together for life."

"You mean like husband and wife?" Judge Hunter asked, a smirk flitting briefly across his thin lips. The rumpled-looking man in the back of the room coughed loudly, and I turned around to see him doubled up over his notebook, a hand over his mouth.

"I think that is a legitimate comparison, Your Honor," Jason confirmed. "At least to some extent."

"I see," said the judge. "Are you a homosexual, Mr. Preston?" he demanded, shooting a reproachful glance in my direction.

"In the statements, which are part of the file you have before you, Your Honor, it is clearly disclosed that Jason and I are both gay men."

"My dear Lord," the judge mumbled, leaning back in his chair. He pinched the bridge of his nose between the thumb and index finger of his right hand. "Mrs. McCleerey, how could you lead these two young fellows on in this way, not to mention little Andrew here?"

"But, Your Honor," Mrs. McCleerey objected. "There is no law forbidding adoption by same-sex couples in our state. It seemed to me that the benefits were pretty clear-cut for a hard-to-place child. A permanent home is absolutely critical to his development, and it is my feeling that these two gentlemen can provide that home. Besides,

Your Honor, you yourself said that Mr. Collier and Mr. Preston come very highly recommended.''

Mrs. McCleerey astonished me with the forcefulness of her argument. I would never have thought she had it in her. I looked at Andrew, who was sitting next to her. He stared fixedly at the floor, his small body tense and completely immobile. I wanted very badly to give him a hug at that moment.

"Mrs. McCleerey," Judge Hunter continued, "how could you possibly expect a petition for adoption to be granted that seeks to place this child in a situation that clearly would jeopardize his normal psychological and sexual, not to mention moral, development?"

"I beg your pardon, Your Honor," Jason interjected. "I don't see why—"

"Just a moment, please, Mr. Collier," Mrs. McCleerey interrupted him, holding up her left hand, as if to say "I'll handle this." She stood up and took two resolute steps toward the dais. I couldn't believe my eyes and ears! Was this the same Mrs. McCleerey we had walked in with? "Judge Hunter," she addressed him firmly. "To a small degree I can understand your skepticism. I was a little skeptical myself at first. But I have done considerable research, and I must say, at this juncture, that I sincerely and very deeply resent your implication that I would attempt to place a child with unfit parents. Your Honor, there is absolutely no significant evidence that homosexual parents endanger a child's development any more than heterosexual parents do. Every professional study done on the subject conclusively supports the perception that children who are raised by homosexual parents are no different, in any meaningful developmental way, from those raised by heterosexuals. Furthermore, studies have also concluded that there is no difference between homosexuals and heterosexuals regarding their ability to be good parents. These are the facts, Judge Hunter—documented, statistical facts.''

"Mrs. McCleerey, you will please resume your seat," the judge sharply ordered. Returning his glasses to his nose, he leaned forward in his chair and glowered at us. "It is the opinion of this court that the so-called gay lifestyle is manifestly incompatible with the objectives of child adoption as set forth by the legislature in the laws of this state. It shall not become the business of this court to encourage or legitimize said lifestyle in any way, especially by placing an innocent child in the custody of two announced homosexuals. The petition is denied on the basis that it is not in the best interests of the child. Andrew is remanded to the care of the Department of Child Welfare Residence at Willow Haven.'' He banged his gavel once sharply on the desk, collected the file and strode briskly from the room.

"Why, you old son of a . . . ,'' I heard Mrs. McCleerey mumble under her breath.

I was stunned into speechlessness. Jason was so furious that I could see the veins bulging in the side of his neck. Andrew continued to sit silently as before, still staring motionlessly at the floor. It almost seemed as though he had expected what had happened.

"Can he do that?!'' Jason demanded, turning his blazing eyes on Mrs. McCleerey.

"I'm afraid he can,'' she confirmed, with a little shrug.

"Just like that? You mean that's all there is to it?''

"I'm not a lawyer, Mr. Collier, but I think you can appeal this decision,'' she said as she gathered up her files and placed them in her briefcase. "It would be very unusual to do so, but I believe it can be done, and I for one would like to see it happen.''

I knelt down in front of Andy and took both his hands. "Well, I guess you have to go with Mrs. McCleerey for now, pal.''

He looked at me with big, sad eyes. I hugged him good-bye. "I imagine you'll be wantin' the basketball back,'' he said.

"Of course we don't want the basketball back,'' Jason answered, crouching down next to me. "That's your basketball. All the stuff we gave you belongs to you and nobody else. Remember that. The only thing you have to worry about is bringing everything with you when you come to live with us for good. OK, sport? Now, come on, give me five.'' He held out his right hand, but instead of slapping it with his own Andy threw his arms around Jason's neck and refused to let go, as though hanging on for dear life. It took a lot of coaxing and cajoling before he reluctantly agreed to accompany Mrs. McCleerey to her car. They stopped at the door, and Andy turned to say his last good-bye. He wiped his nose on his sleeve, waved one final time, then took Mrs. McCleerey's hand and left us.

"Come on,'' Jason said, loosening his tie. "Grab your coat and let's get the hell out of here. We're going to pay our lawyer a visit.''

In the corridor we encountered the strange little man in the fedora. "Hello, fellas," he said. "I'm Roger Bigsby, reporter for the *Post-Dispatch.* Wonder if you fellas might like to make a statement for the press."

"No comment," Jason said, as we brushed past him.

"Guess you guys are just a couple of victims of circumstance," he called after us.

I stopped short, turned around, and walked back to where he was standing. "No, Mr. Bigsby," I said. "You haven't got that quite right, have you? It's Andrew who has been victimized here. No one else. Just that little nine-year-old kid. That's all. And the circumstance that he's a victim of is one of pure, blind, stupid, hateful prejudice. You can print that in the *Post-Dispatch*, if you like."

Of course we never will know for certain, but I shall always believe that it was Judge Hunter who put Roger Bigsby onto the scoop of his life. Why should the press show up at what was, essentially, a simple adoption hearing? Why only Roger Bigsby? Could it, perchance, have had anything to do with the fact that family court judges are elected, not appointed, in this state and His Honor was up for reelection on the Tuesday following the hearing? Perhaps that was the "circumstance" that Bigsby thought Jason and I were victims of. In any case, Bigsby's story appeared at the bottom of page one of the *Post-Dispatch* on the morning following the hearing. The headline read: "Two Homosexuals Attempt Legal Adoption of Boy." The story was written like an exposé, comparable to something in a checkout counter tabloid. Life, for Jason and me, became slightly more complex after that. Letters to the editor, a few of them extremely rabid, began to appear in the paper on a daily basis. Most of these epistles praised Judge Hunter for his valiant defense of innocent youth and condemned the two of us with righteous biblical epithets. One letter even demanded that the Board of Health revoke our license to run a restaurant, stupidly claiming that gay people should not be permitted to work in the food service industry because of "the threat of AIDS." A few letters favorable to our position did appear. One, which I cut out and saved, was from a woman in a tiny rural crossroads. She reminded her readers that many American Indian tribes considered gay men to be *manitous,* people of great spiritual consequence, and that special friendships between two men were often consecrated among the Iroquois and the Sioux.

Business at L'Île-de-France dropped off slightly, but we lost none of our best customers, many of whom were very kind and encouraging. What was lost was our anonymity and privacy. We had to have our home phone number changed and unlisted because of the prank calls, and one night someone spray-painted the word "FAGS" in big red letters on our garage door. Of course, there was some hate mail as well, but none of the brave bigots of Springfield ever confronted us directly. Within three weeks of Bigsby's story the furor had started to subside. Our lives had undergone a profound change and, though it had been pretty rough at times, at least we now had a fair idea of where we stood in the little community we had called home for five years.

With the help of Mrs. McCleerey and our lawyer, Tom Dowland, himself a gay denizen transplanted from Kansas City, we prepared our appeal of Judge Hunter's ruling. A three-judge panel, of the State Circuit Court of Appeals, considered such cases. We had to file our brief with the Clerk of the Court of Appeals and then wait for a date to be set for the judges to render their decision. Our argument was straightforward, simple, and legally sound: that Judge Hunter had put his own personal, adverse reaction to Jason and me as gay men above Andrew's welfare and in so doing had ignored the intent and goals of adoption, which are to find good parents for children who need them. Within a week of filing our brief with the court we were informed that the judges would render their opinion on December eighteenth.

WE were not permitted to see Andrew during the six-week period between the first hearing and the appeal, but we kept in touch by mail. He wrote to us at least once and sometimes twice each week. We answered every letter, of course, and one evening I tried to telephone but was not permitted to talk with him.

The tension became almost palpable, as the days dragged slowly by. Jason, who has always been known for his easygoing nature, would sometimes fly off the handle over the smallest things for no apparent reason. He seemed always to be looking for ways to vent his frustration.

It was the Saturday night following Thanksgiving. I was working in my shoebox of an office in the basement of L'Île-de-France. Jason came down and changed into a waiter's white coat and black trousers.

"Wow! It must really be busy up there tonight if you're going on the floor," I said, looking up at him. He was very serious, and his face wore the gloomy deadpan with which I had become much too familiar over the past few weeks. "What's wrong, Jason? Did something happen upstairs?"

"I just fired Bill Morgan," he said flatly.

"You did what!?" I asked in total astonishment.

"I said that I fired Bill Morgan. You got a problem with that?"

"What did you do that for?"

"Because he was late for the third time this month."

"But, Jason, he probably got stuck at his day job. Sometimes they keep him late. He explained that to us weeks ago. Not to mention his thirty-mile commute."

"That's not my problem, or yours. I need people I can count on."

"People you can count on!" I exclaimed. "Bill Morgan's one of the best waiters we've ever had! He's got customers who specifically ask for him, for Christ's sake."

"Say, listen," he said, pointing a menacing finger at me. "You just stick to your papers and bookwork down here, OK? What goes on upstairs on the floor is my concern. That's always been the division of labor around here, in case you might have forgotten, and it still is."

"Oh, is that right, Mr. Mouth of the Midwest?" I said, pushing my chair away from the desk and getting to my feet. "In case you might have forgotten, I also happen to own a sizable chunk of this little enterprise, and I don't appreciate being addressed as though I were nothing more than the goddamned bookkeeper. So," I huffed, tossing my pen among the papers cluttering the desk, "when you're done waiting tables tonight you can just truck your tired ass down here and finish paying all these damned bills and posting them to the right accounts. You can't fire me, the way you did our best waiter, but I can sure as hell quit." I started to push past him out the door, but he grabbed my arm and jerked me around roughly. I was suddenly enraged. I extricated myself from his grasp and shoved him away from me. We exchanged angry stares for a few seconds before I turned and started for the stairway.

"Where are you going?" he demanded, but his voice had lost some of its combative edge.

"I'm going to the house, and when you come home tonight, *dear*, please don't bring your miserable attitude with you. I've had it!" I screamed. With that I stomped up the stairs and slammed out the back door, as the kitchen staff looked on in complete amazement.

I had left the restaurant without my jacket, and by the time I completed the eleven-block walk to our house I was nearly frozen solid. A half tumbler of neat Bourbon had a definite warming effect, but it also gradually helped to transform my anger into anxiety and then a dull depression. I went to bed and lay there mindlessly watching some stupid television talk-show host desperately trying to be clever until I couldn't stand it anymore and switched off the set. I heard Jason come in at two A.M., but I pretended to be asleep. He crawled into bed and snuggled up next to me.

"Are you awake?" he whispered.

"Your feet are cold," I said. "Go away."

"Cold feet, warm heart. Isn't that the way it goes?"

"It's cold *hands*, warm heart," I corrected. "I'm not interested in your hands or your feet or any other part of your anatomy right now, so why don't you just roll over there to your side of the bed and go to sleep?"

"Aw, come on, Craig. Can't we talk for a little while?" he pleaded. "I'm really sorry. I don't know what got into me."

"What's going on with us, Jason?" I asked, rolling over onto my back. "Everything is in a big uproar all the time now. I feel tense, you feel tense. We're all the time sniping at each other. Tonight really scared me. That acute awareness that makes us tick. It's in jeopardy. We could lose it. I thought we could face anything as long as we had that thing, that connectedness, that bond or whatever. Anyway, tonight, for the first time ever, there was doubt in my mind that we were going to make it, and it scared the hell out of me."

"It's this big blowup over our wanting to adopt Andy," Jason said. "It never leaves my mind. The whole thing is so unfair, and I feel so frustrated and impotent because there is so little we can do."

"But we're doing everything we can," I reminded him. "We're appealing. That's all we can do right now."

"Yeah, but who's to say the appeals judges won't have the same opinion of us as Judge Hunter, and a hell of a lot of other people, as we have come to find out. Oh, you were right. You said something like this might happen. I just never could have imagined what it could do to me, or to us. Good Christ, at times I almost feel like some kind of pariah or something. And it absolutely makes me nuts. What right have they got to make me feel this way?"

"But letting it destroy us means letting them win," I reasoned. "Don't you see that? It means letting the bigots and the religious fanatics have the victory. Their goal is to destroy us."

"But what if we lose the appeal, Craig? What if we don't get Andrew?"

"We will simply have to cross that bridge when, and if, we come to it. We have a very strong case. Tom said so, and Tom's a good lawyer. Until now, there has been no legal precedent in this state for this kind of an appeal. So, there is no more legal reason to be pessimistic than there is for being optimistic. This isn't just about us, you know. It's about every gay or lesbian couple who ever hopes to be allowed to have custody of a child. I think it's better to consider the thing in that light. It's the same for any minority, for any group that's 'different.' Some random act of hatred against a black person is not just directed at him; it's directed at all black people."

"Still, it's Andy we should be most concerned about. I'm not interested in being a hero or a martyr to some social movement. It's Andy I care about."

"But wanting to adopt Andy means that you want to be allowed the enjoyment of a right that straight people are permitted without question. You are demanding equal treatment under the law. That makes you part of a social movement whether you like it or not."

"I suppose you're right," he sighed. "You so often are. It's depressing."

"You should have learned by now to bow to my superior intellectual powers," I teased.

"Let's not get carried away here," he said, laughing slightly. "You're not still mad, are you, I mean, about what happened earlier? I really am sorry."

"I'm sorry, too," I confessed. "I shouldn't have lost control like that. It was stupid. I should have been more understanding."

"Let's try to treat each other a little more gently from now on," he said, as he leaned over to kiss me. "OK?"

"OK." Then, "I love you, Jason."

"I love you, too. And don't you forget it," he replied softly. "Oh, and by the way, I called Bill Morgan to apologize. He'll be in tomorrow night."

WHENEVER it snows, as it did the morning of the eighteenth of December, Springfield reminds me of the town in Frank Capra's sentimental old chestnut, *It's a Wonderful Life*. The many tall Federal and Victorian houses, with their ornate wooden trim, look to be made of gingerbread topped with a layer of white frosting. The downtown shops and restaurants, even the banks and the courthouse, appear cozy and inviting, and the people seem friendlier, almost jolly. Remembering how much little boys love the snow, I imagined Andy's excitement as I gazed at the winterscape beyond our bedroom window. One way or the other, I thought, this is going to be a Christmas we will never forget.

The small courtroom was completely packed when we arrived, and the crowd spilled out into the corridor.

"Who are all these people?" I asked Jason in astonishment.

"I don't see too many faces I recognize," he replied.

When we entered the room the general hubbub subsided. Andrew, Mrs. McCleerey, and Tom Dowland were already seated, their backs to us, behind a table facing the high bench. Andy turned around as we were making our way up the central aisle. When he saw us he smiled broadly and gave us two thumbs up. We had no more than sat down when the three robed judges, two men and a woman, filed in and took their places on the dais behind the high bench.

Judge Rebecca Carter presided. She banged her gavel once and said: "This is a panel of the State Circuit Court of Appeals meeting in Springfield to publish its opinion in the appeal of a decision, rendered in Family Court by Judge E. Maxwell Hunter, denying a petition by Mr. Jason W. Collier and Mr. Craig L. Preston, joint petitioners, for the legal adoption of Andrew David Metz, a minor in custody of the state. Are all parties present?"

"They are, Your Honor," Tom replied.

"This is a unique case," Judge Carter began. "There is little precedent to provide a guide in determining the proper course of action. The mandate of the Family Court in adoption cases, however, is quite clear. It is to review petitions for adoption and decide whether or not to grant those petitions based upon two criteria. They are the same tests that must be applied when rendering a decision on appeal of such cases. Was the prior decision based upon the recommendations of the adoption agency, and was that decision rendered in the child's best interest? In deciding if a given placement is in the best interests of the child, that placement must also be balanced against the available alternatives. The lower court made its decision based upon the idea that the lifestyle of the joint petitioners was incompatible with the purposes of child adoption. Judge Hunter took this decision despite considerable professional statistical evidence to the contrary as presented by the adoption agency in its recommendation. Furthermore, whether or not homosexuality, as such, is viewed as being encouraged or legitimized through the placement of children for adoption with individuals who are *announced* homosexuals is totally irrelevant to this case and should not have been made part of the lower court's decision. Finally, in balancing this placement against the available alternatives it is apparent that Andrew's interests would be much better served if he spent the rest of his developmental years in what is clearly a stable, functional household among people who want and care for him rather than being shunted back and forth between foster homes and child-care agencies. It is the decision of this panel that the lower court stands in error and should be overturned. The joint petition to adopt is therefore granted on appeal.''

The room erupted in a commotion of whoops and bravos and applause.

"Does all that stuff mean we can go home now?'' Andy shouted above the din.

"That's exactly what it means, sport,'' Jason laughed.

"Hot damn!'' Andy said, smiling broadly, his two thumbs pointing skyward.

Everyone laughed and cried and hugged and kissed one another. I even saw Tom, who prides himself on his lawyer's lack of emotion, dabbing his eyes with a handkerchief. People slapped us on the back and shook our hands and wished us all well and Merry Christmas. One woman, who sported a gay pride button on her mackinaw, said she had driven all the way from Cape Girardeau.

"In this blizzard?!?'' I exclaimed in astonishment.

"Nothin' stops me in my four-wheel drive,'' she declared, pounding me heartily on the back. "Besides, it was worth it! History in the makin'.''

Jason stood up on a chair and invited everyone to L'Île-de-France that night to celebrate, and I do believe they all showed up. We gave them *Soupe au Pistou* by the vat, a ton of spicy *Saucisson Provençal* with uncounted loaves of delicious French bread, devastating chocolate cakes called *Reine de Saba*, and champagne by the magnum. Jean Pierre, our very serious and sometimes temperamental chef from Montreal, was persuaded, after several glasses of champagne, to sing French cabaret songs. His wife, Juliette, accompanied him at the piano.

In the midst of the festivities, Jason tapped his spoon on the side of his glass. "My friends, thank you all so much for being with us. Craig and I are overwhelmed by your kind support. Now, I would like to introduce to you the reason for this happy occasion." He lifted Andy onto the table. "This is our son, Andrew, and we are very proud to have him with us at last."

"A toast to Andy," cried the woman from Cape Girardeau, raising her glass.

"To Andy," the guests replied.

"Speech, Andy, Speech!" Bill Morgan shouted.

"They want you to say something," I coaxed. "Make a speech."

Andy glanced first at the expectant guests, then at Jason, then me, and back to the guests. "You guys are funny," he declared with a shy grin. "You guys are really funny."

And everyone laughed again.

Found Cure One

Terri L. Jewell

To burns or sores
   of any kind,
      sweeten if desired.
Make a bread-and-milk poultice
   in the usual way.
   Take four ounces of white wax,
   of wild indigo
   to swelled female breasts.
It is a perfectly innocent plant.

Bad Ass

Terri L. Jewell

I am no gospel child
shouting lost regards
to invisible men
and ivory crosses
veined in gemstones,
velour robes
red as party eyes.
My belts sweep no
pale, atrophied thighs.
I squat bold as neon,
dance to hoof beats
of mustangs,
screech like dry ice,
thump out promises
with sugarcane stalks,
grunt blue as lies.
My sweat carves out valleys,
wells like sweet water
at the edge of my spine.

I am black as boxcars
bringing oils from Tunisia,
lovers curried hot

into earth creased over
from your momma's dreamworld.

from *Hannah Free*

Claudia Allen

HANNAH Free *is the story of Hannah, an independent spirit, and Rachel, the homebody she loves all her life. The play opens in a nursing home where an elderly Hannah is not allowed to see a comatose Rachel who is just down the hall. Denied Rachel, Hannah visits with Rachel's spirit, and they bicker and remember the love that began when they were girls. During World War II Hannah had left the Midwest to join the military and was stationed in New Mexico.*

Act II, Scene i

[*Lights rise on Rachel composing a letter to Hannah circa World War II*]

RACHEL: You keep after me to write you more than three sentences. It took me half an hour to find a pencil, but now here goes. The ground is frozen. We've had snow. The Canada geese are on the lake, taking a rest on their way south. I walk over and listen to them honk; I feed them cracked corn when I can get it. Marge is too interested in boys anymore to go with me. The boy she likes is going into the Army as soon as he graduates. It's hard to believe there's a war on as I'm standing by the water watching those geese take flight, calling out to each other. I read where they mate for life. I miss you, Hannah. I wish you'd stay home, but at least this time I know you're doing war work: you're not just running away from me. New Mexico sounds beautiful, but I'd miss my mulberry tree out back and my lilac bushes hanging over the driveway. You've been having dinner with the same woman all the time. What's that mean, "dinner"? I thought you were going to war; instead you're going to dinner. Well, I'm not knitting you any more warm socks, even if you are in the service. You're down there "having dinner" while I'm up here alone, squirming in my sleep. Well, I know people read your mail, so I won't say any more. Just know that I don't appreciate having to take long walks in the cold while you're down there—eating. You should be knitting me socks. At least this time you left to serve in the war. We can pretend it was patriotism and not just wanderlust. I listen to the songs on the radio and I think of us. Hannah, I don't know how many more times I can let you leave me. At least I'm busy. I'm working at the hardware store, bookkeeping. The man who used to do their bookkeeping is in Italy. And that little Price boy who used to deliver the newspaper? His mother just got word. I'm so thankful you're not overseas. I think of how I used to send you away, then stay up all night and pray. Now I pray for you to come back. Be careful in New Mexico. Watch out for snakes. Check your boots. Come home soon. Was this long enough? I've never written such a long letter. You know I love you, but I'll say it anyway.

In and Out of Harm's Way:

The Lesbian/Gay Graduate Scholar and the Academy

Pamela Olano

Prologos

IN a move inimical to postmodern theory and the pur-
ported impossibility of claiming any subject position, I offer here an
investigation of "subjects" both constructed and real—subjects mediated by culture's rejection and by the university's ambivalence and
fluctuating support. It would be naive for any lesbian or gay individ-
ual or group to assume that she/he/they could simply engage in academic pursuits on any college campus. The waters of academe are not
calm or inviting—indeed, there is a storm raging both within and
around homosexual students.

Before you is a conversation—voices speaking from the closet, the
structure that, according to Eve Sedgwick, has defined lesbian and
gay oppression in this century. The voices that speak from the pages
to follow are those of colleagues who populate this very crowded
closet to which I, myself, often retreat—sometimes in fear, sometimes
in anger, often to rest. Their responses were gathered via written
communication through an almost surreptitious "underground" of
coded and carefully sealed envelopes. Confidentiality was assured. All
participants are currently graduate students in programs at a major
midwestern university. All respondents expressed surprise at the dif-
ficulties they encountered in honestly addressing the questions, in
coming out of the closet even for an anonymous study.

I represent herein the daily personal drama of claiming a homosexual identity. I attempt to avoid myth or universalizing conclusions.
The voices, however, do suggest to me the classic Greek tragicomic
format. My respondents are the players; the closet, the framing device
or backdrop of the amphitheater of the play—the university. The
Chorus offers context; The Sphinx commentary. The plot is not only
my own; it is the story constructed by the lesbian and gay graduate
scholars who are engaged in the creation of their academic careers—

a creation that at times seems more like the unraveling of the carefully knitted fabric of homosexual identity. The characters wear masks—their names are The Lesbian, The Gay Man, The Professor, The Chorus, and The Sphinx. All comments are as actually reported.

I imagine this "gay play" as an act in five *epeisodiae*, spanning the postbaccalaureate interval of two to eight academic years. The episodes present the issues raised by the responses to my survey. These issues form the core of the drama.

PARODOS: *We tell ourselves that it doesn't matter, that we are just like everyone else—until we hit the wall of homophobia, until we try to incorporate who we are into what we do, until we speak the word* lesbian *or* gay *or* homoerotic. *The silence can be deafening. But we are here, ten percent of the population. Invisible to some, struggling for recognition as individuals, building walls around our identities that enable us to move through the university, making decisions to reach out, to come out, to stay out. Considering the options and the consequences.*

Episode I: The Deception or "Passing for Straight"

Stasimon

THE CHORUS (led by lesbian writer/painter, Mary Meigs): *The entire future of a lesbian, or any gay person, lies in the few seconds of coming out, and the freedom one gains comes with a new experience of unforeseen penalties.*

THE LESBIAN: Each week, my seminar has a new guest speaker. Each week, we go around the table and introduce ourselves and our areas of interest. Each week, I have to decide whether I will "be" a lesbian scholar in an unknown context. Each week, I stand poised on the brink of acceptance or rejection . . . or worse, of silence.

THE GAY MAN: Do I come out to my colleagues, professors, students? That's a tough question. I come out to them when it's pertinent. When we're studying a topic that I have a particular angle on, I do come out. For example, I raise the question of whether or not a book/character can be read "homosexually." Sometimes it's not met with much enthusiasm. I was in a gothic novel class and I brought up a possible homoerotic connection between Frankenstein and his monster. The professor didn't exactly scoff at the idea, but he didn't encourage me to continue along that kind of thinking.

THE LESBIAN: I don't generally come out when I do teacher-training seminars throughout the state. I figure other aspects of diversity are enough for people to handle.

THE PROFESSOR: Are you sure that a lesbian topic is a valid subject for research in a seminar on the women's movement?

THE SPHINX: *Silence.*

Episode II: Sexuality and Sensibility: The Inseparable Self

Stasimon

THE CHORUS (led by poststructuralist critic Elizabeth Meese): *The lesbian [or gay] subject is not all I am and it is in all I am.*

THE LESBIAN: Many people take offense at my remarks. "We all have sexualities," they say. "True," I reply, "but you are allowed to assume that we all operate out of the same position of desire. I *never* make that assumption. I've always got to weigh the possibilities."

THE GAY MAN: My sexuality is always at issue in my seminars. It influences the way I perceive the material I study, the work I choose to pursue, the way I respond to my colleagues and professors. Being gay, and wanting to survive in the academic world and the world at large, I have to be conscious of gender issues, sexual preference issues. I feel I have to work harder than the average heterosexual student at what I study because society is geared toward the heterosexual population.

THE LESBIAN: I see my colleagues in class squirm at the thought of having to talk about sexuality and bodies. I have often tried to pretend that I don't have either. But then comes the devastation of someone cruelly saying, "He or she sounds like a faggot or a lezzie." I know that tone of voice. It is not inviting dialogue.

THE PROFESSOR: Is sexuality the only issue here? I feel that you are trying to silence me as a white heterosexual woman.

THE LESBIAN: I would say that my projects are all highly personal because I can't seem to do intellectual work unless it "gets me off" in some way. In this sense I would have to say that my lesbianism is central to everything I do.

THE GAY MAN: I can feel tension in the air when a seminar addresses issues of sexuality. In a recent seminar there were a number of people who felt compelled to diagnose or try to explain the same-sex relationships in Shakespeare's work while accepting without question the heterosexual couplings in the play. One of the lesbian students asked one of the women why she felt the need to diagnose or figure out why persons of the same sex were attracted to one another. The woman became very defensive, proclaimed that it was not meant to be a homophobic response and that furthermore she didn't understand the issue.

THE SPHINX (as Gloria Anzaldúa): *We lay enclosed by margins, hems, where only we existed.*

Episode III: The Closet Dance

Stasimon

THE CHORUS *"Coming Out"—out of the closet. A decision all lesbian and gay people face. "Premeditated" and mediated by many factors: safety, atmosphere, necessity, the topic being discussed. It is a choice never unconscious.*

THE LESBIAN: I was told by some of my younger lesbian friends that I was not "out enough" in my classes. They don't remember the '60s and '70s when lesbians and gay men were disenfranchised from jobs, administrative positions, apartments. My memory is very clear. I sat in seminars at women's studies conventions and absorbed "strategies" to use if I was ever "outed" in my school. "Don't ever resign" was the biggest piece of advice. "Hide" was the subliminal message.

THE GAY MAN: Politically, visibility is essential to our very survival. Heterosexuals need to understand that the project is antihomophobia and not find-the-hidden-fag-in-the-picture.

THE PROFESSOR: I didn't know you were gay. You don't look gay.

THE GAY MAN: I was in a proseminar on Byron and Blake taught by an "old-guard" faculty member. While I was talking with him in his office one day about paper topics, he asked me about my graduate work and what I did before graduate school. In the course of the conversation, I told him I was gay. Then he asked me if I thought Byron hated women. He said he knew the idea that all gay men hated women. I assured him I did not agree. The whole interview was slightly strange: on one hand, I appreciated him taking an interest in me and my life, yet I felt patronized, and I know I was treated differently that day because I was gay.

THE LESBIAN: Don't let anyone tell you that the classroom is a "neutral" space. Sure, it's safe if you are straight. You can even talk about "gay and lesbian rights." Just don't try to exercise any. When you do, you get the message: "Sure, be queer . . . but be quiet."

THE GAY MAN: My worst experiences are probably when a faculty member makes a homophobic/inflammatory remark. I feel as though I must choose between responding at that moment (awkward, given the power situation) or else stew in silence for the rest of the quarter. I have done the latter too many times.

THE LESBIAN: People assume that my love of women means that I love all women, and so I am simultaneously a threat (to their safety—both heterosexual women and men alike) and some kind of icon that is identified as "the woman-identified woman." Actually, visibility is a double-edged sword. Almost damned in both directions. Sometimes I get very confused.

THE SPHINX (as Toni McNaron): *I am a lesbian in my study and classroom as well as in my bedroom or kitchen, and no one can uncover me in any room whatever, because I no longer hide.*

THE LESBIAN: I surprised myself by quickly eliminating the only lesbian faculty member as my adviser. Why? Maybe because I'd have to be too "present"—really all the way out of the closet. I wouldn't be able to move back and forth between my lesbian identity and my presumed heterosexuality. Guilt by association, or something like that. So now I'm challenging myself to risk—this is a personal battle for which, unfortunately, I get little in the way of visible support from anyone. So many of the battles that lesbians and gays fight are fought in solitude. That's probably why there is so much substance abuse in the homosexual community.

THE GAY MAN: Sometimes you are identified as gay just because you bring up the issue of sexuality when no one else seems willing to; sometimes you are identified as gay just because you bring up gay issues. That's fine. That can work sometimes, and it offers a little protection. Small seminars seem more supportive, although they can be indifferent to gay and lesbian issues. Indifference can be good or bad, it seems: good because they won't impede you, bad because they won't help you.

THE LESBIAN: I'm always interested in how people come out. Some of my lesbian colleagues use the same technique again and again. It's like their calling card. What's even more curious is the way I anticipate their coming out as much as my own. Going from seminar to seminar, we acknowledge each other's anxiety by making eye contact during the "announcement." Sometimes it's like an avalanche. Once one person breaks the ice, others will follow. Sometimes it's a race to see who does it first. Don't get me wrong; this is no fun-and-games type of thing. Actually, it's never fun. The hardest times are when you go to a new class, look around the table, and realize that you are the only lesbian. Suddenly, it's not a question of how to come out or when, but *if* you even should. Yet, how can you *not*? I really don't want to be a spokesperson for all lesbians and gays, but it's not that simple. My silence can be traitorous—to myself and to other homosexual students. My silence is really a kind of death.

THE SPHINX (again as Anzaldúa): *To survive the Borderlands*
   you must live sin fronteras *[without borders]*
   be a crossroads.

Episode IV: Community

Stasimon

THE CHORUS (led by researcher Jeffrey Weeks): *Identity is not a destiny but a choice. But in a culture where homosexual desires, female or male, are still execrated and denied, the adoption of lesbian or gay identities constitutes a political choice. These identities are not expressions of secret essences. They are self-creations, but they are creations on ground not freely chosen but laid out by history. So homosexual identities illustrate the play of constraint and opportunity, necessity and freedom, power and pleasure. Sexual identities seem necessary in the contemporary world as starting points for a politics around sexuality. But the form they take is not predetermined. In the end, therefore, they are not so much about who we really are, what our sex dictates. They are about what we want to be and could be.*

THE GAY MAN: I find the general climate in the English-Composition-Creative Writing realms in which I work to be basically homophobic. This is the homophobia of the "good liberals" who can speak out against abstract bigotry much better than they can speak to (or listen to) a real live queer among them. In creative writing workshops, my openly gay work is often greeted by conspicuous silences. When I find another unexpected queer or two in one of these classes, it creates that feeling of community, if only by contrast.

THE LESBIAN: I don't find much in the way of a lesbian community, or even a women's community if you come out as a lesbian. I'm either the token gay person in my classes or I'm a curiosity. I was appalled when, in a poetry seminar where we read several lesbian poets, not one word was mentioned about how their sexuality was influential to their work, their imagery. Finally, I once again took on the role of lesbian educator. I pressed the issue. I was met with silence. Was it possible that these highly articulate graduate students did not have the language to discuss lesbian sexuality, identity, existence? Did I have the energy to do this service again? My importance and my existence is diminished every time someone is silent. Finally, one woman spoke. She described the lesbian imagery in the work of Audre Lorde as "like two sticks rubbing against each other." I responded "Yes, and rubbing two sticks together creates a fire." She hesitated and said, "That's not what I mean." But I already knew that.

THE GAY MAN: As a gay man working in a graduate program, I feel mentor-less!! There are gay graduate students, lesbian faculty and graduate students, but where are the out gay faculty????????

THE LESBIAN: Community is a problematic thing. As a feminist, I want to believe in something called the women's community. As a lesbian, I don't really experience it. Maybe it is because everything becomes so sexualized. If I'm in a women's community, I'm viewed as a radical lesbian feminist. If I'm in a homosexual group made up of gay men and lesbians, I struggle as a woman in a male-female hierarchy that is oftentimes identical to "real-world" situations. Most people don't realize that being "gay" is not necessarily a community-building asset, even among homosexuals. As a scholar, I don't expect any more support from gay men or lesbians than I do from straight folks. There's a lot of internalized homophobia out there . . . and in here, too.

THE SPHINX (as poet, writer, and literary theorist Judy Grahn):

POLICEMAN: *Have you ever committed any indecent acts with women?*

LESBIAN: *Yes, many. I am guilty of not loving her who needed me;*
I regret all the women I have not slept with or comforted,
who pulled themselves away from me for lack of something I

had not the courage to fight for, for us, for our life, our
planet, our city, our meat and potatoes, our love. These are
indecent acts, lacking courage, lacking a certain fire behind
the eyes, which is the symbol, the raised fist, the sharing of
resources, the resistance that tells death he will starve for
lack of the fat of us, our extra. Yes, I have committed acts of
indecency with women and most of them were acts of
omission. I regret them bitterly.

THE GAY MAN: I find more often than not that I feel isolated as a
scholar, partly due to the discomfort of colleagues and partly due
to the defensiveness long ingrained into a fat femme boy. But
many institutional practices function to keep me in this position.
Most appalling of all is the lack of out gay male faculty on a campus this size and in a state this purportedly "liberal"—and in this
English department in particular. Is there even a never-married
male on the English faculty? Are we feeling a little paranoid about
guilt by association?

THE LESBIAN: The atmosphere *never* seems affirming to gays and lesbians—except in some women's studies classes. Sometimes it seems
benign, and sometimes discriminatory in that ignorant remarks are
made or the topic is avoided when it would seem relevant.

THE GAY MAN: Heterosexism exists everywhere. It's taken for granted. I
have to be aware of that and try to correct it where I see it, if I want
to continue in academics and live with myself. I'm not trying to be
super-fag or savior of all gay and lesbian academics; I'm simply trying to carve out a place for myself in the world I've chosen to be
in. I think that anytime any gay man or lesbian is open about their
sexual preference in a seminar, they are helping every other gay
man and lesbian.

THE SPHINX: *How do we build community? With blood and guts and tears*
and sharing and risk taking. How does one find the lesbian and gay com-
munity? Luck.

Episode V: Classroom and Career

Stasimon

THE CHORUS (led by Sarah-Hope Parmeter): *In our fantasies, we could*
present reasons for coming out to every principal, chairperson, and PTA in

the country. We explain the benefits our honesty has for our students and
PEOPLE GET IT. *Our students and their parents start saying, "We want our*
gay teachers to be open. We expect it. Because we want the best education we
can have." Gay teachers can put their full energy into their teaching in-
stead of into hiding. Students with gay family members no longer feel they
have anything to hide. Our classrooms become communities where diversity
is prized. And lesbian and gay children grow up being proud to be who they
are, knowing that some of the most respected figures in their lives share
their identity.

THE GAY MAN: There doesn't seem to be any uniform way to deal with
the question of whether to come out in class to students. In the
AIDS course I'm teaching, I identified myself on the first day of the
class. My two teammates are a gay man and a straight woman. Several of the students in the class are gay, lesbian, or bisexual. The
atmosphere in class is very supportive and affirming, though one of
the straight female students wrote some very homophobic things
in her journal. My female colleague is trying to deal with her.

THE LESBIAN: Sometimes, I just sort of come out "naturally" to my
students, in remarks about "my partner . . . she."

THE GAY MAN: My colleagues and my professors, yes, I usually do
come out to them. My students, not so much. I really have no
clear-cut reason why. If they ask me what I study, I tell them about
my work in gay studies. I often give assignments that explore gender issues and gay and lesbian issues. Perhaps it's a matter of sharing my personal life with students. It feels somehow inappropri-
ate. I'm not sure I can explain. If the issue of my sexual preference
arises, I'm open about it. But if not, I don't stand up and proclaim
myself. That would feel unnatural to me, like preaching, and I
don't like to preach. I don't want to be looked at like some sort of
curiosity: "Oh look! There's that fag teacher I had." I want to be
remembered and respected, I hope, for the quality of work I do as
a student and as a teacher. My sexuality is an important part of my
life; I don't want it overlooked. But I also don't want it to be the
only lens through which others see me. I feel as if I am contradict-
ing myself all over the place.

THE LESBIAN: I don't come out to my students, generally, but I find
that I'm wanting to do so more and more. As my scholarship
struggles to make sense of *the lesbian,* I am more and more becom-

ing a lesbian. I know that sounds like a weird thing to say, but what I mean is that I think the psychological/social or the academic/ real or the she/me split is trying to heal itself.

THE SPHINX (as Audre Lorde): *Each of us is here now because in one way or another we share a common commitment to language and to the power of language, and to the reclaiming of that language which has been made to work against us. In the transformation of silence into language and action, it is vitally necessary for each one of us to establish or examine her function in that transformation, and to recognize her role as vital within that transformation.*

THE LESBIAN: I probably will *not* work on gay and lesbian theory. It seems controversial enough to concentrate on feminist studies. However, I may change my mind, if I ever get the time to contact the lesbian network [in my department] I recently heard about. It's really scary to do it alone!

THE GAY MAN: I'm currently working on a long group of poems that address definitions of names society has come up with for gay men . . . . When I started the project, I was a little frightened to confront the terms in my work. But I felt I needed to do the work, needed to take some of the terms and strip them of their power, redefine them. I realized when I started the project that heterosexual (and some homosexual) people might react negatively to it. I also realized that I might have trouble trying to publish the poems, and if I did succeed in getting them into print, they might be a problem for me when I seek work as a professor . . . . But I have to write about what I know, and I know about my experiences as a gay man. There didn't seem to be any choice really, if I wanted to be honest with myself and with my work.

THE LESBIAN: "You will have to do something unusual to make up for your lesbian work." This was the reply to my question about employment possibilities when I finish my degree. I laughed. Apparently the professor didn't get the fact that being an out queer is unusual. There was just too much irony in that advice.

THE SPHINX (again as Audre Lorde): *The fact that we are here and that I speak now these words is an attempt to break that silence and bridge some of those differences between us, for it is not difference which immobilizes us, but silence. And there are so many silences to be broken.*

Exodus

As the play ends and the audience departs, I am left with the echoes, wondering if these voices will be heard. Theirs is not simply a play in five episodes; the words represent lives. There are faces behind the masks of The Lesbian, The Gay Man, The Sphinx. And undoubtedly, we are *in harm's way.*

THE CHORUS (led by Adrienne Rich): *It means that most of the time I am eager, longing for the possibility of telling you. That these possibilities may seem frightening, but not destructive, to me. That I feel strong enough to hear your tentative and groping words. That we both know we are trying, all the time, to extend the possibilities of truth between us. The possibility of life between us.*

Epilogos

Perhaps my "gay play" is, in fact, a trilogy in keeping with the Greek tradition. As Part One, this essay presents the plot; Part Two may demand further complications. I look forward to Part Three where a successful resolution benefits the members of a diverse university community—a community in which we may all be *out of harm's way.*

The Players

Anzaldúa, Gloria. *Borderlands*/La Frontera: *The New* Mestiza. San Francisco: Aunt Lute, 1987.
Frye, Marilyn. "Plenary Address." National Women's Studies Conference, Akron, Ohio, June 1990.
Grahn, Judy. *The Work of a Common Woman.* Freedom, Calif.: Crossing Press, 1978.
Lorde, Audre. *The Cancer Journals.* New York: Spinsters, Ink, 1980.
McNaron, Toni. " 'Out' at the University: Myth and Reality." In *Lesbian Studies: Present and Future,* ed. Margaret Cruikshank. New York: Feminist Press, 1982.
Meese, Elizabeth. "Theorizing Lesbian: Writing—A Love Letter." In *Lesbian Texts and Contexts: Radical Revisions,* ed. Karla Jay and Joanne Glasgow. New York: Feminist Press, 1990.
Meigs, Mary. "Falling between the Cracks." In *Lesbian Texts and Contexts: Radical Revisions,* ed. Karla Jay and Joanne Glasgow. New York: Feminist Press, 1990.

Parmeter, Sarah-Hope. "Four Good Reasons Why Every Lesbian Teacher Should Be Free to Come Out in the Classroom." In *The Lesbian in Front of the Classroom: Writings by Lesbian Teachers*, ed. Sarah-Hope Parmeter and Irene Reti. Santa Cruz, Calif.: Her Books, 1988.

Rich, Adrienne. *On Lies, Secrets, and Silence: Selected Prose 1966-1978*. New York: Norton, 1979.

Sedgwick, Eve Kosofsky. *Epistemology of the Closet*. Berkeley and Los Angeles: University of California Press, 1990.

Weeks, Jeffrey. As quoted in *Growing up Gay in the South: Race, Gender, and Journeys of the Spirit*, James T. Sears. New York: Haworth Press, 1991.

Part III

"Every Last Drop":
Writing Desire

Michelle Paladino, "Mary Jo and Bert"

Mimosa

Carol Anshaw

THE usually hushed gallery rings and lights up like the inside of a pinball machine. The carpenters are here with clattering scaffolds and thwanging hammers. Three people from Graphic Design are adhering small, impeccably correct title cards next to the canvases. There are also two guys the museum hires as lighting consultants. They bring with them more scaffolding from which they dangle and toss around cables thick as Amazon snakes.

In the midst of this, Renata is trying to sound utterly sincere as she speaks to Steve Palm, the artist whose canvases are the subject of all this hyperactivity. He is unhappy, silent, and broody.

"We can rehang the entire show, if necessary," Renata says, putting a hand lightly on his forearm. "Rehanging is not a problem." It would actually be a huge problem, and he knows this. They both know rehanging is not an option. She goes on anyway—"What's important is that *you* feel good about everything"—then waits for whatever mechanisms Steve Palm will have to go through to get back to okay. Sometimes her job irises down to just this, a detached kind of waiting for others to come around to her point of view.

Renata finds a moment to sneak back to hide in her office. "Any calls?" she asks Joan. Joan wears black clothing and powdery white Kabuki-like makeup and has a diamond stud in the pierced side of her nose. Renata hired her for these affectations, thinking they might indicate someone more interesting than the cardiganed secretaries the museum personnel office has a seemingly endless supply of. Joan, though, has turned out to be cardiganed within. She has a life that revolves around a computer programmer husband and their weekends spent with puzzle maps and thermoses of coffee, driving around the suburbs of Chicago in auto gymkhanas.

Joan holds out a ruffle of pink While You Were Out slips. Renata takes these and sees one is from Kimberly, and her spirits buoy. After the phone number, Joan has written "Sounded like she was calling from bowling alley."

Renata closes the door, sits down at her desk, slips her shoes off onto the carpet, and dials the number, which is not a bowling alley but the shipping department of a small plant that makes trophies and metal plaques. Kimberly heads up this department. She loves her job.

"Yeah?" a guy answers and, when Renata has asked for Kimberly, yells (without moving the receiver away from his mouth) "Kimber-leeeeee!" And then there is the sound of the dropped receiver clattering again and again against the wall. Renata reads half the catalog on a ceramics show before Kimberly rescues the receiver at the other end.

"Yeah?"

"It's me," Renata says.

"Oh. Well, listen. I can't make it tonight. My brother's coming over with his wife and their new baby."

"Maybe you could come by later. After they've left."

"Maybe." Kimberly doesn't like to commit to assignations, or keep them once she has, or show up on time when she has decided she will show up at all. Renata knows enough not to pressure and so just accepts this change in plans and hangs up.

And is astonished and thrilled when—hours after she has gone to bed and fallen into a racy, surface sleep—she awakes to the sound of a key in the lock. She pretends to be unwakened. She doesn't really want to talk to Kimberly, doesn't want the light switched on for a showing of pictures of the new nephew or the suggestion that they get up and make sundaes. (Kimberly is a pageant of impulsive gestures.) If she keeps her eyes closed and her breathing even, she will hear clothes falling and feel sheets parting and get the Kimberly she wants, naked and needy.

THEY met several weeks ago at a bar. It was late. Renata had gone to two gallery openings, then dinner with two ancient married pairs of collectors. A truly deadly evening.

Afterward, at the bar, she watched Kimberly dance with a big-hair-and-lipstick girl about her age. That is, about Kimberly's age, which is nineteen, as opposed to Renata's, which is forty-one. That night Kimberly was in leather, her hair gelled back. She looked like Garbo coming out of the sea. Renata caught her between dances, asked if she could buy her a drink.

"A mimosa," Kimberly said. Something in the way she said this made it clear she had given thought to her drink, to having one.

The drink didn't establish any connection, though. Kimberly went back to dancing, this time with someone tall and thin and wearing beat-up khakis and a white T-shirt, a camp-counselor look Renata knows stops the hearts of many women but does nothing for her. It is only girls like Kimberly who perform a sort of sexual photosynthesis around Renata, leaving her suddenly without enough air available for breathing.

Kimberly seemed to know everyone in the bar, as if tonight were a party to which she had invited them all. It was only after last call that she gave any indication she was aware of Renata's presence.

"We could talk. Or something. We could go to your place," she said. "I live too far for one thing."

The other thing, which Renata didn't find out until a bit later, was that Kimberly still lives at home. Now when Renata calls, she leaves messages, either with Kimberly's mother or on an answering machine that features the voice of Kimberly's father and the barking of the family dog.

THE night of the opening of Steve Palm's show, Renata is in the staff ladies room, fluffing up. She asks Joan, "Do you think this dress is too conservative?"

"The hickey undercuts it," Joan says, tapping a spot on Renata's neck just below and behind her ear, then lends her some concealer.

Renata supposes Joan, like everyone else at the museum, thinks she goes with Greg Berger, a straight-looking gay collage maker who offers Renata protective coloration in exchange for the opportunity to cozy up to people who might be helpful to his career.

After the opening, to which Greg has come as Renata's escort, she drops him at the apartment of someone new he's seeing, then drives by the bar where she met Kimberly. She does this most nights. If she doesn't see Kimberly's car, she goes by two other bars, then out to the edge of the city where Kimberly lives—a low-to-the-ground yellow brick house, the inside of which is limitedly observable through a picture window framing the huge chrome base of a table lamp, the backs of two armchairs. The driveway handles a revolving population of cars, one of which is Kimberly's black CRX, which takes a $300 nip out of her monthly paycheck and is one of the major reasons she expresses for still living at home, where her parents charge her only $25 a month rent for her room. Renata has guessed (perhaps incorrectly) which window in the house is this room. If the CRX is in the drive, Renata cuts the engine and sits watching for a while—the house, the CRX, the darkened window—before making the long drive home, where she can rest knowing Kimberly is not out, riling up the night.

Tonight, though, the CRX is in the parking lot of the bar where Renata met Kimberly. She can't just go in and assume that Kimberly will be happy to see her. Kimberly enjoys impulsive gestures only when they are hers. Everyone else should be the rising and setting of the sun, the phases of the moon, the progression of seasons—a calculable backdrop against which Kimberly can provide the weather.

Renata pulls into the lot and parks at the far end. She is prepared to wait until the bar closes, but within the hour Kimberly steps out, jaunty on her pins, an astronaut emerging from some chamber that has been distorting gravity, subverting balance. She is holding onto the arm of the person who has won the Kimberly prize tonight. Renata barely registers this woman, who exists only in that she is occupying the space immediately adjacent to Kimberly, which precludes Renata from occupying this space herself. The dilemma reduces itself to one of emotional physics.

She doesn't need to follow this vignette any further but does anyway, tailing the car they get into—one of those jeepy boxes set high on oversize tires—a few miles to a neighborhood with next-to-no parking, where Renata sits in the dark of her car, watching Kimberly and her new friend walk into one entrance of a courtyard building. Lights come on briefly in a third-floor apartment, then go off.

FOR a year and a half, Renata saw a capable therapist who worked hard to help her tear loose from the relentless, exhausting necessity to be in love with one Kimberly after another. And together, she and the therapist were successful. For two years following therapy, Renata was not prey to any futile attractions. The problem was, she wasn't prey to any attractions at all. Deprived of her obsession, no other, more regular tropisms then became available to her.

"MY parents want to meet you," Kimberly says one afternoon about a week later when she is painting Renata's toenails, having talked her into staying home from work. Renata, in turn, called the metal shop, pretending to be Kimberly's mother with news of her daughter's stomach flu.

"Oh," Renata says. "Sure." She tries not to convey any emotion along with these words. Within, she is thrilled at the invitation, even as she is appalled at the idea of going through with it. Kimberly is one of the new breed of babydykes—out to her family practically since puberty—while Renata's relatives are still hoping she meets Mr. Right. And so there is no cover connection to pretend to. She can't come in as Kimberly's French tutor or life-drawing instructor. Renata wonders exactly how Kimberly *has* described her, what word she used to designate Renata's position in her life. Having been brought up to Kimberly's parents gives credence to Renata's pinpoint focus. It means she has a place in the small universe of her obsession.

"Do you have Nintendo?" Kimberly says, out of bed and poking around in the videotapes stacked on the bottom of the TV stand.

"No," Renata says. "I don't have anything. I don't even have cable."

"You should," Kimberly says. "When you need TV, you need enough of it. Cable gives you enough."

She's restless, Renata sees. On the near edge of boredom, a brink Renata does not want to let her slide over.

"Bring me some ice cubes from the refrigerator, will you?" Renata says.

"What for?"

"Crush them down a bit. I'll need little pieces."

Kimberly does as she's told. She's surprisingly obedient for some-one so ruthless and willful.

When she is back, Renata gives her permission. "You can take those off," she says, tugging at a bit of elastic, as she puts shards of ice into her mouth, takes another between her fingertips, and begins.

"IT's always nice to meet Kimberly's friends," her father says, offer-ing a hand and standing with the temporary stoop of someone just out of a recliner. It's his hair that makes a strong first impression: it's thick and bristly and randomly combed, like a young Kennedy's.

"Mr. Lazar," Renata says; she hasn't been given a first name.

Kimberly's mother doesn't let this particular awkwardness happen. She dusts Renata into the living room with small, fanning motions of her hands as she says, "Call me Nikki. We're not much for standing on ceremony here."

Renata sees in an instant what she hadn't predicted, also now sees she could have only *not* predicted it by propping up a lead sheet of denial—that these two people are younger than she is. Only by a couple of years, but still.

"Kim has told us so much about you," Nikki says, sitting down, then jumping up again to offer corn chips and guacamole. She is health-club thin, her limbs exposed by the rolled-up sleeves of her "JUST DO IT" T-shirt, her black spandex tights.

Mr. Lazar is bringing in a bottle of wine. With the other hand, he has his fingers laced between the stems of wine glasses. Renata has no idea what this "so much" about her has been composed of and so has no clear response available. She tries smiling as though all the information preceding her has been fascinating and complimentary. She feels suddenly overwhelmingly old. She feels her hair going white, then yellow. Her gums receding, her cheeks lapsing into wattles. Like an unsuccessful escapee from Shangri-La. Like the aging admirer in *Death in Venice.* And, of course, like Humbert Humbert.

THE conversation doesn't stall out so much as it never really reaches liftoff. The Lazars are undergoing the trauma of kitchen renovation, and Renata contributes her own handful of horror stories on the experience. Which only seems to worsen the situation. The more common ground they find, the more ludicrous it seems that Renata should be sitting across the living room from them, their daughter sitting on the floor at her feet. The going gets particularly rough when Nikki asks Renata if she has any children herself.

Kimberly is the only one who seems to be at ease. She sits at Renata's feet and also accepts a small plate filled with tortilla chips her mother has predipped in guacamole for her daughter and in neither position indicates the slightest discomfort.

Renata, on the other hand, listens to Mr. Lazar explain his business, which is the moving of items both heavy and fragile—grand pianos, alabaster urns, and such. In this context he has met a few art collectors and runs their names past Renata who, in not recognizing them, feels like a prospective employee unable to provide references. She has, she realizes too late, only after she has drawn blood, been gnawing at her cuticles, a habit she broke in college. She also finds a glob of guacamole on the knee of her white linen pants.

"You should get that off," Kimberly says in an overurgent tone, as though something has happened that will require a tourniquet, the raising of feet above the victim's head. "I'll show you where the john is. Get you a washcloth."

She takes Renata down a narrow hall, their footfalls absorbed by a thick, pale blue cushion of carpet. When they reach the bathroom at the end, Kimberly gives Renata a light push inside, then follows and pushes the door shut behind them with her back. She is slightly taller than Renata, also bigger boned. And so she can create the physical impression that she is swooping Renata up into her arms.

Renata closes her eyes as she feels first the lips, then the teeth at her neck. It is absurd and regrettable that in moments such as these Renata feels her most authentic self. Which means the rest of everything must be shaped to the absurd contours of this fascination.

THERE is a meeting of all the museum's curators and department heads. State funding has been cut again, which means positions will also be trimmed, along with salaries. Everyone has been expecting this; it's no surprise. But now they can all see the axe above them, beginning its fall.

Enid, the museum director's secretary, scuttles in through a side door of the boardroom. "I'm sorry," she says in her rangy Australian accent, then signals to Renata that she should step outside.

Renata tries to imagine what could have happened, what terrible news awaits on the other side of the door, what could have persuaded Enid, who takes her job as seriously as a sentry in a turret, to interrupt this uninterruptible meeting. Renata imagines some nameless piece of bad news, sees herself crumpling onto a chair, being instructed by Enid to put her head down between her knees.

"It's your mum," is what Enid actually says, and Renata's heart slips inside her. Her mother is seventy-four and has high blood pressure. Renata just talked with her two days earlier, though, and she sounded fine. "There's been an accident, I'm afraid. She was hit. By a cement truck apparently. Someone called from the hospital. A nurse in the emergency room. Frightfully noisy. I couldn't really hear all the details."

Renata doesn't have to look down at the slip of paper Enid is handing her. She already knows what number will be written there. For months to come she will have to make up reports of her mother's progress, her recuperation for Enid and the others who will be solicitous.

Moments later, behind the closed door of her office, she shouts into the receiver, into the background din, "What? What is it?"

There's a long pause, filled in with racket, then finally, "I just don't like it when I can't get you. They say you're in a meeting. I mean, what does that really *mean*?"

Renata explains that occasionally—in this case, for instance—it means she is actually in a meeting.

"Well, I don't like it, though. Sometimes I need to get hold of you."

"Like now," Renata guesses, but she is wrong.

"No. This time is just a test. Like for the Emergency Broadcasting System. This time there's only a tone." Kimberly imitates the tone. It's amazing how long she is able to hold it without taking a breath.

Semiotics

Mary Jo Bang

The night speaks its obsessive language
of shadow and light. Your face between
my hands is luminous, mad arrangement
of shimmering surface. Of course, real

truth lies buried, illegible. You are
nothing but silhouette against quivering
moonlight until you begin to undress:
breasts echo the *o* in once, the beveled edge

of every distant star bobbing in blue
darkness. I worry your long hair, wind it
round my veined wrist. It is tonight.
We are each held captive. You remove
vesture of fig and frock, exposing nakedness
and meaning—mine for the naming.

Bonsai

for Troy

William Reichard

It's about what is left
after the roots have been cut
clean away, what remains
after limbs have been pruned,
dwarfed by the lips of our sweet scissors,
the blades of our small knives.

And we have constructed ourselves
in this same way, trimming back
families and familiars to bare essentials,
pruning back all that we've come from
to all that we desire. We have constructed
our lives along the lines of the reductive,
waiting after every stinging cut
to see if we can live without that
particular branch, that puny limb.

It's about what can be bent,
branches cowed into curvature,
aesthetics dictating nature,
and you and I watching those
square porcelain pots for a day
or a decade and maybe nothing will change,
maybe one new leaf in the space
of eighty years, one new shoot. And yet,
we wait, learning slowly
the distance through which we can push ourselves,
the subtle growth of trees.

Goliath

Galleria dell'Accadèmia

Jim Elledge

No one particular
muscle nor vein, not the erect
nipples nor relaxed left
thigh, not a frontal
view nor one from behind, but these
together, the body
              whole.
                 How his
balances—half eager, half
reluctant; flirting,
denying; fluid, tense—
perfectly coy: the head cocked
left, tilted so that,
sighting the giant, his
come-hither stare skims the forehead,
grazes the hair. The right hip
juts out where the hand
palms a stone.

           Like Goliath,
but smaller even than
this boy-king, I circle
him then circle back, wondering
whether to flee or stand
ground, all the while
wanting to lay me down at his feet.

To One of Two Boys on a Bench

Oz Park, Chicago

Jim Elledge

You're sure, absolutely, you're the only one to
dream sweat trickling down another boy's
cheek, a snail's sleek trail slipping to his shoulder
blade, to the hard nipple-tip where it dangles,
a diamond all star-glint. Then a door-slam or the
alarm and you're awake, thirsting.

                    When you make
the basket, and he pats your rump as he heads
down court, you're sure you're the only one to go
deaf to the world's clatter, the cartwheeling
cheerleaders, angels hosannaing at Armageddon:
Rah-rah, O blessèd among Man.

                    But look close. Maybe
not now. Someday. Years from now, years pot-
bellied, gray at the temples. Lean again into his
Sea-Star blue eyes, lean as if over the edge of
a wishing well, not into a bull's-eye darkness but
a sky lit round, lean until your silly hair
that never lies flat no matter how hard you brush
turns dizzy, sizzles, threatens suicide. Look
close. Stare for all you're worth, for the blood he
sent thumping against your rib-slats, your teeth:
eyes reflected, simply two stars among
                        hundreds.

Boxers

Joseph Like

Naked backs and shoulders
shine as they crouch toward
each other. Blunted hands raised
to prevent anything from getting through
to swollen lip or eye as they
lean in, then dance away.

On the padded square,
they circle the ring
and play by gentlemen's rules;
no punches below the belt—
no holding your opponent—
when you lay your man out on the mat,
walk to the nearest neutral corner
and wait for the count—
when the bell sounds, go home—
when it sounds again,
come out fighting.

Each time they wrap arms around
and still wild limbs, feel
chest rise against chest,
they could be mistaken.

Every hold, now an embrace.
Each punch, a reaching out.
One head thrown back, one
nestled on the other's shoulder.
A hand, on the small of the back,
slips down silk trunks,
the other against the chest—
hangs on or pushes away.

Chene-Ferry Market, Detroit

(c. 1975)

Don Mager

This building is drab like a bunker.
Its twice-a-week business huddles one end.
Food-stamp buyers and a few farmers
trucked down from eastern counties, mostly men.
Obedient, lacking inflection—
none of them even dicker. If these
are garden-variety everyday men,
then they should join up as potatoes.
Some dark heat keeps them going, though, I suppose.

But eroticism is color,
skin, abundance—lavishness spilled
on sawhorse-jerried tables under
their steamy white, thermos-coffeed
breaths. Their fingers are chilblained and chafed
in knit gloves, knuckle-length cut open.
They sort, count, weigh, as if honied
sweetness, spiny juice, pungency, or burn,
might in this market be imbibed by touch alone.

But are their fingers touched by Eros
as they arrange produce for shoppers?
I move two ways in this hubbub space;
shopper to carry sacks to my car,
and cruiser whose lilted eyes prick, spar,
and lure: bright onions, parchment peeled, moistly
aglow and magenta; roots scrubbed bare
in squeamish bundles, parsnips, parsley,
ginger; fuchsia-flushed turnips; sprig-leafed celery;

and the ebony-purpled eggplants.
I glide across their aura, adrift

from stall to stall in a mesmered dance;
then abrupt to choose, a quick thrilled lift,
I seize, buy, and bag. Fruit is stuffed
till damp sack starts to tear; parrot-green
polished apples; limes; a bark-rough
pineapple, juice-scent full to its skin;
casabas; grapefruit; pears; tangerines.

But the aura is mine, nerves teased wide,
the tick and spark of a small charged cloud,
plectrum-fine sensors, deft with spider glide,
soloing me through the drab crowd.
The passion of color erects toward
my eyes; scents dive at nostrils that snare
and engulf; and the ice-stung air hoards
a bright pitch as if the whole place were
shimmering with spun harmonics, distant and rare.

But of course I am merely buying
produce—sweatshirt, denim jacket, boots,
a matter-of-lone-fact man pushing
along, intent on both task and its
event. What my eye investigates,
spars and returns with a radiance
to widely lure and invigorate
my own impeccably cocky response
(the eye at the halo hole of its dance).

Especially when it's another man.
Yes—even here—hoisting pineapple crates
down, him, with extravagant full-blown
hair, and eyes whose sudden flash creates
white stars reflected in deep black pits.
The light gyre and glance of his hips
restlessly keeps a private hushed heat.
How delicate to embrace, then slip
my tongue between his grape-skin and ripe full lips,
delicious to beckon him follow
me now.

Oh lamentation! Oh hate!
bitterness, numbed, scarred, and unspeakable.
Men who hold in their infantile guts
the gnaw and need to own others, but
cannot, not quite ever, not in full,
so always are cheated at their white
core, where they turn on a spit, spiteful
and frozen. Oh lamentation! how awful

to stalk a woman, wrestle her down.
Men scream out with knotted, puny fright:
"Bitch . . . bitch . . . if you call for help I'll pound
your face in . . . kill you . . . rip your cunt out . . . "
Oh lamentation! At home at night
what terror to be the volcanic flash
that erupts their furied drive, to beat
and batter cowering wives, and to crash
slamming fists again and again into torn flesh.

Oh lamentation!—
                    But here my aura
is fetterless. It sparkles a man
who double-glances me, and then turns a
wonder-stunned and teeth-white-as-stars grin.
Sure, he is flattered that I watch him,
for he hoists down his crate with impudence.
His pineapple's juice-scent full to skin
dives at my nostrils. My nerves' expanse
at this cold bright noon stretch to field and frame him.
The potential is shaped. The brisk space
has opened. Blood drums. I could enter
the charmed circle, dive into his face
approaching to ask, has he the time, or
to offer help. But brightly sprung under
the charm of his fleet exchange, I stride
toward the door and the sunlight's flashing blade,
still keen to that blunted raw anger,
lamenting its slow sad spread through the world.

At the door, whiteness. My eyes squinny.
Anticipation of my death floods me—
not premonition—rather, story
launched with clear focus, a simile
to this noon's gathered fragility
as if whiteness has hushed even blood.
My lilted ease and serenity
is sustained like a long modal chord
beneath chime and vision. Exactness unfolds.

> *I am seventy-five, hair and beard still*
> *full—both impudently white. I wake*
> *to frost-thick dawn, my lover nestled*
> *with his chest warm along my back.*
> *I rise from bed, graced by the simple fact*
> *that we made custom fresh again last night*
> *as the old knowledge of each erotic*
> *pulse unfurled skin to its full delight.*
> *I lie my lips upon his brow, blessed by habit*

> *then pull on my sweatpants, socks, and shoes.*
> *At the porch step, running enters me*
> *as it does each day, long legs, down through a*
> *street whose sun tipples the red trees.*
> *Again my upraised face grabs in the*
> *bright air, across bridge and through the hushed-*
> *with-birdsong woods. Deer graze watchfully*
> *in the roadside grass and twisted brush.*
> *At island end, red on water, the sheer rush*

> *of fire swells and my body's action*
> *quickens toward sudden poise; here, again*
> *I feel my whole thrust reach toward the sun,*
> *greeting. I slack the long strides, ease down*
> *breathing. Eyes reach into trees again,*
> *to high-scanning gulls, earth crust lichen.*
> *The event of sight is suddenly born.*
> *I walk through dark woods whose early sun*
> *is soft, and on a log with hoary bark, sit down.*

My pulse is surging its resilient chime,
and that moment stops its muscling clock.

At the market doors, plucked from the dream,
my eyes blink the sun in and I wake
to stiff fingers, and a stiffer neck.
I stride to my car, fumble the keys,
completely splitting the half-torn sack,
turnips lost in snow, and feel extravagant ease.
At the center of the wild hollow hum, stillness breathes

even as I slam the trunk and glance up.
Bull's-eye grin; he's watching me—watch him.
Surprise. He's parked those crate-hoisting hips
in the doorway. Snow has already spun
a nimbus on his blaze of ebon
hair. Perhaps he has read my dream-pause
in the snow as beckoning. Might have been;
this time wasn't. Serenity does
nothing but be its breath. Needs are what tease.

Welcome to Beth Homo

Lev Raphael

BARRY flung one end of his knee-length wool *tallis* over his shoulder as if it were a lush sable stole, and Steve smiled.

Barry said to him, "Maybe we should start our very own synagogue, Beth Homosexu-el. Beth Homo, for short." And Barry held his head up like Huck Finn declaring he *would* go to hell. "And *everyone* could join the Sisterhood! What do you think?"

Barry had been about to put his blue velvet *tallis* bag away that Saturday afternoon, but had suddenly unzipped it and whirled out the impressive black and silver striped ivory prayer shawl, entering its folds like a magician about to perform a fabulous escape. When Steve clapped appreciatively, he said, "Thank you. Now you may kiss my fringe."

Just then, through the open windows, they heard the roar of what must have been another Ohio State touchdown. It was going to be a terrific season, but without Steve. He hadn't attended a single home game this fall, unlike his freshman year, when he painted his face red and white and left every game hoarse, exhausted, triumphant. The camaraderie in the student section was electric: on the warm days most guys didn't wear shirts, and the heat of their skin when he'd pummel friends and even strangers after an interception, a great pass, or a terrific second effort was all he could ask for. College football is almost a religion in Ohio, more so than anywhere else in the Midwest, Steve thought, and he worshiped happily, not having to let anyone in the stands know that privately, he also belonged to what David Bowie once called the Church of Manlove.

This fall, however, Steve was spending all his Saturdays at the Hillel co-op, which wasn't far from his dorm, to go to *Shabbat* services at Hillel's Conservative *minyan* with Barry, have lunch, and then fuck in Barry's room on the second floor in the former fraternity house.

Steve's first time there, Barry had fondly pointed out that what was once a lounge and now used as the chapel was on one side of his

room, while the men's room was on the other. "That's me all over—
between the toilet and the Torah!" His room was hung about with
purple paisley Indian coverlets, like someone's idea of a dope den in
the '60s. All it needed were Janis Joplin and Jimi Hendrix posters, but
Barry had nothing on his walls to distract your eye from the filmy
purple cloth, and the way it set off his dark eyes and skin, as if he were
some silent-screen vamp lurking in a dusky fur-lined boudoir, and every shadow and fold deepened his mystery.

Steve had actually come to Hillel to hear a faculty speaker address
the rising incidence of anti-Semitism at Ohio State. Dorm room doors
were being smeared with swastikas, Jewish books had been vandalized
in the main library, students were getting crank phone calls, and letters were appearing with increasing frequency in the student newspaper that declared the holocaust a fabrication of "The Jewish Media," so wasn't it time to shut up about it already?

Partly to quiet his anxious parents back in Cleveland and partly to
still his own nagging sense of helplessness, Steve went to the lecture at
Hillel, his first appearance at any campus Jewish event. It proved to be
a disappointment until he met Barry. There were lots of people there,
mostly Hillel nerds—the kind of guys who dressed and looked as if
they were still high-school outcasts. At the midpoint, Steve went looking for a bathroom, but the one downstairs was occupied. He rushed
up the stairs to the second floor, where there was an Out of Order
sign on the public restroom. Desperate now, he pushed open the
heavy door marked Private, Co-Op Members and Their Guests Only
and gratefully saw a little Men's Room sign.

Inside the blue-tiled bathroom, his urgency blurred and shifted.
Standing at one of the sinks, drying himself off from a shower, was a
sullen beauty with the body of a varsity wrestler. He was a dirty blond,
with milky freckled skin and a very fat and heavy-looking cock that
almost completely hid his balls. Steve tried not to stare from over by
the urinal, which he was leaning into, hoping that he could finish
pissing before he got a hard-on. The guy didn't say hello, didn't even
seem to notice Steve, just tightened his towel around his hips and
padded out into the hall when he was done. Steve zipped up with
a sigh. But he wasn't alone: a silky, sarcastic voice said, "Don't be
impressed by our Jim. His cock's the only big thing about him. It
dwarfs everything else." That was Barry, smiling, standing in the other
shower, which Steve realized had been running until that moment.

Steve shrugged. "If that's the dwarf, call me Snow White."

"Oh, I *like* you." He smiled. "What's your name?"

They exchanged names. Steve liked him, too. It was easy. Physically, Barry had the shy sad grace of one of those beautiful and commanding dark-eyed imperial figures in a Byzantine mosaic: long face, hands, nose, everything. In fact, his dark good looks (though not his height) came from a Sephardic grandmother, Barry told him later.

They chatted, Barry completely and beautifully nude, a towel rather exiguously draped over his shoulder, Steve leaning back against one of the sinks. Barry looked like a runner.

"So, Steve, aren't you going back to the lecture?"

"Nothing new there," he said. The speaker had struck him as boring and lacking in presence. Steve had vaguely wanted more than a report on the status quo, but he couldn't have explained what that would be. "How about you?"

Barry shrugged. "I don't go to meetings or rallies—it's a waste of time." Then he said, "I'm right next door." Steve followed him.

Steve was not at all prepared for what happened. He expected Barry to push him inside, lock the door, and jump him. But Barry was a very slow and gentle lover. They hugged and kissed longer than Steve thought he had ever kissed anyone, as if Barry wanted him to always remember the feel of his thick, firm lips. Each time Steve's hands strayed from caressing Barry's hair or his back, Barry murmured, "Slow down," and gradually Steve did let go.

That afternoon, he felt as if he were lost in some eighteenth-century palace, passing through an enfilade of rooms, the high double doors—painted with tender Watteau-like scenes—swinging open by themselves, one magnificent, gleaming, lavish high room following another. Barry made him feel exalted and relaxed. As Charles Ryder says in *Brideshead Revisited*, he was "drowning in honey, stingless."

Barry later got out Perrier from the tiny refrigerator in his closet, sliced a lime, and they sipped from their glasses in the silence of old friends.

They were on their sides, facing each other. They leaned forward to kiss now and then, lips cool and wet from the drink.

Steve heard some kind of hum behind him, and when he reached back to touch the cotton-covered wall, there was a kind of vibration under his hand. "Plumbing? Electricity?"

"It's the power of the Torah," Barry said, smiling. "The ark is right on the other side of the wall. I'd love to hollow out the wall and hide in there sometime, and when they opened the doors during the service I'd pop out!''

"I would kiss you, if they carried you around."

"Kiss me anyway."

He did, after which he couldn't help saying, "I wish I were like you." Steve gestured at Barry's long dark penis hanging down across his thigh, the thick head resting on the sheets.

"Oh, please," Barry said. "You have a *lovely* cock."

"But I'm only average."

"Honey, it's not just the jewel, it's the setting." Barry patted his cheek. "You're a very sexy man. Enjoy it! Oh my God, you're blushing."

In his midteens, Steve had often been told he looked like a chubby Al Pacino, the adjective canceling out for him the glamorous image, and though he was not unsuccessfully trying to lose weight, he'd been hesitant about taking his clothes off in front of Barry, whose body was so finished and so trim.

"Listen," Barry said. "There's six rooms in the co-op, but Carol got mono and had to go home last week to Chicago. You could move in, if you wanted to."

He didn't. He explained that he wanted to stay in the dorm his entire four years at State. Why would he ever want to leave the constant show of male flesh, men padding around their rooms barely dressed, even naked, unconscious of how much a gift just a glimpse of beautifully defined pecs could be for him. The descriptive words themselves excited him: definition, separation, vascularity—so cold and mechanical in the abstract, but signaling such richness in the flesh.

And Steve's roommate, Thomas, had the most casual relationship with clothes—pulling himself out of them as soon as he got back from a class, a meal, a date, wandering around in silky black bikini briefs like John Travolta's in *Saturday Night Fever*. The briefs were a great choice, Steve thought, because Thomas even looked a bit like Travolta (though he was somewhat more intelligent). His casual nudity—as if they were in Florida and not Ohio—knocked Steve out, made studying very difficult at times. Dressed for the gym, Thomas was a stunner—wearing spandex biking shorts with mesh panels that revealed a ripe high butt while clinging to his runner's quadriceps.

Thomas always got into bed nude, and from the very beginning of sharing a room with him, Steve had been unable to look away completely from the muscular thick body on which dark hair curled and boiled like the arabesques of a Baroque ceiling. Steve was fascinated by the nighttime shaking of the bunk bed above his, which went on for weeks. Thomas would hardly wait until the lights were out, then he would go at himself as if he were speedboating across a finish line, ending with a sharp stifled gasp.

One night, Thomas started *before* he climbed up into his bed. He prolonged the casual loving stroke and lift lots of men give their cocks as they change, while he stood there at the foot of the lower bunk.

"Wanna jerk off?" Thomas asked.

Steve nodded and pulled back the sheet. Thomas lay down next to him, closed his eyes, and began pulling on Steve's hardening cock so vigorously that Steve came before he wanted to. Thomas groaned just as quickly and went up the ladder. Steve wanted to lick his hand, but he knew that wasn't entirely safe.

The next night, their thighs were touching when they jerked each other off. Thomas felt his balls, and when he was about to come he slid sideways to rub his cock along Steve's thigh. The night after that Thomas flipped over onto him and rubbed on his stomach as hard as if he wanted to dig a trench. "I know what you want," he said a week later. Did he? Did Steve? They never talked about it, never did anything except at night, late, when no one would call or knock on the door. Though mostly they rubbed off on each other, Thomas's eyes were always closed, and he never took Steve's hand. If Steve tried to touch him or even raise the subject during the day, Thomas would stare at him with all the furious contempt of an untalented writer reviewing a book that seemed to mock his own lack of achievement.

When Steve was done talking about Thomas, Barry nodded a few times and finally said, "Thomas must be pretty hot if you put up with all that."

He didn't know how to answer. What he had with Thomas wasn't much of a relationship, but it *was* a relationship. His first, really.

"Or maybe you're just neurotic?"

Steve looked away, stung, but he had to smile when Barry added, "Sorry. My parents are both shrinks—sometimes I can't help myself. I wish they'd been something else—like bakers . . ."

"Right," Steve said, "and then you'd talk about my buns. Don't worry. I'm an English major, and things always remind me of books or plays."

Barry set his glass on the floor and then slowly ran his index fingers down the sides of his cock as if he were a model on one of those game shows, stroking, displaying a prize.

"What does *this* make you think of?"

"*Long Day's Journey into Night.*"

"Let's go," he said.

STEVE'S parents were proud of his regular attendance at services, especially since his brother Ronnie had married a Roman Catholic. Steve's stock in the family had risen steadily once Ronnie started dating her. Though Steve's brother was a lawyer, had always been a B+ student or better, he was no longer the star, and all Steve had to do to maintain his position was not cause trouble.

So he was certainly not going to tell them that he was gay. In high school, Steve had seen openly gay guys—or some who were just suspected of being gay—have their lockers vandalized, get beaten up in the parking lot or the locker room. One very effeminate kid, who never talked to anyone, so enraged the captain of the basketball team that he poured gasoline on the kid's head during lunch and threatened to take out his lighter. This was after *An Early Frost* had played on national TV and news reports were talking of "a new openness" about homosexuality in America. What Steve saw was open hatred and disgust.

Barry was lucky in a way. "My parents always knew," he said. "I was a queen at three! Clomping around in Mom's pink nightgown with all the ruffles, and when I was twelve she found me in the attic wearing this old dress of hers—layers of black and white chiffon, kind of like that dress Grace Kelly wears in *Rear Window*. Isn't that an incredible movie? The first time I saw it, I cried, I burst into *flames!*"

"But what did your mother say to you about the dress?"

" 'Lunch is ready, honey—time to change.' "

That was the same year Barry first had sex, of a sort. "We were getting work done on the house in Shaker Heights. Sauna, gazebo, bowling alley—who cares? Work to me meant workmen, burly, sweaty workmen, bending over, stretching, cursing, the whole deal. And I would hang around this one guy, Nick, and ask him kid questions like what kind of car would he drive if he were a millionaire, because I couldn't stay away. I mean, with those low-riding jeans he had a crack that could have done more than launch a thousand ships—honey, they would have all stayed *home*, all those Greek warriors, to get one sniff, one little *lick*. I'm talking deep, mysterious, the way Africa was supposed to be, or Garbo, take your pick.

"Now listen carefully, because here's where it turns into—thank God—a *Man-date* fantasy, and *not* a rueful every-gay-man-has-one story about The One Who Got Away. Because our Nick left the door to the guest bathroom open, and I just happened to come by and he just happened to have dropped his pants somewhat to pee, instead of using his zipper, and that ass, or most of it, anyway, was gleaming at me like the Hope Diamond. I know, you're going to tell me about Marie Antoinette and how the Hope Diamond didn't do *her* any good—but we'll let you eat cake later. Right now I am declaiming. I stepped in, shut the door, and—can you believe it?—he just backed right up to me and started rubbing. Bliss! I grabbed his shlong and came in my pants, but I did not decide to pursue a career in home design."

"Wow," was all Steve could come out with.

Barry wriggled his shoulders. "Just call me Scheherazade."

And Steve was his captive audience, seduced by the muscled slim dark body, the penetrating mournful eyes, his hands, his lips, his cock, and the flashes of camp.

Barry told him lots of stories, not to keep disaster away, as the Indian princess did, but to draw him even closer. It worked.

—Like when he went to a Turkish bath in Jerusalem and found ten fifteen-year-old boys jerking off in front of a mirror in the locker room. Steve would probably have blushed and turned away, but Barry claimed to have applauded and then helped them keep time: "*You* know, like one of those beefy cretins beating a drum for the slaves pulling oars in a galley? And we certainly got up to ramming speed!" Later he wandered the bath as if lost in a fantasy version of *Ben-Hur*, with beautiful men in towels lounging in and by a pool, some sprawled on stone slabs, being oiled in more and more exciting ways, watching men watch men, like endless mirrors of desire.

—And the time he was cruising in Jerusalem on *shabbos* with a friend in the *gan*, the park, near the building housing the Chief Rabbinate, and a little black-suited, black-hatted man, *tzitzit* and *payess* flying, rushed past them and screeched to a halt like a cartoon character. "Honey, you could almost *taste* the dust and practically *see* the skid marks vibrating in the air above his pious little head." The man turned to look them up and down, checked his watch, and then shook his head sadly and raced off to services!

—And if Steve thought *Barry* was big, Barry showed Steve pictures of his cousin Moshe in Eilat, who looked amazingly like Gregory Harrison. "Thank God for a Polaroid—no developer would return these, they'd go on sale at every KY-Mart in the country!" Moshe and Barry shared a room, and they could only make love at night because Moshe stayed hard for three hours after he came and couldn't get dressed. "It would just *loom* there like the Ghost of Blowjobs Past, like a *zeppelin*. Spooky!"

"Would you want to live in Israel?"

"With all those Jews? I'm not sure."

Steve said Barry was the first Jewish guy he'd had sex with.

"What!"

"Well, didn't you go to bed with, like, Arabs when you were in Israel?"

"No way. They always wanted to fuck me, and I said forget it. They were just too big."

Bigger than him? Than Moshe? The image of that excited Steve, and Barry edged down the bed to take Steve in his mouth. Barry murmured something in Hebrew, and when Steve closed his eyes he realized that they were words right before the end of the Amidah prayer, *tzuri v'goahli*, my rock and my redeemer.

When Steve was very hard, Barry stood him up and got behind him. Not being able to see him, Steve felt a strange little thrill of danger, as if they were driving on a road covered with just enough snow to make the lanes invisible. Barry's hands stroked his hair, his arms and chest, palms lightly brushing his nipples, which he had discovered through Barry were incredibly sensitive; no one had ever touched or sucked them before him. Barry must have crouched then, because his cock slid between Steve's thighs, under his balls, and when Steve reached down, his hands took both their pricks, rubbing, pressing. He began to feel that all of that flesh was his, and he was lost in his body as he had never been with Thomas or anyone else.

"Do you want to be inside me?" he asked, the words of this new question emerging like rabbits from a magician's hat, each a tame and white surprise.

Barry's answer was to draw him to his bed. "You know what we need to do?" he asked. "To be safe, I mean."

"I've read the pamphlets."

"Honey, let's write ourselves a *book*."

STEVE didn't move out of the dorm, but he started studying over in Barry's room and staying for dinner. Even though he helped cook and clean up, no one in the co-op seemed to like him or care that he was around. No one was friendly to Barry or him. Two of the women, Jane and Sandy, were graduate students deep into studying for their comprehensive exams, so they mostly talked to each other or sat in a stunned and prohibitive silence through meals. When Barry and Steve cracked a joke, both of them seemed to shudder the way someone seriously ill might do, passing happy healthy drunks on New Year's Eve.

Blond Jim was only sociable with Cleo, the third woman, who dressed like a drunken biker, Steve thought. Barry called her Miss Faux because "Fake!" was her favorite term of derision. The co-op members were all fake Jews, of course, but then she seemed to think that Judaism itself was a fake religion. Once she overheard Steve asking Barry to attend a pro-Israel rally, which he wouldn't go to alone. Barry declined because he said that services every *shabbos* was enough Jewish commitment for him. She laughed and shouted at them, "Praying to *what*? Some bullshit phony asshole God? You don't believe that shit—you're just faking it!"

"Bullshit" was her other favorite epithet. From Barry's room, Steve sometimes heard her down the hall shouting on her phone, or maybe just to herself, the word "Fake" alternating with "Bullshit!"— her voice like a slapping unoiled screen door. He couldn't imagine her as a landscape design student—wouldn't she be constantly ripping shrubs up to hurl them at people she disliked?

She certainly despised Barry. Another time at dinner, Barry was dishing some girl's hair on campus, and she hissed, "Faggot! What the fuck do you know about hair!"

"Darling," he said, "faggots *invented* hair."

Jim and the other two looked at them as if wishing they were dead. Did they have to keep causing trouble, did they have to be so gay? Steve assumed that meant being gay *at all*. They did not talk about AIDS, which at State still seemed like one of those bloody civil wars in a Third World country that most people couldn't find on a map. For Steve and Barry, it was hardly more immediate: no one they knew had AIDS or had tested positive, they'd never been to New York or San Francisco, they didn't subscribe to any gay publications.

Except for meals, he and Barry were rarely with the co-op members for any length of time, which seemed fine for everyone, including Rabbi Meyer, the Hillel director, who was an ardent Reaganite. Meyer was always looking at him and Barry as if they were some burdensome project in home repair he didn't quite have enough money to take on. Meyer frequently complained that none of the people in the co-op really cared about doing anything Jewish, let alone *being* Jewish. Each program or fund drive he tried to start there never worked. The fact that Barry regularly attended services didn't seem significant to Meyer, who counted Steve and Barry for the *minyan* but never called either one of them up for an *aliyah*.

And Rabbi Meyer resisted any attempt to be drawn into discussing gay rights, or the question of gays and lesbians as rabbis, or even considering that Judaism's view of homosexuality could change. Barry kept making programming suggestions to cover these issues, but Meyer said, "It's not a problem we have to deal with. And there aren't those kind of students on campus anyway."

When Barry told him that, Steve exploded. " 'Those kind!' What're *we* supposed to be?"

"Freaks, I guess."

"Why do you put up with this? It's so ugly."

"The dorms are better? Ever try putting up a Star of David or an El Al poster on your door? See how long it lasts. Or go to a gay bar in town and let them hear your last name. Watch their expressions when they say, 'Are you Jewish?' " Barry's last name was Shlomowitz, and he'd been frequently asked why he didn't change it to something "normal."

Once at a bar in town Barry had heard someone tell this joke: "What's the difference between a Jew and a pizza? Pizzas don't scream when you put them in the oven."

"Steve, nobody flinched! Some people laughed, and one guy said, 'That's so gross.' I walked out."

They were sitting on his bed, where before mentioning Rabbi Meyer, Barry had been telling Steve about giving a ride to an Israeli soldier who looked like Sal Mineo, and how they went to a nude beach. Steve reached across now and took Barry's hand, brought it back to rub the long, dark fingers through his hair.

"Thomas and I have sort of stopped," Steve brought out, having wanted to say that now for an hour.

"What happened?"

"A couple of times, I said no—"

"—and he got the message. Does this mean I can carry your books home from school?"

"I think I was sort of hiding out being gay—you know, just having sex, in a room where no one would ever know anything."

"We're some pair."

"How? What do you mean?"

Barry sat up, his back against the cloth-draped wall, looking so still with the wild purple print dancing behind him. "We're *both* hiding out. I've been thinking about how I never want to go to anything Jewish that you bring up—meetings, whatever. Neither one of us does anything gay, like the dances, the Lesbian/Gay Council rap sessions. Nothing. We're hiding out."

"And you haven't met my folks. I haven't met yours."

Barry nodded. "Sometimes I feel like I'm still up in the attic, dressing up, with nobody there, just me and an old mirror."

"Remember what you said about Beth Homo? Why don't we start it? Not a synagogue, but find some more gay Jews, lesbian Jews. Don't tell me there's just you and me at a school this big."

"Would two bisexuals equal a full member?"

"I'm serious!"

"I'm not, not often. Well . . . I am about you."

"There're all these other student organizations; why can't there be one for us?"

"But what would we do?"

Steve didn't know.

Barry shook his head. "Steve, I don't think I could be *that* Jewish, or *that* gay."

Hearing those words, Steve realized he could have said them with as much honesty. He thought about how often he'd been glad he had red hair, blue eyes, and freckles, could even pass for Irish, and glad his last name wasn't Cohen, Schwartz, Feinberg, but White, an Ellis Island gift; about all the friends whose Jewish jokes he hadn't objected to; all the films and books on the Holocaust he'd avoided; all the images of bearded black-hatted Jews on television he'd been repulsed by; all the discussions about Mideast politics he'd pretended not to care about; all the silence and lying, years of it, years of dimly hoping somehow that he wouldn't exactly *have* to be Jewish—and yet snatching up books on Jewish history or novels by Jewish writers, reading them with the furtive embarrassment and confusion of little kids talking about sex.

It was the same with being gay. There was the way he had circled Gay Literature sections in bookstores, hovering, nervous, terrified someone would see him, report him, announce on the loudspeaker: "There's a faggot in Aisle Seven." He'd snatched up Andrew Holleran's *Dancer from the Dance* with relief when it showed up in one store's Fiction section but been afraid to buy it because the paperback had a bare-chested man on the cover, and he'd even thought of trying to steal it. Steve bought six other books as camouflage. He read books like Holleran's in secret. Seeing any gay character on television made him wince, no matter how he or she was portrayed: Steve felt humiliated and exposed. It only took one article or a brief news report about AIDS to spoil his entire day. Even if he hadn't read the article or had turned off the radio, the TV, the assault had touched him and humbled him.

Steve tried telling all of this to Barry, who didn't move to hug him or even take his hand.

"I feel the same way," Barry said, eyes down. "Basically."

And they sat there in silence, not looking at each other, like the only two kids at a prom who have no date but are ashamed to even smile at each other, too miserable to dance.

Agrology

Terri L. Jewell

We met in Arkansas.
    You invited me to till your loam
    sift for seed with delicate vision
my tongue dipping litmus to gauge your hollows.
We smelled the grasses,
        chewed vanilla pods of climbing orchids
        emerged cress and pomegranate
to fall and sprout again.
When earth rumbled, peaked into your shoulders
the thick bows of our lips composed musics
        Ashanti, Kikuyu, Fulani, Ibo.
        We met in Arkansas.
Your buttocks rained a moister substance
soaked fertile rows down to bedrock.
        Our roots enwrapped excuses
        crushed them to inert powder
as we lie spent and fallow
vows of rebirth hot behind our eyes.

Wire-Rims

Jeannette Green

I. 1937

The black curtain of her hair fell into her eyes
and she pushed her glasses up.
She ran along the halls barefoot and sliding.
She sat behind the water-closet door laughing into
the curling cup of her hands. Laughing until her
sleeves were wet with tears. She wouldn't find her
standing so still with her mother's cotton dresses
and her father's Sabbath day suits.
She moved away from the slow heartbeat of her lover's
footsteps.
She shrugged the blouse from her shoulders and the
skirt collapsed willingly at her feet.

She caught her in the cold pantry.
Steam pouring from the slick and tang of her body. Her
lover's hands on her body like rainwater in the
tide. She pulled the cold steel glasses from her
face and gave herself over to the
blindness.

II. 1942

The world
Ripples
Flexes
Cringes
and her glasses wait cold for her on the loose puddle
of cotton and wool at her feet.
Her shaved head nods in the clinging snow and she
covers the twin tents of her breasts.

A thread of urine spirals down her leg and her toes
dig deeper into the yellow slush.
When she sees her mother she will tell her to check
the ovens, check the ovens MarMar something is burning.

She hears a train coming, a shower would be good. Clean.

Sucking Off Jamie

Robert Klein Engler

It was the time
he returned from
Costa Rica, tan
and ripe as a berry.

He called me—
we went to dinner,
then back to fall
together on his futon.

He told me how
he would swim
far from shore
in the warm, blue sea.

He could see the white
stretch of beach and
the green palms—his feet
never touched bottom,

and the azure sky was
as empty and forever
as one man could know
it. I listened to his pulse

beating like the surf,
tasting the salt he swam
through; I listened,
at a loss to say but this.

Hot Summernight Cloudburst Rendezvous

Antler

The two boys embracing in the thunderstorm
Don't care if they get drenched,
Don't care if as they strip each other
    their clothes drop in lightninglight
        into puddles
    and are kicked laughingly into the mud.
It's the first time they've kissed each other,
The first time either of them ever kissed
    a boy
And neither has ever kissed
    a girl
And neither ever kissed before
    with his tongue.
They had no idea
    how passionate
        passion could be—
    they can hardly believe it,
That merely putting their lips together
    could be so . . .
        ah.
For a moment they stand apart
    silently gazing at each other
        in the flashes and thunder,
Centuries of Boyhood, Aeons of BoyLove
    proud in their playful smiles,
Knowing just what they're going to do,
    even though they never did it before,
Knowing that before long
    each of them is going to jack off
        the first boy he ever jacked off
    besides himself,

Knowing both of them can come
    and giving in, giving themselves
    to boyfriendship's ultimate gesture,
Knowing they both know
    how to jack off real good
    and aren't going to stop frenching
        while they whimper toward the brink.
Sure, it's beautiful
    to see a boy you love
        ejaculate in the lightning in the rain,
Crying with pleasure while the thunder thunders
    and the sky ejaculates millions of raindrops
As you squirm in rapture
    on the muddy grass
        under the tossing trees.

Negative

Charles Derry

THE synapses in my brain are working overtime. Connections are being made, memories uncovered. Things are moving very fast now; I can barely keep up with the changes. My windshield is dirty, and when I push the washer button to clean it, a charge of adrenaline surges through me and I feel my heartbeat high in my neck and under my tongue. Back and forth, the wipers slash. My neck, my tongue, the node under each of my arms. I remember a day, I think in 1957, I was seven years old. I was sitting in my Uncle Tony's Studebaker with my father. Studebakers are history now, dead— you don't even see them in the vehicle graveyards all along Route 68. I was sitting in the backseat with my cousin Frankie, and it started raining. We saw the rain through the front and rear windows, only not through either of the side windows. Frankie was the slower of us, of course, to realize that it wasn't rain but washer fluid from the car's windshield washer tank, which dispensed the fluid from above, not below. "You stupid kid," said Uncle Tony to his son. "But why isn't it raining on the sides?" Frankie persisted. He was always slow, living up to his father's expectations. Even today, at forty, Frankie is slow—still living with his mother, and fat, ignoring the now-grown son he fathered out of wedlock, staring, when I last came over to visit, at the photograph of his alcoholic father, long dead. The funeral for Uncle Tony was a somber affair, not sad but reserved, with a sense of things unsaid, and so many knew about the rumors that in his later years he was not to be left alone with any of the young cousins or grandkids. Uncle Tony liked them to sit on his lap while his hands wandered; and at the funeral those who had lap-sat looked at him in the casket, and no one cried, no one spoke, because he was finally dead and a scandal avoided. And now I remember even that Uncle Tony's father had killed himself—an old Italian man who refused to face the fact that he was too old to work in his garden. Does it run in the family, I wonder; will Frankie, following his father following his own father, be the next? And more and more connections are being made, things moving fast, going back and forth like the windshield wipers on my car and the memory of the day so many years ago when my father and I sat with Uncle Tony and Frankie in the old Studebaker while a blue sky shone above and birds sung in the beautiful old trees in the old Italian neighborhood. Is it because I'm dying?

I read in the paper today about the actor B——, who died yesterday of AIDS. An interview with those close to him—a wife, a child—suggested that he had acquired the disease from his drug use. He couldn't handle fame, she said, but a friend of mine in New York, long dead, used to tell a story late at night about his affair with B—— and the necessity for discretion.

There are lies all around me. I look at my skin, I see the rash (no, the skin is not purple, they are not lesions), and those I work with look at me with sympathy. "Uh huh," they say, with a sigh of sympathy and a smile, and I lie to them, smile at them; no, I am not worried, no, this little blot on my face means nothing (and actually, the doctor says no, it really does mean nothing). When I was ten years old, my grandmother held up her hand to me in our kitchen. She rarely visited, and it was my fault, of course, that she didn't. I didn't need her, she said, not like her little favorites Joey and Carlo (Carlo killed in Vietnam, Joey hustling in Las Vegas after pushing her down the stairs, the family lost touch). Her skin was like a cooked clove of garlic, almost transparent, delicate, faintly odorous. "I really have a lot of wrinkles, don't I?" she said. "I used to have such beautiful hands." And she had—I saw photographs. We looked at them after her funeral, though what she died from I can no longer remember. My father did not attend his own mother's funeral. He was allergic to the perfume in the flowers and spent the three days sitting in his car in the parking lot outside Biondo and Sons' Funeral Home. Years later when my father died, we used a different funeral home and asked that no one send flowers. Nosek and Sons was really much more beautiful, with a pond in the back, and ducks, and swans, even, unless I am misremembering because of my illness.

The doctor's office is in a largely abandoned strip mall. My mother used to take me to a shop there for orthopedic shoes. The doctor's shoes are Reeboks, and I study his feet when he comes into the room. They are definitely not flat like mine. He knows enough not to let his patients wait, and when he comes into the examining room with his big feet, he says, "No, no."

It is just like the last time, the doctor says, "No, the test results do not show any infection; your test is negative." But he knows, of course, that there is a window, that were I infected in the past week, for instance, the infection would not yet show up in the test. And so I have him schedule another test for three months later, just in case. Like the last time.

The rash on my leg is as dry and scaly as ever. It isn't purple, but it won't go away. My other doctor, the dermatologist in the old building they are about to tear down, gave me some medicine, which I have been using now for over nine years; as long as I use it faithfully, my skin remains under control. Nine years is a long time, and I know the scaly patches aren't really lesions, although in the last week, the leg started bleeding. Does that mean anything? Is it just more of the old rash or had I brushed against some poison ivy the day I was walking along the nature trail?

The man I had met there had wanted to make love to me, but I had said, "No, no." Actually, that is not exactly right. The man I had met there had wanted to make love to somebody, and I had been there and available. "No," I said to him, "no." Certainly not in public.

He said that the trees and flowers provided a natural ambiance of their own and that the surroundings were the whole point of the love-making. Still, the fear that I could be caught was so palpable that I knew I could never enjoy it. It was autumn, and the leaves were rotting and beautiful. When I was five years old, at a huge family picnic at Tinkers Creek Park, my cousin Angelo issued a challenge. "We're climbing up the big hill," said Angelo, and all forty of my cousins followed, until Angelo said, "And if any of you little guys get stuck along the way, we'll leave you there to rot!"

It was autumn and beautiful, and the trees were everywhere except along that huge steep hill. It was so bare, even of brush, that climbing it without anything green or living to cling to for support seemed almost impossible. And to me, it seemed like a mountain. Too afraid to go on the expedition, I stayed behind. As my cousins all hiked up the hill, I waited anxiously, wondering what would happen and listening for news of the first casualty. Some went up only a little way and then rolled back down, only to start up again. Some made it up halfway, and then, paralyzed with fear at how high they seemed suspended, were afraid to proceed in either direction. At the top of the hill, Angelo laughed and rolled boulders down the hill, aiming at various cousins, who screamed in fear. "It's the survival of the fittest in the jungle," Angelo shouted, and then added a stirring Tarzan yell while beating his breast. At the funeral of Angelo's mother only last month, I saw Angelo again for the first time in over two decades: fifteen years of drug use had taken their toll, and he looked gaunt, used up, walking like an old man, barely able to climb the five steps into the Kettering-Smith funeral home, let alone a small mountain. And for a moment I wondered whether he had contracted it, too.

I hope that the man in the woods has not. I know that people will lie about these things. Orgasm is a powerful motivator; it is for me. If I had a lover, I would not have to take walks in those woods and pretend to enjoy the trees, although perhaps that is disingenuous and I would anyway.

Afterward, in my bedroom, the man from the woods looked much less attractive, and in the yellow light of a sixty-watt bulb, I could see wrinkles and shadows. We talked about things unsaid. Eventually, passion was exchanged, and all was accomplished safely, but then when I looked at my leg, the skin seemed red; it had been bleeding. Had a drop of seminal fluid come in contact with it?

Later, I rubbed some lemon juice into my leg to discover whether the wound was really open. The first time I didn't feel any burning sensation, but the second time I rubbed, I did, unless the burning was the result of how hard I had been rubbing. My mother used to make "lemon aid" for me during the summer when elementary school was not in session. The neighborhood kids and I would play in the wading pool in our backyard, pretending to swim. The pool lining was blue, and there were brightly colored fish lacquered on the corrugated metal pool frame. Richard Sindelar would sit in the pool with me, and once Richard told me that he would give me a dollar if I touched his penis. I didn't, of course, because I knew that those kinds of things were simply not done. Years later, in high school, I suddenly realized that Richard Sindelar had moved out of the neighborhood, though I couldn't pinpoint the precise moment we had stopped being friends. He had become a juvenile delinquent, a neighbor had said, and was stabbed by another teenage hoodlum in a fight over a girl. Did a stab wound feel like lemon juice on a scaly leg? Last year, when my mother cleaned out her garage and threw out the wading pool, she was reminded of Richard Sindelar. "Oh, I wanted to tell you," she said in the same tone she would use to tell me that the paperboy had delivered a wet newspaper. "Your friend was on the news the other night for eating the private parts of some men he had killed. Or maybe it was just someone who looked like him."

When I get into my car after my news from the doctor, the humidity seems greater than before, and I feel as though I am drowning in that wading pool. I want to scream (when I was seven I was allowed to scream or when I was five or when I was ten, but I am almost forty, my birthday is next week), and I think no, people will hear.

I think no, but if only I can get through the next three months, till the next test, till the next one.

I am drowning. I am drowning, and the wipers in the car are slashing back and forth. My synapses are tired making all these connections, and maybe later I will finally smile, watching some reruns of old television programs where everyone laughs a lot and wears nice clothes and ordinary shoes, and no one will say a word about any of it, not a word.

Brother Balm

Gerard Wozek

*"I refuse to become a seeker for cures. Everything that has ever helped me has
come through what already lay stored in me."*
Adrienne Rich

Our prodigal brother has come back from the city.
A city that has stripped him of his erotic power,
condemned him for his innocent passion,
named his love as an unnatural act,
shackled him to secrecy and shame.
Weary, our brother has imbibed their words,
their poisonous prognosis, their fetish
with a death that seeks to conquer him.
He limps back from the city, shunned as a leper,
speckled with fever and sores,
so we circle around him.

He is spattered with the milky saliva of our kisses.
We run our hands over his sweaty back,
then dollop him with cool swamp water.
Smearing earth and moss over his blistered shoulder,
we wrap him in fig leaves soaked in mugwort and cypress.
We circle around him.

Screams are lodged somewhere in his throat,
so we take turns rocking out his stifled cries.
Comfrey and tulip petals are dabbed over his eyes,
and plum-colored bruises seem to fade.

There is healing in our linked hands and arms
as we blow light into his solar plexus.
Singing the lost sonatas of doves and pelicans,

we fan him dry with palm leaves and wind bracelets of
shells and shark teeth around his neck and wrists.

We light candles to honor the gentle spirit that offers us
this meadow, the waves, the star-dusted prairies,
the oceans and rain, the span of summer sundowns.

We bait the angels with dances and chants,
we smudge the air with prayers and sage,
consorts of butterflies, servants of light,
we sit and cry into the moon and our vision of healing
begins to take root.

Our brother begins to breathe calmly,
and he takes over the serpent of his own erotic power
which coils around him like a safety net.
He joins our circle where we name him comrade,
spirit warrior, brother.

We circle around. This is the gift entrusted to us.

We have no one to thank for this but ourselves.

Survival

Karen Lee Osborne

I

TONIGHT she sleeps in a crevice. She curls on a bed of scattered leaves and pine needles, seeking comfort in a slice of the mountain. The snow has stopped as inexplicably as it began. Who would have thought so much snow could fall on a California mountain? "Do you realize we expect snow tonight?" the woman at the ranger station had asked. "No problem," Miranda told her. After growing up in Illinois, she wasn't worried about a few flakes on a California mountain in March. Until she woke up the next morning and found it had covered her tracks. She started hiking down anyway, not knowing where she was going. She followed a creek. Surely it would lead her down the mountain.

The first night away from her tent she slept at the base of a tree. Nearly froze. Last night she found the crevice. Now she shakes her legs and arms and stamps her feet to keep them from freezing. The ground is still damp. But the snow is gone.

II

In my dream she is calling my name, and I do not know why. She hasn't called in weeks. In my last letter I told her of a friend who is dying. Tonight, another woman has spoken to me in my solitude, and her voice has followed me home. She makes me want to listen again. Her phrases touch nerves, set off sparks. After months of silence, sounds shock me. When I cry out in pleasure now, a different name is on my lips.

III

Not Miranda. Miranda is freezing on a California mountain. She has not eaten in three days. They are hunting her now, with dogs. She does not know this. She is nearly delirious. She follows a creek, her secondhand running shoes gripping the rocky bank. She can smell herself. A rank odor like a mildewed basement. Today she will take the creek as far as it goes, and it will lead her down to the city. When she gets there, she will bathe with warm water. Someone will bring her a clean towel. Her feet will come to life, will feel pain again.

IV

I cook with pleasure, as if preparing sacraments, and serve my love breakfast. She is lovely, and wise. Wiser and stronger than Miranda, I think, or perhaps only in a different way. She loves Chicago and will never leave. She is tall and walks with the grace of a woman who knows what she wants. I believe I will love her more than I loved Miranda, and longer. She carries me out of the cold rocky cell I've been in, and I rise, easily, my heart opening again to city, lake, sky, wind.

V

Miranda navigates the second waterfall that signs have marked "impassable." She has been bleeding all day, soaking her underwear and jeans. Along the inseams dried blood has frozen in ridges. She believes there are no bears here. When her mind tries to imagine bears, she ropes it in. The firm discipline of a cowboy. A pioneer. She can hang on. She climbs from tree limb to rocky footing to trunk and limb again. Her jeans have saved her ass. The first time she slid and fell on the rocks, she scraped a patch off the elbow of her jacket, but her jeans didn't tear. Another fall cut them on the thigh, but they protected her.

VI

Tonight, I have trouble sleeping. I awaken, cold, and touch my new lover. I turn on my side, begin breathing deeply to calm myself. One long breath in, through my right nostril. Hold. I am not certain I want to enter these rapids, this change. She has pledged her love. My desire surges through me, an apparently indestructible force that will carry me right through into a new life, the life I have always wanted, a life Miranda was not quite ready for when she loved me. But I know it is Miranda who led me to this water. "Don't leave me," she begged at the end, but she had already left, needing to be free. I exhale slowly, deeply. I have let Miranda go, she who taught me how I deserve to be loved, and I am not with her now to carry her down from that mountain. I sleep again and dream. I hear Miranda calling my name, but I do not know where she is. Then I dream we are preparing for a trip, packing food. She looks at me, her face drawn, her lovely, fair forehead creased in pain. "There is not enough," she says. "Not enough for both of us." I leave the food with her and watch her walk away, alone.

VII

Miranda has not known where she is for four days now. She has been tracking the creek downward, knowing that the water will lead her to where she wants to go. But today her journey halts. The third waterfall really is impassable. If only she had some rope. There are no trees, no ledges, no breaks in the rock where she can get sure footing. Her feet are like bricks someone has tied to her legs to weigh her down. Has she come so far only to die alone? She has a knife in the pocket of her jeans. If she collapses, if the vultures come, she will act while she still has strength. She will plunge the knife into her heart so that she will not have to endure what they would do to her alive. But still there is time. She has at least one more day. She will sleep here, near the falls that have stopped her. Tomorrow, if she has strength, she will backtrack and try another canyon.

VIII

In my dream I am dancing with Miranda again on a smooth marble floor of black and white tiles. It is slippery, but in Miranda's arms I am not afraid. She knows how to move.

IX

It is daylight. She has been semiconscious for some time. She splashes her face with water and tries to wake up completely. She drinks the creek water, not caring whether it will make her sick. It is cold and yet somehow no longer painful to her mouth. She would drink more of it if her stomach would accept it. She looks toward the other canyon, but when she starts to walk, she stumbles. She is too dizzy. Her feet will not go where she wants them to. She sits down again.

The trees rustle, louder and louder. After what has seemed a very long time, she realizes it isn't trees at all but a machine. A helicopter. She stands, slowly, and begins to wave. Yes, they see her. They have found her. The helicopter lands and a man in a park uniform comes to her. She tries to tell him not to be concerned about all the blood; she's just had her period. She knows she stinks, but she has been too cold to dare bathing in the icy water. He brings her a plastic bottle, motions to her to stop talking and drink.

Down at the ranger station where, six days earlier, she had left her car, she is helped out of the helicopter. Two handsome women in park uniforms are waiting. Miranda sees their quads defined against the fabric of their pants. They are the most beautiful women she thinks she has ever seen. They are waiting with food and drink and bandages. She still stinks, but she can't resist: "I need a hug." The first woman, tanned, healthy, strong, with thick reddish hair like a fox's, comes to her and wraps her warmly, smell and all. Miranda begins to cry.

X

When I learn she is safe, I understand that it is time. In my dreams she no longer calls my name.

"Are you all right?" Miranda's parents ask. The park people, her friends, the reporters, the nurses have all asked the same thing.

"Yes," she tells them.

I watch a strong and gentle wind smooth the wrinkles from the lake, caress the sand and rocks. Inside her apartment my lover moves across the warm wooden floor and comes to me. Before she asks again, I answer.

"Yes."

Every Last Drop

Allison J. Nichol

Fair warning. On your eightieth birthday,
when you are feigning brittle breathlessness,
I will remind you of promises made this large
October day. That when we reached the outer
boundary we would shimmy ourselves into skin

tight lime green stretch pants, cherry red
toeless tennis shoes, lavender lace bustiers.
Waddle, arm in arm, proud and fat as cows
through thick suburban shopping malls
eating melted chocolate ice cream

with our fingers. Smearing the remains
on our crotches like old blood. Stick
our tongues out at startled blond
sales clerks as they refuse us access
to the expensive furs. Cause commotion

in fine jewelry popping diamond rings
into our mouths, spitting them out
with no excuse but the smiles
of two old women performing
the reckless magic of dying angels.

Part IV

"Faithful Past in Continuous Present": Text/Context

Genyphyr Novak, "Scott McPherson, Danny Sotomayor, and Scout"

An Interview with Scott McPherson

Owen Keehnen

"Now I am 31 and my lover has AIDS. *Our friends have* AIDS. *And we all take care of each other, the less sick caring for the more sick. At times, an unbeliev- ably harsh fate is transcended by a simple act of love, by caring for another. By most, we are thought of as 'dying.' But as dying becomes a way of life, the meaning of the word blurs."*

—Scott McPherson's program note to Hartford Stage Company's production of *Marvin's Room,* December 1990

WHEN Scott McPherson died from complications due to AIDS on No- vember 7, 1992, the theater was robbed of a talented young play- wright. Scott's major work, the absurdist, poignant, and brilliant *Mar- vin's Room,* received numerous accolades, including the Outer Critics' Circle Award, the Drama Desk Award, the John Gassner Playwriting Award, and the Dramatists Guild's Hall-Warriner Award. Scott was liv- ing every writer's dream and living with AIDS. Yet despite his illness and the death of his lover, activist and political cartoonist Daniel So- tomayor, in February 1992, Scott never became bitter. Instead, he struggled through his illness with a strength and humor reflective of his *Marvin's Room* characters.

Sadly, Scott McPherson leaves behind only a small body of work. Besides *Marvin's Room* and its screen adaptation, Scott wrote only one other play, *'Til the Fat Lady Sings,* and a screenplay for Norman Lear's Act III production company called *Legal Briefs.*

When I began to update the introduction to this interview for *Re- claiming the Heartland,* I decided to go back and review the tape as well. I hoped to add a couple of questions that had been edited, a little something to reveal the real Scott, not just "the brilliant play- wright of *Marvin's Room,*" but the caring and wise, funny and whim- sical man known to his family and friends.

The tape began with the loud, sniffing sounds of Scott's dog, a boxer named Scout. The sniffing was followed by numerous calls of

"No, Scout" and "Stay, Scout" by both of us and then laughter as Scout knocked over the tape recorder. Next came about twenty seconds of indistinguishable sounds of shuffling and muffled movement and muted conversation. It became quiet for a second, and then there were a couple of distinct "Ahems" and the interview seemed to officially begin.

The first question I asked went something like this: "Congratulations on winning the uh . . . uh . . ." I had trouble remembering if it was called The Outer Critics' Circle Award or the Critics' Outer Circle Award, and I flip-flopped a couple of times before asking Scott which one it was. His response was, "The Critics' Outer—no. Wait. The Outer Critics' Circle Award. Yeah, it's the Outer Critics' Circle Award. I always get that confused, too."

I didn't notice or record the exchange when I originally transcribed the interview. It was trivial. But when I reviewed the tape for this anthology, with more than a year's passage and Scott now gone, the opening snippet seemed much more significant. Suddenly what was really going on was quite apparent. I could tell that Scott knew what the award was called, but rather than simply saying, "It's the Outer Critics' Circle Award," he feigned confusion and tripped himself up just so I wouldn't feel bad about not being sure of the proper name. It was a small but accurate glimpse into the casual sweetness of the man.

OWEN: Congratulations on winning the Outer Critics' Circle Award yesterday.

SCOTT: Thanks.

OWEN: Has the critical and commercial success of *Marvin's Room* come as a surprise to you?

SCOTT: Yeah. When I got done writing it, I will admit that I liked it and I felt really good about it. At that time I was working at a warehouse in Schaumburg, and I wrote a lot of it out there, which is why I was eventually fired. I wrote this play on the back of their commission reports. I was hoping maybe Lifeline would do it since they'd done my other play. If I was ambitious at all, I was hoping to have an Equity production of it, but that was as far as I was thinking. Then a reading was arranged at Steppenwolf, and then all of a sudden there was all this momentum behind it.

OWEN: What did you learn from writing your first play, *'Til the Fat Lady Sings*, that you were able to apply to *Marvin's Room*?

SCOTT: There is a lot of similarity between the plays, but there are also great differences. *Fat Lady* was big and sprawling. There were scenes with twelve people on stage at the same time and a lot of slapstick—very broad, bold, and farcical strokes. When I wrote *Marvin's Room*, I wanted it to be more of an etching, distinct fine lines with no excess. But thematically the two are similar and the sense of humor is similar—almost as if the same person wrote both.

OWEN: Uncanny. As a former actor, did you write *Marvin's Room* more through an actor's eyes than a playwright's?

SCOTT: I think so, but I think I write mainly from an improviser's point of view. When I first got into acting, that's what I wanted to do. When I write, I usually just think, "What happens next?" Like in the first scene of *Marvin's Room*, Bessie is at the doctor's office, and I thought, "Now what would happen next?"—and the answer was she'd go home.

OWEN: So rather than diagramming, you write with the momentum of what you have previously written?

SCOTT: Yeah, more exploratory than anything.

OWEN: How much of your personal life overlaps into your writing?

SCOTT: In surface ways, a lot. My grandfather was named Marvin, and I had an Aunt Ruth and an Aunt Bessie. When I sat down to write, it helped to focus on these real people so I could get started, but as I wrote, they changed so much and the situations were fictional, so they didn't resemble the real people at all anymore. I always intended to change the names, but I never ever did.

OWEN: So of course your family thinks it's about them.

SCOTT: Oh, sure.

OWEN: Aside from this, how do you build a dramatic character?

SCOTT: I think first I try to find some sort of comic tic and work backwards from there to make the tic grounded and part of a full-fledged character rather than just a gag.

OWEN: On the surface your characters may read as jokey, but—

SCOTT: Thank God for the actors, because they bury it all in a complex character.

OWEN: That's overly humble—the complexity of your characters is evident in just reading *Marvin's Room*. Your dialogue is fantastic; did you get it from a family of storytellers or something?

SCOTT: No. I don't know. I never really thought of having a knack for it. Again, maybe it's all flowing from the "What happens next?"

momentum. The important thing about doing that is finding the voice of each character.

OWEN: What was your main consideration in adapting the *Marvin's Room* screenplay?

SCOTT: I tried to take the characters and the story and remove the theatrical conventions. I tried to come into each scene visually rather than through dialogue. In movies you can say so much with the right image.

OWEN: Who's doing the film?

SCOTT: Robert DeNiro's production company, Tribeca, and, as of now, Miramax is the distributor—but it's changed before. It's attracting the attention of a lot of actresses because the play has two very strong female leads in their forties—and there aren't many film roles like that.

OWEN: Who's after the film?

SCOTT: Names fly around. The latest is Meryl Streep. Debra Winger was very interested for a while.

OWEN: Who would you like to see in the film version?

SCOTT: My first choice would be the stage cast, especially Laura Esterman, because she is so great in the role. She's taken the character so many places I never dreamed of and seems totally inherent to the part.

OWEN: Who would you want if you had to choose a film actress?

SCOTT: Dianne Wiest would be my first choice. She's somewhat like Laura. Laura has a certain goofiness about her that belies the tragedy, so she sort of bubbles along on top, though all these things are happening to her underneath. Yet, despite the goofiness there is a great strength, and I think Dianne Wiest has that quality, too.

OWEN: What are you working on now?

SCOTT: I'm working on a screenplay for Norman Lear's company called *Legal Briefs*. It's a screwball farce that can only happen in the movies.

OWEN: What writers do you admire?

SCOTT: Raymond Carver, David Mamet, Joe Orton, Beth Henley. And I admire Arthur Miller, partially just because of who he is. I read his autobiography, *Timebends*, and felt he said a lot of really good stuff. One thing he said, and I'm probably horribly misquoting, was that "you know you've written something good if it makes you feel embarrassed—because you've really revealed something about yourself from someplace deep."

OWEN: Do you view life as a black comedy?

SCOTT: I view it as black. I don't know if I have a world view as much as I just try to survive. I always felt that if I just wrote seriously without the humor that everyone would say it was bad. If you can be funny and entertain, you can get away with much more.

OWEN: You wrote *Marvin's Room* when you were first diagnosed—

SCOTT: With HIV.

OWEN: If you were to write the play now, after living with AIDS, what, if anything, would you change about it?

SCOTT: I wrote the play even before I met Danny [Sotomayor]. And then we met and . . . as he became sicker, a lot of my energy went to trying to help him, and I would sometimes be sick. It was so weird. It was like my life was catching up to the play in the same ways. I felt good when I saw *Marvin's Room* in New York and realized that what I'd written about, that experience, was true.

OWEN: It's so weird to think of the play as a precursor.

SCOTT: I know. A lot of articles say I wrote the play while taking care of Danny or I wrote the play between bouts of illness while being sick with AIDS, which is not true at all. I was still totally healthy. I was HIV-infected, but I hadn't experienced a single symptom. I hadn't yet met Danny when I finished it.

OWEN: Your life is so divided. On one side you're experiencing every writer's dream and on the other side dealing with the loss of Danny and living with AIDS. How does that all come together?

SCOTT: Well, it makes the awards and attention and stuff sort of meaningless, what with Danny dead, and even before then with just being sick. It kind of takes the wind out of your sails. Having audiences still laugh and be moved by the play brings me enjoyment, and that has not faded because of personal things, but all other stuff I don't find very exciting. Maybe if I were healthier and Danny were still here.

OWEN: When someone leaves the theater after seeing *Marvin's Room*, what is the overall impression or impact you want the play to have?

SCOTT: It might sound stupid, but I just hope they had a good time at the theater. I hate to be bored at the theater, which a lot of times makes me go for the humor. And I guess I want to make people see the value of caring for other people and that caring in and of itself offers a reward. It's a valuable thing.

Clytemnestra's lament

for L. M. H.

Edward Thomas-Herrera

Ten years
ten wretched years
ten long wretched years of nothing but good news
    interminable letters filled with warm and friendly tidings from
      the Trojan front

    (greetings Wife that's what he always called her she hated it
      when he called her that
    greetings Wife soon we will deliver the hostage Helen and set
      sail for Greece
    once again our forces have proven victorious in battle
    how's the weather there it's a little nippy here
    give my love to the children
    yours truly Agamemnon)

ten miserable years of falsehood and pretense
    playing the faithful wife the dutiful queen the cheery keeper
      of the hearth
    to a boorish ungrateful testosterone-besotted sensitivity-
      challenged cad
    who would rather run off and fight a ridiculously pointless war
    than help her raise a quartet of troubled preteens
ten insufferable years of sacrificing to the Olympian gods
    praying for the safe return home of the fighting sons of the
      Peloponnesus
    all the while secretly hoping that some priestly oversight some
      divine whim some sacred loophole
    would keep her soldier boy far far away for an extended
      period of time if not permanently

How Clytemnestra longed for
    the day when a teary dutiful messenger
    covered with the sweat and dust of a distant journey
    would arrive at the palace gates bearing the black news of a
        great hero's fall in battle
how Clytemnestra longed for
    the day when she could don her widow's veil and weep
        bitterly
    at the sight of a mighty warrior's armor-encased corpse
    stretched out in state on a flower-strewn bier
how Clytemnestra longed for
    the day when she could mourn the passing of a husband and
        father
    pretending to be so grief-stricken that on cue her faithful
        Nurse
    would restrain her from leaping onto the funeral pyre
    while flames consumed the lifeless body of a man
    she had forgotten how to love so long ago
    (afterwards
    sobbing and inconsolable
    she would retire to her chambers
    where Aegisthus would be waiting
    freshly annointed with oils a kylix of rich heated wine in each
        hand
    his noble manhood primed and ready to celebrate their love
        once again
    on the same bed where years before she had surrendered her
        maidenhead
    to bring forth a dynasty of Mycenaean kings)
how Clytemnestra longed for
    the day when an impressive marble stele
    depicting the valiant king's final moments
    would proudly commemorate the occasion
    of her emancipation from matrimony patriarchy and
        servitude

Ten years
ten lovely years

ten wonderful years of not having Agamemnon around
    unshaven unbathed reeking of wine and horses
    forcing her into performing wifely duties headache or no
    climbing into bed for a little matinee performance wearing
        his muddy boots
    then asking her to play hostess inviting the troops over for
        dinner and debauchery
    (you could've at least given me a little warning I have to
        notify the kitchen staff
    what I told you last summer they were coming over)
ten marvelous years of no man telling her what to do
    happy years of peace and quiet law and order
    a city-state run like a highly efficient household
    the streets neat as a pin the municipal budget balanced
    the newly renovated agora beautified with seasonal blooms
    military expenditures diverted toward food and clothing for
        the needy

ten incredible years of sweet Aegisthus
    young handsome smelling of cedar and myrrh
    funny romantic sensitive vulnerable considerate and caring
    wherever however whenever she wanted it she called the shots
    they would indulge in frenzied lovemaking on a lonely
        Aegean beach
    and she would experience truly passionate kisses and multiple
        orgasms
    then watch the sun come up over the sea while he read his
        poetry to her

    (you know I'm really impressed that you could find a word
        that rhymes with Clytemnestra)

ten eye-opening years of growth and change
    coming out of the kitchen
    coming out of the nursery
    coming out of the bedroom
    realizing she didn't need a husband to make her happy
        even if he is a rich and powerful warlord

realizing her full potential as a parent as an administrator as
    a human being as a woman
realizing how everything was just so much nicer when she was
    on her own

three thousand six hundred and fifty days not counting February
    29ths
    and now it was all about to come crashing to an end today
    in the worst-possible-case scenario the war was over
    Agamemnon was coming home

    (back to walking ten steps behind
    back to being the little woman
    back to standing in his shadow)

    (she had to think of something)
    (quick)

open heart

Kitty Tsui

a languorous autumn day
in a sun-filled apartment
on the banks of lake michigan,
the home of lola,
born in the year of the ox.

she has offered to do a reading.
i am seated on the floor,
a circle of hearts before me,
stones from
the beaches of the windy city.

i talk about the tour—
three cities, eight days, four shows.
hard, intense, exhilarating, and exhausting.
then the march on D.C., meeting
hundreds of thousands of like-hearts.

i talk about the rejection,
the struggle, the pain of being with another.
i cry, my heart open,
remembering abandonment and separation,
the loss of my grandmother and my best friend.

lola asks if i do stones, crystals.
no, i reply, not remembering
all the hearts i've found on beaches
since anita's death:
shell, stone, bark, mother-of-pearl.

ngay yow sum, she says.
in a literal sense, you have heart.

idiomatically, you are caring.
yow sum, have heart,
yow sum, thoughtful, caring.

the chinese language so full of hearts:
ho sum, good heart, kind.
seung sum, sad, broken-hearted.
hoi sum, open heart, happy.
siew sum, little heart, take care.

tiem sum, sweet heart,
seung sum, open your heart,
ho sum, good heart,
siew sum, my heart, *yow sum,*
have heart, *hoi sum,* open heart.

Faithful Past in Continuous Present

What Endures: Visiting the Edith Lewis-Willa Cather
Cottage on Grand Manan

Linnea Johnson

She loved faithfulness.
—Stephen Tennant, *Willa Cather on Writing*

I

THE Grand Manan Museum displays Willa Cather's small
table on which sits the Oliver typewriter she used while at Grand
Manan most summers between 1922 and 1942. It has an open bank
of keys arranged like butterfly wings. On the table next to this typewriter sits the Bernice Slote–Lucia Woods pictorial, colored yarn
strands marking pages with photos of this island, home to Cather as
no other place since Red Cloud, Nebraska. To the right of the little
table sits a small rocker unmarked as a thing of Cather's but that
matches in tone her footstool tucked under the small table. This writing table is no more than a couple of feet square on four plain legs—a
thing easily moved from indoors at an upstairs attic window to a grassy
lawn sloping to the Bay of Fundy on a flawless, cool, and sunny summer day of writing. In the typewriter is a list of Cather's novels, those
written wholly or in part on Grand Manan asterisked: *A Lost Lady*,
1923; *The Professor's House*, 1925; *My Mortal Enemy*, 1926; *Death Comes
for the Archbishop*, 1927; *Shadows on the Rock*, 1931; *Lucy Gayheart*, 1935;
Sapphira and the Slave Girl, 1940.

To the left of the typewriter, just barely on the table, is a quotation
in primer typeface reproduced from Edith Lewis's memoir, *Willa
Cather Living*:

Ever since the writing of *One of Ours* [1922], Willa Cather had found that island . . . a great resource, an increasingly congenial place to work . . . the
beautiful silence, accentuated instead of diminished by the sound of the sea

on the shingle, the wind blowing the alder bushes, rain on the roof, the songs of hundreds of birds, was tranquillizing to the spirit, seemed to open up great spaces for it to roam in. (192)

Above the table and typewriter, book list, quotation, rocker, and footstool is the Rinehart-Marsden photographic portrait of Cather in which her arms come through embroidered jacket sleeves, her hands resting in front of her. Above the Cather portrait is a photograph not of Edith Lewis, with whom she lived on and off Grand Manan for nearly forty years, but of a friend of Cather's from Grand Manan, one Dr. Jack Macaulay.

Next to this modest display and not intended as part of the display is a large picture window beyond which lies a meadow of lupine, daisy, and iris, and the sea. The landscape taken together with the Cather display seems a musical chord, a resonant portrait of why Cather, with Lewis, so frequently summered on Grand Manan.

In her preface to *Not Under Forty* (1936), Willa Cather writes, "The world broke in two in 1922, or thereabouts" (15). Nineteen twenty-two is eight years after the Vorticist movement began, 1922 seeing the publication of both *Blast* and the *Egoist*. Dada has begun. Pound is writing. Stein is writing. Pasternak and Pirandello are writing; it is six years after Henry James died, a mere four years after the World War ended. Nineteen twenty-two is the year Mussolini marched on Rome, Proust died, Eliot published *The Waste Land*, and Joyce published *Ulysses*. Edith Sitwell writes *Façade* in 1922; Hesse writes *Siddhartha*.

It is about this time that Cather, nearing fifty, must have, more than ever, looked for the enduring—a kind of inexplicable faithful past set in continuous present. Perhaps such hardships as experienced on Grand Manan—no electricity and poor food—looked suddenly appealing to Cather: "It was a sort of Robinson Crusoe life," wrote Edith Lewis in *Willa Cather Living* (193). The Modern, which Cather rejected, had yet to be thought, much less enacted, written about, or lived (through) on Grand Manan.

How necessary it must have been for Cather to find the kind of felicitous space she remembered from her childhood, her youth, which she wrote into her novels—that sort of landscape Cather said she'd found writing about her character Alexandra, that "home pasture," she'd called it, inscribing the same into Carrie Miner Sherwood's copy of *O Pioneers!* (O'Brien 208-9). With Edith Lewis, the enduring intimate partner of her adult life, Willa Cather began frequenting Grand Manan in 1922, just when the world, for Cather, broke in two.

Grand Manan (Ma-'nan), New Brunswick, is the largest island in the Fundy archipelago lying between Maine and Nova Scotia. It is a cliffed rock about twenty miles long and, in places, eight miles wide. Its people have historically made their living on the sea. While Grand Mananers no longer build ships, many of the twenty-five hundred or so residents continue to mine herring weirs. Weirs are large, circular log-and-net offshore corrals that trap herring moved into them by the dramatic push of Bay of Fundy tides. Marion Marsh Brown and Ruth Crone note that Cather

first learned of the island when she was doing research in the New York Public Library during the winter of 1920-1921. She mentioned to Miss Overton, a librarian there, that an author needed a quiet place to work. Miss Overton had a suggestion. Four of her friends, she said, had vacationed on a small fishing island in the Bay of Fundy and thought it probably the quietest place in the world. One of them, Miss Jacobus, had been so enamored of the island that she had returned and bought property there. Now she had started a small summer place, Whale Cove Inn. Perhaps it would satisfy Miss Cather's needs. (5-6)

Summers now there are two ferries making the two-hour trip several times a day, from Blacks Harbour on the New Brunswick mainland to North Head on Grand Manan. Lewis remembers "a five or six hour trip" to cross the Bay of Fundy "on a small steamboat which sailed twice a week from St. John's, New Brunswick" (128). The resident population has remained fairly constant over the past several decades, and there continue to be guest accommodations at inns, B&Bs, cottages, and a hotel. Though there are certainly more summer people who own their own cottages on the island now than when Lewis and Cather summered on Grand Manan, still, the island does not seem touristy and does seem, if not remote, then removed somewhat from the run of things.

The summer weather on Cather's "flowery bowery isle" (Robinson 129) is hot sun, cool air, cold nights, daylight in July stretching from maybe 4 or 5 A.M. until 9 or 10 P.M. Fog and sun and rain blow on and off the island for hours at a time each day. Mosquitoes moil about for a couple of hours around dusk, swallows diving, feeding on them, clearing them away. Evenings are for lobster on the dinner plate, conversation and reading, a birch fire snapping in the stove. Nights not pillowed in fog are a blaze of stars.

The southern part of the island has the most and densest fog, which can cause wildflowers separated by less than ten miles to be two weeks or more different in growth and bloom. It is the profusion and variety of wildflowers along with the astounding cliffs, woods, and sea that create the Grand Manan landscape.

Though the weather was perfection to me and the absence of lardy knots of tourists was more than I had hoped for, I was on the island to see the Cather-Lewis cottage. I have been reading Cather since I took a class on her taught by Bernice Slote at the University of Nebraska in the mid-1970s. I continue to read Cather, though these days I tend to read more about her than by her. And I find that reading anyone in situ—Cather or Faulkner or Twain or Jewett—illuminates and vivifies the work, the writer, and the reading.

Willa Cather, through Bernice Slote, enabled me to read differently a landscape I felt was devoid of detail, of interest. I was restless, then, living in Nebraska, having left my home in Chicago. I thought there was nothing to see in Nebraska. To me Nebraska was the absence of landscape: water, trees, buildings—where were they? Everything I knew to look for wasn't there, in Nebraska. Through Slote's class, through Cather's narratives, I began to see where I was living. If I couldn't read city, or read myself fitting my fingers around boles of birch in gold-coin fall woods, still, in Nebraska, I could read land never built on or cut by a plow. I could gather late-summer ground cherries ripe inside tiny three-sided paper lanterns. I could read and walk through the "spring snow" of cottonwood groves. In Cather, as in Chicago and in the Russian fiction in which I grew up, landscape and weather are narrative carriers of myth and continuity and art—the spine and song and spirit of story.

Then, as now, I look for women active in fiction. As a writer, I look for artists in fiction. As the daughter of a Swedish immigrant, I look for people who sank new roots into new places. As a sane and joyful person, I look for positive images of artists, immigrants, and women. Also, because I am a woman, I read unlike the way most critics read and am enabled/forced to read for myself. Cather was one of the first women I read. If Cather does not direct her female characters' attention and love toward the love of a good man, neither does she direct their attention and love toward women, but she does direct passion toward their art. And, if Cather's immigrants are not industrial city workers like my Swedish father, neither are they anomic, rich

Fitzgeraldian white boys imploding from ennui. Cather's work, for me, is still satisfying.

One lucky Monday morning in July 1989, I went to the Grand Manan Museum and found the archivist, who was busy with Canada Day activities. I introduced myself and told her I was writing a piece about Willa Cather on Grand Manan, asking when might be a good time to speak with her about the museum's Cather collection. The archivist said there wasn't much to tell and that when I had seen the Cather typewriter display I had seen the museum's Cather collection, though as soon as she got the kids singing "O Canada" she'd be happy to talk with me. Of course, she'd give me directions to the cottage then, too, although she said I certainly didn't need her for that, as just about anyone on the island could get me to that cottage.

II

. . . you must find your own quiet center of life and write from that. . . .
—Sarah Orne Jewett (Lewis 66-67)

INSTEAD of directions she volunteers to take me there. She has some time, she says; she'd like to see the place again.

From the museum in Grand Harbour we drive north, turning onto Whistle Road just south of North Head village. Less than a mile up the road, where a red oar is secured to a tree trunk, she turns onto a path through the woods. The archivist pulls into a meadow up next to a car parked there. I pull my car up next to hers. We are at Whale Cove Cottages, she tells me as we get out of our cars; this is where Cather stayed before having her own cottage built, "just north of here," she says. This is a three-building compound, two cottages to the north of a large mowed meadow, the inn to the south of it. We are looking for the innkeeper, a woman who as a girl served meals to Cather and Lewis at the inn.

When the archivist spots the innkeeper, she asks me my name again, then introduces me to the innkeeper, saying that I am interested in Cather and am writing something about her and Grand Manan; she has brought me to see Orchardside cottage here before we walk the few hundred feet through the woods northward to see the cottage Lewis and Cather had built. The innkeeper and the archivist haven't seen each other for a while, apparently, and they chat about the place, the archivist's mother, and generally about what beautiful weather we're having. It is perfect weather, the blue sky outdoing itself in blue, a cool wind to keep the sun from biting, an eternal sea chipped with diamonds, wildflowers to gather by the armful.

The first thing they remember about Cather is that she didn't like anyone even canoeing on the ocean in front of "her" property, something she could have seen only from the cliff or maybe from her attic writing space. Her cottage is set back about two hundred feet, and the ocean is probably one or two hundred feet below the cliff, they note. The archivist remembers Cather—but it was probably Lewis, the innkeeper corrects—who shooed kids away from her cottage and who ran, white hair wild, to the edge of the cliff, pushing the air away from her with her quick hands, pushing away intrusion. "Had to be Lewis," the innkeeper says. "Cather had that auburn hair, Lewis had the white."

She continues: "And when they first put in that weir Miss Cather complained at dinner how she hated it, but then she got so she would tell everyone all about the comings and goings at the weir." They laugh. I laugh.

I wonder about Lewis and ask if she was with Cather much. The innkeeper, who by this time has invited us in out of the sun into the house behind the Orchardside cottage, says, "Oh, yes, they were mostly always together. Then we thought maybe Lewis was her secretary. Now everybody thinks they were lesbians." She mentions that some members of the Cather family are particularly "touchy" about "the subject." I note that both Lewis's job and Cather's secretary were back in New York.

The innkeeper says it doesn't matter and adds, "Nobody thought anything of it back then, even if it were true. There were a lot of single women traveling together then." Indeed, in the 1920s nearly all the Whale Cove Cottage guests were unmarried women, who, as Brown and Crone note, "were feeling new ground . . . were leading the lives they wanted to lead" (34).

"And who cares?" says the archivist, meaning it kindly. I say I think it is important, why miss it, and leave it at that.

We are invited to see the inside of Orchardside as well as the inn's dining room later; now the innkeeper asks the archivist if she'd like to show me the Cather-Lewis cottage (she says, "Miss Cather's cottage"). She knows the Cather niece who owns the place now, who entrusts the key to her, and says it's likely she wouldn't mind our looking at it as long as we don't disturb anything. People, she says, are peeping around there all the time; she finds it honorable that I ask permission before I go over there.

Cather and Lewis last summered on Grand Manan around 1942. They had planned to go back after the war. Cather (b. 1873) died in 1947, and Lewis, despite her intentions to the contrary, didn't return. Lewis (b. 1882) died in 1972, in the Park Avenue apartment they had shared.

The innkeeper says the cottage now doesn't look on the inside anything like it looked "when Miss Cather had the place," that the museum has "what stuff the family didn't want," passed from Lewis to the Cather family at Lewis's death. I've seen all that in the display at the museum, haven't I? Both the archivist and I say yes. The thirty years (1942-1972) and more of inattention has necessitated the partial rebuilding of the place. Along with the recent rebuilding efforts, the family has "updated" it. "You'll see," the innkeeper says, handing the key to the archivist.

We walk the path a few hundred feet through tall spruce woods past a path veering southeast to another cabin, barely visible, and I notice yet another cabin northwest of our path. The archivist says that there are more cabins in these woods than it appears: "None of these were here, of course, when she was here." "She" is Cather. Rarely does anyone say, in person or in text, Cather *and* Lewis.

The archivist orients me, her hand making the shape of the quarter-mile lazy "C" this road makes down from the paved road, Whistle Road, this road that our path has just joined. "Nothing but this road goes this far in, from the inn on." This dirt road has been cut all the way down to the Cather-Lewis cabin. We go on, taking the left fork and find it, ell of the house toward the path, front of the house facing east toward the sea.

The cottage is a full cape, eastern cedar shingles weathered grey where they have not been recently replaced with new honey-colored ones. Cather describes this cottage in a 1944 story, "Before Breakfast," one of her last stories and the only story she set on Grand Manan. In the story this is Henry Grenfell's cabin:

The cabin modestly squatted on a tiny clearing between tall spruce wood and the sea—sat about fifty yards back from the edge of the red sandstone cliff which dropped some two hundred feet to a narrow beach—so narrow that it was covered at high tide. The cliffs rose sheer on this side of the island, where undercut in places, and faced the east. (*The Old Beauty, and Others*, 142)

Edith Lewis wrote of this cottage:

> It was in the summer of 1925 . . . that we decided to build a small cottage on Grand Manan. Willa Cather felt that it would be an advantage to have a sort of summer camp where she could come and go at will—where she would not have to make arrangements in advance, keep set dates, etc.—and where she could live with complete independence. . . . It stood on a sloping hillside, about fifty yards from the edge of the cliffs, in the middle of an open meadow, and was surrounded by a semicircle of spruce and birch woods. It was rather a rough little place, with many inconveniences; but it came to have not only comfort but great charm. Above the living rooms was a large attic from which one could look out over the cliffs and the sea. There was nothing in it except a few trunks, and her chair and table. (130-31)

Today there is scaffolding against the south side of the house where the setback ell begins. We notice that someone has recently re-roofed the cottage. The archivist gestures at the trees and shrubs in front of the cabin: "None of the bushes were out front then—grass clear out to the edge of the cliff." We try the key in the lock on the front door to the ell, then in the lock to the main front door, where daylilies grow to the sides of the stoop. Around back, we try the side door of the rear-protruding ell, but the innkeeper's key unlocks the dutch door to the kitchen. Chives grow along the kitchen stoop; a few feet back there remains a retaining wall, overgrown now, made from large oval stones.

It is wonderful to be here, turning the knob of this back door, anticipating entrance into this house. I remember sitting upstairs in Cather's Red Cloud, Nebraska, house writing a poem, a journal entry, one fine May morning. I remember Bernice Slote opening the cellar door on the Pavelka farm in Webster County, Nebraska, that cellar door transformed by Cather into Ántonia's cellar door out of which ran Ántonia's bright stream of lively children. I remember having tea in Bernice Slote's apartment one spring day and her showing me and the rest of the class Cather family scrapbooks. I remember the connecting sensation it was writing there, being there, touching those things, the fabric of reality and fiction and place a tight weave.

Inside, the kitchen has been remodeled. To the north of the kitchen is a bathroom that has recently replaced a small bedroom.

The small bedroom formerly had not opened into the kitchen but only into the larger bedroom in front of it.

In front of the kitchen is the living room in which stands the central chimney, one hearth for the living room, one for the bedroom next to it. These four rooms form the main house, the east rooms facing the sea, the attic above.

To the south of the living room stands the ell, a long vaulted-ceiling room that closes off from the main part of the house and that has its own doors to the outside, one east to the sea, one at a ninety-degree angle to the dutch door of the kitchen. A half-bath has been installed on what would have been a service porch when Cather and Lewis were in residence.

We look around a while, touch nothing, walk from room to room, returning to the living room. "No charm left," the archivist says. "Nothing like when Miss Cather was here. There were Mexican rugs then, and old Oriental ones. Simple pieces," she says, "and not many of them." The archivist had found the writing table now in the museum "right over there," under the living-room window.

With an attic in the house, Cather wouldn't often have written in the living room. Lewis noted: "Willa Cather looked forward fervently to her attic at Grand Manan" (153). We find the attic door just inside the kitchen door and start upstairs. The treacherous pie-cut and steep steps up to the attic remind me of the ones to the attic in her childhood home in Red Cloud, Nebraska—steps built for mice feet and for feet accustomed in youth to such hazards.

The attic hasn't been redone; it is a relief from the updating of downstairs and is likely the only part of the house Cather and Lewis would recognize—those bare rafters and random-width, unfinished floorboards. Besides the New Century cast-iron cookstove, there is very little else in the attic. A small stack of nondescript bricks sits near the stove. Not much else.

What there is in this attic, however, is familiar. There is a goodly pitch to the roof and there are windows at each end of the attic. This is the kind of place not readily subjected to change. Even in a small house like this, which is being redone inside and out, the attic hasn't been touched. The table and the Oliver were up here. This attic is reminiscent of the attic in Red Cloud and perhaps of her writing room at the top of Isabelle McClung's Pittsburgh house where she wrote early in her career, then too sharing rooms with a woman whom she loved passionately. This attic is also like the top-floor room (adjacent to Edith Lewis's room) at the Shattuck Inn in Jaffrey, New Hampshire, where Cather wrote during so many falls after so many Grand Manan summers.

As we begin down the attic steps I look around a last time and notice a small floor plank of unstained pine across which is stenciled some numbers and the words, "Edith Lewis." Cather and Lewis must have finished or patched the attic floor with packing crates. "Look," I say to the archivist, "look at this."

Back at Whale Cove Cottages, the innkeeper shows us around Orchardside, its nameplate rusting on its front door. Its site in relation to meadow, cliff, and sea, as well as its design and floor plan are a template for the cottage Lewis and Cather had built, the one from which we have just returned. Orchardside has not been updated and has more of the feel I expected from the other cottage. The table and bed Cather and Lewis used remain in this cottage, not out of reverence for Cather's memory but because bed and table are still serviceable, are still being used. "Cather wrote in this bedroom," the innkeeper says, "though she liked the attic here and at her place, too." A woman and a man with several small children seem to be spending the summer here reclaiming Orchardside from the ages, intact and true to its aged self. I like it here.

On our way across the open, mowed meadow, the innkeeper mentions that "your teacher, Professor Slote" spent some time at Orchardside some summers ago, "with her friend, Miss Virginia Faulkner, I believe." I look back toward Orchardside again.

At the inn, the innkeeper shows us the dining room where Cather and Lewis took meals. "There were six square tables in here for diners," she says. "Her [Cather's] table was over there," under a sloping roof by a north window.

The dining room lies as a rear ell at the west of the main inn building. It has a low, low ceiling. The inn, and especially this room of it, is unusual, looking as if it has been washed ashore, moved here from an ancient charming European seacoast village. The room is beautiful, though sunk now into the ground and needing to be lifted somehow back up onto its sills. The innkeeper is thinking of having the ell bulldozed. "It's the bulldozer or the checkbook," says the archivist, "for most of these old places."

Along the dining room's north wall is a long, low window above the baseboards, perhaps six feet long by two feet tall. On the south wall is a window and a door out. To the west is the doorway to the kitchen. The east wall holds shelves on which are displayed blue willow plates. Through the doorway on this wall lies the living room; beyond its deep ship's bow window is meadow, cliff, and sea.

It was, the archivist tells me, her own grandmother who owned all the land along this particular curve and stretch of coast for several miles, and who must have sold the land to Miss Lewis. It was Miss Lewis who signed the deed. "Of course," she adds, "it was Miss Lewis who organized things, did all the running around."

III

Whatever is unnamed, undepicted in images, whatever is omitted from biography, censored in collections of letters, whatever is misnamed as something else, made difficult-to-come-by, whatever is buried in the memory by the collapse of meaning under an inadequate or lying language—this will become, not merely unspoken, but unspeakable.
    —Adrienne Rich, " 'It is the Lesbian in Us . . .' " from *On Lies, Secrets, and Silence*

VISITING the Edith Lewis-Willa Cather cottage on Grand Manan is reading *about* Cather while still reading her. To sit on the cliff in front of the cottage reading about that cliff as Cather wrote about Henry Grenfell seeing it in "Before Breakfast" is to come close to that work sensually, dimensionally, and to experience that interlocking matrix that is writing and the reading of writing. To recognize "meadowsweet" as one reads the word in the story is one kind of experience, but to reach over and pick meadowsweet as one is reading "meadowsweet" is an experience close to having Cather type the story into one's own skin.

Similarly, to isolate "meadowsweet" at all is to foreground a piece of background; it is to interrupt the narrative, hold it still, climb into the page, and look closely at all the separate, distinct details that create landscape. It is to play music instead of merely hearing it. It is to notice that landscape equals foreground plus background, foreground plus background a matter of locus and focus.

For me, this accurate read, this holding it still, necessitates situating precisely the location of the cabin as best I can on paper, placing it distinctly where it is. How it sits and what it sits in relation to are important to me as are details of physiognomy. It is crucial to say what is east of what, to make distinct the presence of alder, birch, and spruce, of the writing attic. Similarly, it is important as alder that Lewis be placed where she was. Birch was there. Edith was there. Lewis's name, then and there, on a pine plank floorboard (more plain than the rusting "Orchardside" nameplate, only a bit more plain than Lewis's headstone a few feet from Cather's tombstone in Jaffrey, New Hampshire) vivifies detail and the importance and meaning of detail as it also illuminates some of that very detail. How Cather sat, at what, and in relation to what and to whom are details important to meaning—are important, are meaning.

At once in the work about Cather little is missed, though much is misread and, therefore, is missed. A low point in writings about Cather occurred in a 1982 *National Geographic* photo essay wherein the writer tells of traveling the land of Cather's childhood and books, trying to "understand Willa Cather" (Howarth 74); he mentions famous men who admired her, various wildflowers she loved, the buffalo that were no longer on the Plains in her childhood, Yehudi Menuhin, of whom Cather was fond, and so forth. He ends a paragraph by saying that she had eight brothers and sisters and "a great capacity for love and affection. Yet she never married" (74). This writer says that he has spent years reading Cather, that he knows the landscape of her life and indeed has found "her at last in the land," yet his read of her is off (74). How can he read the buffalo that weren't there and miss Edith Lewis who was? He mentions Lewis not at all.

The most egregious of mistakes made by writers about Cather, however, is not from some unknown magazine writer but, instead, the legion (and mostly male) critics of Cather. James Woodress, the sore thumb of them all, persistently and consistently reads Cather as if through Coke-bottle bottoms, while structurally he professes to clarify or, at least, to convey fact. Indeed, a tiny instance of this usual off-read occurs when he ignores his own notes to read Cather against what he demonstrates he is aware of. On the subject of purchasing the Grand Manan cottage sites his text reads: "Cather made a short visit to Grand Manan Island" (396). His note on this sentence refutes this: "there is no proof I have found that WC actually went to the island [then]" (550, note to 396). Then he interpolates Lewis's memoir, noting that "one or the other of them staked out the location of the cottage" (396). Finally, he (foot)notes that Lewis's name is on the deed (550). Such a little point, but he could have gotten it right. Why ignore what is apparent in favor of speculation? Why not say textually that Lewis bought the land, recognize the Cather-Lewis union, their conjoined lives? Why off-read?

Elsewhere in the same critical biography, Woodress, lacking notes or any substantive base, bluntly asserts: "Cather was married to her art and sublimated her sexual impulses in her work" (125; see also 127). Further, Woodress states that Cather has "an adult bias against romantic love" and that "her greatest failing as an artist is her inability to depict heterosexual adult relationships" (299). On that same page Woodress calls her "a celibate writer." Here, as elsewhere in his criticism and that of others, assertion substitutes for and as information and, if one is not aware of such habitual off-reading of Cather, often displaces other possible interpretation and fact.

The off-read of Cather misses the existence and resonance of relationships between female and female and between female landscape and female authority/writing. What else the off-read misses is what Cather called the "open secret." Passion, Cather wrote in *The Song of the Lark*, "is every artist's open secret" (397). To off-read Cather is to keep the "secret" and to miss the "open."

It is essential to read Edith Lewis in Willa Cather's landscape and life; Lewis is as indwelling in that life as the stenciled pine plank in that attic. Elizabeth Shepley Sergeant, in her memoir of Cather, quotes Cather as saying, "We are what we love—that is all we are" (49). To miss the landscape in Cather's fiction, in her life, is to miss what and whom she loved; it is to miss the detail Cather meticulously created; it is to miss *what is there*; it is to "miss" Cather.

The cottage on Grand Manan is the only home/physical space/landscape Cather ever participated in owning. Willa Cather and Edith Lewis met in 1903, moved in together in 1909, lived and traveled together, and were still together at Cather's death in 1947 (Lewis xi). In a life such as Cather's, where physical detail/landscape *is* The Story, to write about Willa Cather and to ignore or to displace the attic/landscape/detail of Edith Lewis is akin to writing about Grand Manan and ignoring or erasing the sea or weather or the inundation of wildflowers. It is to misread an iris as a lily or as not there at all. It is to confuse the Atlantic with the Indian Ocean or with being not an ocean at all. The landscape Cather wrote *in* is as important as the landscape she wrote *about.* Where she could and did write, with and for and because of whom, informs what she wrote. Nothing else is true.

For Henry Grenfell, Cather's protagonist in "Before Breakfast," Grand Manan is a place where "everything was the same, and he, Henry Grenfell, was the same: the relationship was unchanged" (162). Perhaps Cather saw in Lewis what she saw in Grand Manan—a solid rock, enduring, out of which grows the passionate profusion of particular wildflowers and story—constant, private, and, if not eternal, certainly faithful as waves.

References

Brown, Marion Marsh, and Ruth Crone. *Only One Point of the Compass: Willa Cather in the Northeast.* Danbury, Conn.: Archer Editions, 1980.

Cather, Willa. *Not Under Forty.* New York: Knopf, 1936.

_____. "Before Breakfast." In *The Old Beauty, and Others,* 141-66. New York: Knopf, 1948. Reprint, New York: Vintage, 1976. Page citations are to the reprint edition.

_____. *The Song of the Lark.* New York: Houghton Mifflin, 1915. Reprint, New York: New American Library, Signet Classic, 1991. Page citations are to the reprint edition.

Howarth, William. "The Country of Willa Cather." *National Geographic* July (1982): 70-93.

Lewis, Edith. *Willa Cather Living: A Personal Record.* New York: Knopf, 1953.

O'Brien, Sharon. *Willa Cather: The Emerging Voice.* Oxford: Oxford University Press, 1987. Reprint, New York: Ballantine Fawcett, 1988. Page citations are to the reprint edition.

Rich, Adrienne. " 'It Is the Lesbian in Us . . .' " In *On Lies, Secrets, and Silence: Selected Prose 1966-1978,* 199-202. New York: Norton, 1979.

Robinson, Phyllis C. *Willa: The Life of Willa Cather.* New York: Holt, Rinehart, & Winston, 1983.

Sergeant, Elizabeth Shepley. *Willa Cather: A Memoir.* Philadelphia: Lippincott, 1953. Reprint, Lincoln: University of Nebraska Press, 1963. Page citations are to reprint edition.

Tennant, Stephen. "The Room Beyond." Foreword to Willa Cather, *On Writing: Critical Studies on Writing as an Art.* New York: Knopf, 1949.

Woodress, James. *Willa Cather: A Literary Life.* Lincoln: University of Nebraska Press, 1963. Reprint, 1987. Page citations are to the reprint edition.

Part V

"Moving In/Moving Out": Writing the World

Ricardo Garza, "Two Sailors, June 1991"

Moving In

Terri L. Jewell

Just say y-e-s
and I will come
live with you
bringing only
84 houseplants needing
an eastern exposure
a 30-piece weight-
lifting set
5 sets of South African liberation
sheets with matching curtains
9 pairs of lavender
sneakers with orange laces
23 stuffed armadillos
147 unmatched earrings
1,178 Lesbian Feminist buttons
on-a-rope
12 crates of my
unfinished novel
4 six-foot ceramic breast
plates from Oregon
65 blues 78s from
the 1930s
750 pounds of native quartz
crystal from Kentucky caves
a 30 x 51-inch stained
glass profile of Whoopi Goldberg
my cat Kiku and her hand-knitted
mouse collection from southern France
2 reams of patchouli-scented
stationery
a trunk of silk panties

in your favorite flavors
every note, letter, card, song,
and pressed flower you've sent me
and all the collard greens,
cornbread, red beans, and chitlins
you could possibly ever
want to eat!

Frog Prince, Cape Cod

Jim Elledge

Listen, reader, you don't
know me from Adam, not
how, for nearly four
months, a ghost circled
my bed nightly, chanted ring-
around-the-rosy
until it toppled
dizzy, giggling into sleep
nor how each night
I invented a full moon
sun-bright from within—
no pockmarks, faceless—
sidekick to the real
one, ice inside out.

Beware. I'm honest to a
fault: fingerprints, dental
records, blood type, shoe
size. I lie through
my teeth. I could say
Midnight. Full tide. We
rolled our jeans knee-high.
Waves slicked our leg
hair down. His tongue, my
tongue. His breath,
mine. Clouds parted once
we separated, stumbling
across sand to a wood
fence that held wind at
bay. Back of his neck,
inside of his elbow,

his right sole singed
my lips. Cassiopeia
glared. The Milky
Way, a diamond smear.

I might say *In bed, two*
oceans flooded the strait
between them, became one
no louder than fog
horns, no calmer than waves
wracking shoes. Next
morning—sand, sand
everywhere.

Believe it or not, reader,
magic explodes unexpectedly—
one silent flash then light
chinks in swarms at eye-
level, constellations
buoyed on shock waves—
then a world once in ruin
shudders awake, gets to its
knees, rises out of rubble,
shard, ash. Bridges
untangle themselves, arch
their backs over rivers
that, sludge earlier,
flow again into oceans,
mountains climb into their
peaks, VW Rabbits spiraling
up no-passing zones,
vanishing into the full
moon, and a toad
far from lily pad and pond,
bursts through its
skin and—voilà—at last
there stands a prince
because of what
began as a simple kiss.

Rua de São Pedro, the Alfama: Market Day

Jim Elledge

Cobblestone streets twist, slip
over or under themselves, down then up one
hill, the next, lose their names, take
another, become a spine of
steps without warning, force Fiats and Citroëns
higgledy-piggledy at first rung.

Compasses work here but don't help.

Scents of skinned eels laid out on cardboard-
box scraps and petrol, of rotten
wood and brine mix, thicken,
hunker down over this street that's little more
than alley. Building shadows seep
back into facades as the sun climbs into
its zenith. Fishwives scream
Lisbon's version of blue-light specials.
Gossiping shoppers elbow through
one another. Children play soccer.

Here or there, buildings lean in
over the street until rooftops almost
touch, the boy next door's bedroom
one meter or less from the neighbor girl's
dream of him last night.

Missing Pieces

Nikki Baker

I have a childhood full of holes, episodes of which I have no recollection. A tricky amnesia, sometimes I can call them back—memories materialized from the smoke of a word or a smell, a sound or a picture, calling the past thin-voiced through a fog of time, never quite knowing what will come—fragments and missing pieces.

My mother says this is nothing I have gotten from her side. This forgetfulness is all my father's, my own brand of his weary retreat at the first sign of bad news to the comfort of his bed, an old man curled in the sleep of an infant. My sleep of not remembering. My mother, an iron-haired and iron-willed black matriarch, indefatigable, says, "Wouldn't we all like our lives to be different somehow?" Kitchen-table wisdom: "Everybody want whatever it is we don't have." My mother is revisionist, remembering everything head-on. What she doesn't like, she simply changes, cheerful as pictures of me at places I cannot, without their aid, recall that I have ever been.

She sends me the photo album of our cross-country trip, sends it with a card for my birthday, oddly stiff-faced pictures of me at the St. Louis Arch, Hoover Dam, the Great Divide, the Grand Canyon, Yosemite, places I had always wanted to see, memorialized in heavy plastic pages between the blood-red leather covers. My mother loves photographs, composed, controlled moments of the past. She has captioned them all so I won't forget, dutifully doing for her children what she knows they will not do for themselves. The picture, irrefutable evidence of how things were.

Here she has carefully pasted car keys, cut out of black construction paper, written, "Gallup, N.M. Mom locked the keys in the car with the motor running and the police refused to come," this punctuated by a thick green exclamation mark at the end. The spidery writing in red makes a circle around the paper keys. Next to it there is a picture of my father talking on the phone. This captioned, "You did what?" as if it were someone's high-school yearbook. A joke my mother and I had laughed about like sisters.

ON the sixth day, outside of Gallup we stop for gas. It is a godforsaken place off the infinite interstate between the Continental Divide and the Painted Desert, Navajo reservation land. Night is falling, and my mom goes inside to use the washroom. When she comes back I have gassed up the car because we have to get to Flagstaff before six or they might give our room away. I am hoping to get my own room now after five nights in a twin bed across from my mother's. A good hundred miles from Flagstaff, and it would be good to get on the road.

"I need a Coke juice," my mother announces, what she calls Coca-Cola, which she has been swilling the whole trip. Drinking Coke and picking apart the way I drive, her seat pushed back as far as it will go, right foot working an imaginary brake pedal.

"I'm going to run and get one," she says.

A Coke juice, and my jaw gets tight. I cannot imagine she will run. My mother has gotten fat since her breast cancer, so fat that her head looks small. The extra weight gives her a pushy, swaggering manner, puffed up like a tick. She brandishes this new evidence of her mortality, a club behind the words, "Someday you'll wish you'd been nicer to your mother," bullying.

Now she only complains, "I can't see out of my side," giving me the order to wash the windows while she gets her drink. Rummaging in her still mommy-sized purse, which sits open on the passenger's seat, she takes out her billfold, a Milky Way candy bar, and slams the door so hard it rattles the windows of my new car. She has been slamming doors this whole trip, taking liberties as if the car belongs to her like I belong to her. My shoulders tense at the sound for the umpteenth time today. The car is brand-new, financed on a five-year note, and I don't want to think about all the years I'm going to have to live with rattly windows before the car gets paid off. I would like to say something. I said something about the door slamming in Oklahoma City, and she told me, "When you were a kid, you ruined my stuff." So in Gallup, I dip the window washer in the murky water from the bucket hanging on the gas-pump island and slop the squeegee end over the windshield instead.

Ten years ago after college graduation, the first thing I bought was a car, the means to get away. I hung the tassel from my mortarboard on the rearview mirror. Now that tassel looks sun-faded and tired, fringe swaying slightly to some unseen wind, as I raise the dead, crusty bugs from the window. I scrape the hard rubber thing across the glass, top to bottom, blotting the drippings with a coarse, blue paper towel. When I go to get back in my car the door is locked, even though I have given my mother another set of keys against just this possibility. I can see them in her open purse as I peer through the spotless window, thinking how I should have known to take my keys. My car, my keys.

"Jesus," I am swearing softly by the running car with the damp crumpled paper in my hand. *I should not have trusted her.* Behind the station the sun is sinking, red and yellow, inches by seconds. "Jesus. Shit."

My mother turns around, mouth full of candy, halfway to the Mini Mart when she hears me. "I didn't do it." She says this as my sister and I used to as children, caught at it. She knows, although I have not said what *it* is. *Caught at it. A mother knows. I know you better than you know yourself.*

"The door is locked." I shout across the twenty-five feet that separate me from my mother. The door is locked. Both doors, the self-locking ones, tied together so that one will lock the other. My mother carped on me to get them because a woman alone in the city ought to opt for safety.

"Don't look at me like it's my fault," my mother says.

"Who else could have done it?" Rage comes up on me suddenly, and my voice in the dead night air is startling. Anger. Not about the keys anymore, this small controllable inconvenience. This is for slights only half remembered, brought up like bile behind a greasy roadside meal, reminded by my mother's look and smell, by nights and days in the smothering closeness of her presence.

"Jesus." I am walking around the car, swearing louder now, like crazy, until the attendant comes out and stares. He is young and country, sharp-boned, checking out my fancy gold watch with narrow, black eyes. Night is falling here—wherever here is. The middle of nowhere. As hard as I'm breathing, I still can't get quite a full breath.

"We'll just call the police," my mother says, too stupid to be frightened in the middle of nowhere by the skanky old cars that cruise past slowly, their bodywork looking like rolling dry-rot rust and puttied-over blood-colored primer waiting for a $99.95 paint job, full of dusty-looking men. Red-necked birds circling fresh distress. As if this is no big deal that we are two black *women*, two *black* women alone here.

This awareness comes over me like sudden nakedness, as I have never felt my blackness or my gender before in my usual circles, the places where I go: my genteel downtown office; the white-lesbian functions self-consciously inclusive of women of color.

My father assured me, "You're as middle class as they are," assuring himself—this, years ago in the context of a job I aspired to, now remembered as a snatch of conversation. He listed my features like the options on my new car, here stopped and useless, its exhaust condensing as the night gets colder. "You've been to Europe. Your diction is never going to slip." My father's voice was gloating, he Pygmalion and I his proud creation.

My father is a secret agent, black, black, black, southern working-class field stock, passing through enemy lines, short green lawns and quiet suburban streets. His perfect children are his disguise. My mother his operative, coaching, coaching all the time, how to cross your legs when you sit, how to work in toward your plate so you'll always use the right silverware, the proper way to tweeze your eyebrows, how to marry a nice professional man. Skills carefully learned, stunningly unhelpful in this situation—the middle of nowhere in the falling dark. Marry a nice professional man, and you will never be in this situation, *outside safety*, here with your mother who cannot protect you anymore, who maybe never could anyway.

I am suddenly scared, irrationally panicked as only children really are, and still swearing, borrowing catastrophe when the attendant offers the phone in the office.

"Read me the number. I'll call." My mother, right away take-charge as she always is.

"No," I say. "I'll do it." Unable to stand the sound of her voice and praying that she will not come with me to the phone.

The attendant looks back and forth as if this drama is nothing he's seen before, rocks on the heels of his work boots, runs his fingers through the front of his hair. "I'm closing up at 7:30."

"I'll call. It's my car," I tell him finally, following his blue shirt and the back of his slick black hair to the stale-aired little office.

"We're locked out of our car. My mother and I." I start to tell the police dispatcher when she comes on the line. My voice is as even as I can make it, but tears are starting at the corners of my eyes. "I'm wondering if someone could come out and help us."

"Tell them the engine is running." My mother is shouting, "Did you tell them the *engine* is running?" Talking over the woman I am trying to hear on the other end of the phone. "And be sure to tell them where we are." She reads the address to me from the paper on the desk.

None of this makes any difference. The dispatcher says there's a bad wreck on the interstate south of us and all the cops are there.

My mother is in the corner talking to the attendant, telling him her side, how the door "just locked." Three days ago outside St. Louis, her fruit punch fell out of the holder and knocked the gear shift into low. Her daughter, she says, exploded. She had nothing to do with this either.

He is nodding. He knows a locksmith in town. "But it's going to cost you," I hear him say, since it's Sunday night after seven o'clock and out here so far from town. The sun is gone.

"I'll pay," my mother says. "Since you think it's my fault."

The attendant locks up and leaves. We wait outside by the faint greenish light that comes from the empty office.

The locksmith shows up in half an hour. We measure the time in Coke juice without talking. He's a small white man who looks as though the desert has sucked all the moisture from him. The locksmith takes a Slim Jim from the metal toolbox on his pickup and does violence to the rubber seal around my passenger window, pulling up, pushing down, trying to catch the cable that works the lock with his hooked piece of shiny metal. The third time he tries there is a click. Because I have the cash, I give the locksmith four twenties. Nobody's got change, so he keeps a ten-dollar tip and goes away whistling through a smile like cracking mud.

"I'm going to pay you back. Let me drive now," my mother says. "We're supposed to share the driving," as if this is a rule written down somewhere.

When I don't answer, she slides back into the passenger seat reluctantly. I have turned on the headlights and pulled back onto the frontage road. Driving fast up the entrance ramp to the freeway. Dreaming of separate rooms in Flagstaff, dreaming there are rooms left after all of this.

"Slow down," my mother demands. "I'm not riding with you if you're going to drive like that."

"It's my fucking car," I say, hands tight around the steering wheel, eyes straight ahead at the lights coming up on the other side of the yellow line.

"It's my fucking life. Just slow down," she says again.

I pull the car over until I can hear my tires on the gravel berm, hear my mother shifting her butt in the bucket seat as if the shock of her swearing has stopped the car. She reaches to unsnap her safety belt and, victorious, pulls at the lock on her door. Trucks fly by us on the interstate; their wind shakes the car.

"It's my car," I say, angry again but calm, dry ice. "If you don't like it, you can get out. Get out if you want," I say. "It's your life."

I remember running up the stairs as my father tried to beat me for this smart mouth. He was going to smack me straight, straight, straight with the flat of his hand. My mother caught me, held me there in the upstairs hall so that he could slap me. I was down and cursing when he raised his hand again, "Just know payback, when the tables turn, old man, you're fucked." Aghast, my mother called a powwow around our kitchen table, revising history. *This is not our family. This is not how we are. Your father and I are not hitters.* But for two weeks I went to school with the bruise where my glasses had slammed against my face.

Outside the cars come spaced at lonesome intervals.

I say, "You live your life and I'll live mine."

My mother stiffens. "Best remember what you have I gave you."

"I didn't ask you to."

I remember having just come from a summer job during college, when I was met with the kitchen-table inquisition. While I was away my father had opened a plain white envelope from the Society of Gay and Lesbian Scientists and Engineers, as he opened all mail that was addressed to me, so I would not miss any job opportunities. He paid for this house, and everything in it. Paid good money for his children to be one thing, not to have them turn out as another, an embarrassment. My success is his success, and failure. "You're not really gay," my mother told me, a sideshow hypnotist employing the amazing power of suggestion. "We know you just want to help these people. That's how we raised you. We're proud of that."

Now we sit in my dark car, and I wonder if my mother has rewritten this memory, too, rewritten my life.

I repeat, softly this time, "I didn't ask you for it."

My mother lets out one smug puff of air, turning away. "Do you think you've thought of something new?" she mumbles, more to herself than to me, and turns back again, sharp-eyed.

MY grandfather's folklore comes back, retold in my mother's voice from her stories about the summers growing up on his farm. *Beat a dog, you'll make it mean. If it turns on you, look it in the eyes.* My stomach is knotted up tight, wondering if she will really go along by herself down a dark highway. I wonder if we both wouldn't like to rewrite this ending, leaving us both more choices.

There is a crack as a passing eighteen-wheeler skips a stone across my hood. My mother's eyes are hard and dry, appraising. What they see I can't say; the dome light is off. Outside in the desert I can barely make out the outline of the rocks beyond the yellow circle of my headlights. Whatever she sees when she looks at me, my mother decides to fasten her seat belt again. There is a click as the metal catches. My mother takes the Coke out of the holder below the radio and sucks on the air and ice in the bottom through her straw. I start the engine again and pull the car slowly out onto the highway. We drive like that toward Flagstaff, with no sound but the whine of tires on the flat, dry road. She faces the window, shoulders hunched, resting her forehead on the glass. Her breath making fog as quiet as if she were sleeping.

IN the note my mother sent with this photo album, she writes excitedly about its acid-free paper and the special glue that will hold these photo images unchanged forever. Gallup, New Mexico, will never yellow, never fade. Now this album will always be here to fill in the blanks for me, to paste together the missing pieces of memory—my mother's and my own.

San Antonio Stroll

Allison J. Nichol

We found ourselves by accident
following the stone path that wound
like a rumor just below the city's
surface. Suddenly we were surrounded
by bluebonnets and bougainvillea
bathing naked in the first sprinkle
of spring sunlight. Blackbirds nuzzled

their young in the shade of a shaggy
elm. Water stolen from god ambled
at our feet slow as a late August breeze.
Startled by this unexpected beauty,
you clenched my arm, then released
a soft sigh. I stumbled a smile
that fell forward to your lips, certain
all creation was inviting us to kiss.

coming into light

Kitty Tsui

cruising
at an altitude
thirty-five thousand feet
above earth,
traveling west
from the heartland.
flying
from night-darkness
into light,
into sunshine,
memories of you
linger in my mind.

a chance meeting
at a conference,
conversation,
much laughter, and
a long,
slow tease.
talking about
leather and
black lingerie.
fantasies,
discoveries,
sexual terms,
and sexual tastes.

it is
a long evening
on the sofa
in the living room.

i am having
the most
sensuous
one-night stand
and i'm
not even
touching you.

it is windy
leaving your city
and i am terrified,
remembering
the lurching
earth shaking
the building
i call home
last october
during
the earthquake.

when it is windy
they say
it is
the voices
of the ancestors
speaking.

it is a windy day
in san francisco.
unusually hot, too.
i still fear
hot weather,
have
earthquake weather
phobia,
though experts say
there is no such thing.

but how can
even experts deny

that for the
phobic person,
there is
any such thing.

it is a windy day,
complemented well
by verdi's *aida*
blasting from
the CD player.

i am in recovery
from my many phobias,
self-destruction
and self-hate.
i am
coming
into light,
into sunshine.
and memories of you
linger in my mind.

it is a windy day.
i do not know what
the voices of my ancestors
are saying.

do you?

Low Hangs the Moon

from *Moon over Miami*

Robert Klein Engler

Landing at Orlando in the half rain,
I step outside and look at the sky.
December is split in two—the North,
pine and snow, the South, coconut and palm.
The days have folded on themselves.

Above, seagulls haunt the cloudy air
like circling kites above a field.
They cry down their prophecy of loss.
"Look," I say to them, "don't haunt me.
I only come to loaf and invite my soul."

Later, at the Space Center, I watch
as they serve food children like—
pink hot dogs, tasteless Popsicles.
A girl tongues an ice-cream cone,
a boy fellates a chocolate banana.

It was here earth heard an insufferable
noise, saw fire ruining with fire.
It was pure fire, the fluid essence of heat,
pouring from the Saturn V rocket
in one stream of flame, thick as an ingot.

Yet today the spigots are cold.
Like Roman columns toppled from the forum,
the rockets lie in sections on the lawn.
Nearby, a museum of auxiliaries
stand up like Druid stones.

Empty engines yawn a cave for birds.

Tourists worship them by taking photographs.
Afterwards, they buy newspapers
and shake their heads in disbelief.
What hunger makes a man consume himself?

Everywhere in Florida
the body count makes news.
First six. Now fourteen. Maybe thirty.
The *Miami Herald* for December 30th, 1978 reports:
"Meanwhile, Friday, Sheriff's officers dug up
part of a lot owned by Gacy, but nothing was found."
"We have to check it out, because you never know . . ."

A rocket to the moon has fifteen million parts.
Rabbi Simlai teaches a man has 248 members.
Does a snapping in the brain make a man kill for cock?
Now that he rests in leather cuffs,
how many parts make him whole?

Tonight the damp air hangs down like moss.
A swampy moonlight drapes the bay.
As Florida revolves to calm,
I stand on the white legs of memory
and look across Key Biscayne.
A cool descent of rain adds nails to the night.

The body count is up to twenty-one.
I came here to look into the mirror of my heart.
Other formulas have found me out.
Soon the space shuttle will hang in orbit like a gull.
In some northern cell, the habit that conjured death
circles frictionless about a madman's skull.

The cotton silence of a tropic night descends.
It follows the small rain down.
I followed my passion to this swamp,
like a man following fire to the moon.
Time winnows the gift from my hands.
Past fulfillment, I have nothing more to hold.

Across the bay, the full moon slips behind clouds.
A transparent breath ripples the dark water
as an alien feeling comes over me with a chill.
Suddenly, the moon appears again,
ocular above the blood-black bay,
a low moon, white, with an eye for fire.

Time Lapse

William Reichard

On television, the documentation
of the formation of clouds and flowers,
an archer fish spitting a spear of water
at a fly, devouring it,
all in a matter of milliseconds,
captured on camera in slow motion;
the world is a diorama
for those who know how to watch.

The time I hit my lover,
for example. I am not
a violent man. Yet, one hand
ran out ahead of thinking,
fist open, instinct struck his face.
Or the time my mother cried,
trying to prepare potato salad
during menopause, could not find
the paprika, wanted only
my hand; I walked away.

That camera, that slows the world,
I could use it occasionally,
to harness time, make it easier
to comprehend action, and inaction;
those moments that must be catalogued,
dissected, disengaged from
heart's memory before
we can completely understand them
(if we ever can).

Surrender

Carole Maso

I had come from France where I had gone to write, living on a borrowed $1,000 for months, but I was at the end of my resources: financial, emotional, psychic. Even this life, beautiful and mysterious and charmed as it was, had become intolerable—I was moving every few weeks, uncertain as to what would happen next, house-sitting or caretaking or other more elaborate and difficult arrangements. And the woman, dear Helen, who had over the years seen me through all this—inventing schemes, guiding me, urging me even into each necessary if troubling arrangement so that it might be possible to write my books—four in all then, in one state or another of completion—she, too, was at her wit's end. And so I had decided to accept, yes, the outlandish, impossible offer of meaningful employment by the wild-eyed iron-willed woman I had met a few years earlier at the MacDowell Colony. She, one Lucia Getsi, had predicted on the first day of my residency there—based on very little, only my first novel—that I would teach at her school, Illinois State University (ISU). With no M.F.A., no teaching experience, and no real evidence that the Midwest existed at all, I nodded unworriedly, convinced no such thing would be possible. Two years passed. I went to Provincetown; I went to France; I finished a second novel. But possible indeed it was, and before I knew it Lucia's prediction had come true.

I was destitute, and I had no prospects of publishing. My press, the noble North Point Press, about to do my third book, had just folded, and the New York publishers were less than enthusiastic. What choice did I have? And so once again in sadness, in weariness, my leave-taking began. There had been so many leave-takings already. I would leave France, leave home (New York City), leave Helen, to do a job that I was unconvinced could even be done, in an imaginary Midwest, in a place called Normal.

Landing at the Bloomington, Illinois Airport and looking up into a sky of utter vastness, I felt I was falling upward into a dizzying blue

213

sea. It was beautiful here in its vastness, its flatness, its nothingness. I have never seen anything quite like it. Only vaguely does it recall Arles, which Van Gogh thought recalled Holland. All summer I had walked in lushness, caressed by light, by olive and lemon and fig trees, embraced by gently rolling hills. Because my time in France was coming to its inevitable end, it had become too beautiful there, too painfully perfect. My parting became a kind of unbearable opera of longing. But then, overnight it seemed, there I was in the Midwest, and there was nothing, and the nothingness, the weird, fierce resignation of it was somehow exhilarating. I surrendered in seconds to this void, and like all landscapes I form a permanent bond with, it, at a crucial moment, a moment of crisis, of change, happened to mirror my internal state identically. My remoteness, my desolation. Stepping off that plane, the world was devoid of everything, a clean slate of sky, a nihilism of space, empty, the end, and yet it was oddly beautiful—like my own brand of nihilism.

And so dropped headlong into a strange land, a world utterly alien to me: world of dramatic and violent weather, dramatic and resolute landscape, dramatic and bizarre academia. Weird world of students and faculty and politics and paper. I have not been in school for a very many years. And from this vantage point the university seems as odd and coded and impenetrable as just about anything. Because I am just the visiting artiste, I do not have to go to faculty meetings, but I do anyway for their circus-like aspects. I go to academic parties for the spectacle, the *Who's Afraid of Virginia Woolf* qualities, the bizarre vocabulary, the accents. I roam Normal/Bloomington memorizing middle America. I am a tourist, and there are many fascinating things out there. I come to class in the first week with my findings. At the hospital down the road I tell them there is a stone bench and engraved into the bench is written, "Today we prepare for our dreams of tomorrow." I tell them as students of writing it's going to be tough going, as they can go and see for themselves, because the clichés are literally written in stone.

In my tour of downtown Bloomington I see a radio tower that looks a lot like the Eiffel Tower. How far I think I've come from anything even a little familiar.

Luckily there are a few new friends: a colleague and fellow fiction writer who murmurs "Blanchot, Blanchot, Blanchot," like a prayer, like the way out of here; another who loves the local band Thrill Kill Cult and Beckett. And of course there is Lucia. Having gotten me into this thing, she takes full responsibility. We swim together several times a week. We take trips to Chicago. She saves me with her thousand generosities: her impromptu three-course Italian meals, her gossip, her poems. Also, she is an extraordinary scholar. She allows me to sit in on her German Romanticism class. She lends me the fantastic Novalis translations she has done. It's ecstasy then. Lucia, high-spirited, determined, with her stubborn Tennessee accent, does all she can to cheer me up. She says not to feel so bad—after twenty-five years in Bloomington, she still does not feel at home here.

And there is the woman who the day I arrive has already left five messages on something called Voice Mail. She implores me to let her enter the class. She is older, about my age. She, too, becomes my friend, with caution, because she is my student, and I know from the first day of class that this is a sacred relationship. It's a delicate balance to maintain, and a crucial one. There are only a few things I tell myself in the beginning: work the students as hard as you work yourself, and respect with your entire being that sacred relationship (in other words, no matter what, do not sleep with them). I am so lonely here. Helen, back in New York, shows no signs whatever of visiting.

In a somewhat surprising and unanticipated turn, I end up adoring my students, feel them to be more talented than most of the published writers I have come across, want to celebrate their instincts, their feeling for language, their willingness to try anything with me. They seem unreasonably hopeful, perky, wholesome—but I consider that this may be just in comparison with the French. They are diligent, intelligent, open-minded, and, like the landscape, filled with longing and possibility.

Stupidly and naively and without any real feeling for their actual lives, I come to class one day thrilled with an event from the evening before—a tornado! The weird, green sky, the awful silence, the seemingly backward flying birds. I tell them of my fantasy: to go to the thing's center, to be obliterated, to achieve oblivion. In reality when the tornado comes I have no idea what to do and feel scared. No key to the basement, I stay in my attic apartment alone, the radio saying over and over, take cover. I'm afraid—and there's no one here to die with me. The class is clearly appalled by my comments. What do I know of the grief such phenomena have caused them, their families? Immediately I regret my flippant tourism. The next day I go into a brief but heartfelt apology. I have learned something. What was I thinking? That they had, all these years, remained unscathed? After my apology they slowly begin to trust me. They tell me about cows and corn and the prairie. The semester can begin, finally. I seem like a New Yorker to them: exotic, ridiculous, impractical, and yet somehow credible (it must be the two books), or, if not entirely credible, at least worthy of trust. And I think they enjoy teaching me things, the roles reversed.

Writing classes are about trust, of course, and after a while, in the safe place we have created together they begin writing their dreams, their fantasies, their desires. What many of them write about again and again is a thing many of them have never seen—the ocean. I am so moved by their longing—these children of the Midwest, these children of ISU—cinder-blocked, landlocked. They swim in high water. They never tire. They begin to learn how to write themselves free.

My graduate class at first makes me a little nervous. After all, I have never been to graduate school. I have never been in a writing workshop before. I have never taught anyone anything. But they, too, are unreasonably kind.

Still, something is a little off. I am often lost there, disoriented. The boys seem too perfect, too polite. I am amazed at the heightened, garish sexual fantasies they inspire. And the girls—they're too complacent, too nice. I realize that part of why I'm here is to teach them to be bad, to question, to disobey. Normal: I feel on the edges of town and then out into the countryside, the severity of farmers, rising at dawn, eating dinner at five and to bed. They would not approve of me, these men. There's a certain unreality to everything I see or perceive. Here, where people still eat lots of beef and lots of candy bars and smoke cigarettes, and many, it is true as the French like to say of Americans, are overweight. The fat people for the circus must be grown out here, I think in a dream. And even the university is a paradox, a very unusual place. On the outside it is a lot of ugly buildings plunked down in the middle of nowhere. On the inside there is a gleaming altar to the most innovative and experimental literature in the world. It is taught here, it is valued, it is even published. Illinois State now houses both Dalkey Archive Press and *The Review of Contemporary Fiction*, as well as Fiction Collective Two. And in the Unit for Contemporary Literature, the dream of a literary avant-garde utopia is slowly being realized. In this whole wide country there is no other place that comes close to it. Few places in the world come to mind. And my New York is light years away.

This land of stark miracle springing from the extraordinarily fertile earth. Flat earth. Where each night on the flatlands I dream of a curvaceous woman. She cups water in her hands. And I marvel at the beauty of the cornfields and the sky. Count pheasants. Visit what I've dubbed the Beckett tree, straight out of *Godot*. The land is breathtaking in its austerity, in its uncompromising forever, as gorgeous as anything I've ever seen. A different sort of ocean.

And I fear at times the cornfields and the miles and miles of soybean fields and the sky. We are up to our thighs in corn. We imagine we drink utterly pure, sweet water. Heartland water. Perfect water. But three younger women now, natives of this place, all from the heart of the heart of the country, are stricken with cancer, and I am forced to wonder what it is about. The pesticides in the sweet water? The beloved injected cows, the delicious, the coveted beef? The feed?

This pristine countryside. We drive. I take my class hours and hours away to another school to see the great filmmaker Stan Brackhage, who has turned up to speak and show films. We are examining alternative narrative strategies in my graduate class. Hearing him speak and watching his extraordinary films in the dark, I forget for a few hours how far away I am from home. For a little while I am more at home than I am anywhere else.

I was expecting nothing. Then, after a while I was expecting an extreme provinciality from my central Illinois. But finally I have come to realize that it is no more provincial than one of the minor cities: Pittsburgh or Milwaukee, say. And, in fact, it may be somewhat better, who knows? I joined the Normal ACT UP, a branch that included maybe ten people. But the freezing October night we read the names of those who had died all the way through until dawn there was a legion of people: all ages, all types. All night.

And of Chicago, I recognize immediately that it is a city I might, given the chance, come to love. I find myself more comfortable there than in any other American city I know outside of New York. It seems real—its architecture, its grandeur, its people, its cultural life, its miseries. I find it a relief after the pretty toy of San Francisco, the segregated contrivances of Boston, artificial D.C., sprawling, incomprehensible L.A. And the other cities: Houston, Atlanta, whatever. Who knew?

And in retrospect ISU will be among the best institutions I shall teach in. Schools that now include Columbia, Bennington, Brown.

And it is the first time I will ever be called a goddess. And it is the first time in my adult life that I will be able to pay my bills. Or go to the doctor.

The goddess is waiting again, having gone home to New York and having flown back to Chicago, for her all-too-small, all-too-private plane to take her back to Bloomington. I look for the dark angel I see each time in the propeller's rotating blade. So many hair-raising American Eagle trips that year, flights I was pretty sure I'd never get off alive. They were always cartoonish, it seemed, with drinks flying and ladies crying. Before boarding they would check our weight and the weight of our carry-ons, in order to assign seats. So much waiting that year. The wings are frozen solid again. I entertain the grim possibility that perhaps I have come here to die.

There are many strange dangers. I have always feared the Midwest, I realize that now—known for its clean-cut serial killers, its smoldering, unreadable violences. When I walk into my friendly, neighborhood liquor store I literally see red before my eyes. Sometimes it's only for an instant, but sometimes it's something more prolonged. It's odd because I do not ordinarily translate anxiety or other emotional states into color, and yet the color is undeniable—red. Only much later do I learn of the triple murder that occurred there a year or so before. OK, maybe I, too, have come to die. I can't help wondering.

Or maybe I've come here just to dance: we pile into the truck in our glitter and bows and head for Peoria to the local gay club to watch our friend perform in drag. I am a little smug. I am of course from New York City, and dubious to say the least. In my time I have witnessed more than one crossdressers' convention in Provincetown, that gay mecca, and I fancy myself something of an expert.

Peoria, Illinois. The audience in this grungy club is the weirdest mix: lots of working people, farmers and the like, their wives, businessman types, young lesbians and gay men of all ages. I have never seen such a sight. Our friend appears center stage. It is *he* who is the goddess, with those cat eyes, those cheekbones, that perfect jaw, that smile. His hair is fabulous, his makeup is fabulous, his dress. He, or rather, she, is more amazing than anything I've seen, and she's just my type, too: a young, kind of decadent Bianca Jagger. She bends her knees, blows kisses, does a little turn. And the music begins. I wonder what the French would think. Nothing here is ever quite what it seems. And I must admit I am a little bit in love.

Publication Histories

"Swimming Lessons" by Gregg Shapiro originally appeared in *Christopher Street* 166 (November 1991) and in his collection of short stories, *Indiscretions*, published on computer disk by Spectrum Press.

"On My Way to Lake Michigan Sunrise on the Milwaukee Lakefront Breakwater" by Antler originally appeared in *The Pennsylvania Review* 5, no. 1 (1993).

"A Solstice in Southern Illinois" by Jim Elledge originally appeared in *Nothing Nice*, a chapbook published by Windfall Prophets Press, 1987.

"Salt into Wounds" by Jim Elledge originally appeared in *Sandscript* 19 (1993).

"Canto Faggoto" by Don Mager originally appeared in *Mouth of the Dragon* 2, no. 5 (1975).

"Mimosa" by Carol Anshaw originally appeared in *The Country of Herself: Short Fiction by Chicago Women*, edited by Karen Lee Osborne and published by Third Side Press, 1993.

"Bonsai" by William Reichard originally appeared in *Visions International* 44 (1994).

"Goliath" by Jim Elledge originally appeared in *Into the Arms of the Universe* published by Stonewall/New Poets Series, 1995.

"To One of Two Boys on a Bench" by Jim Elledge originally appeared in *Louisville Review* 20 (1986).

"Welcome to Beth Homo" by Lev Raphael originally appeared in slightly different form as "Beth Homo" in *More Like Minds*, edited by Ben Goldstein and published by GMP Publishers.

"Agrology" by Terri L. Jewell originally appeared in *More Serious Pleasure: Lesbian Erotic Stories and Poetry*, edited by the Sheba Collective and published by Sheba Feminist Publishers, 1990.

"Sucking Off Jamie" by Robert Klein Engler originally appeared in *The Dallas Review* 1, no. 1 (June 1992).

"Hot Summernight Cloudburst Rendezvous" by Antler originally appeared in *Erotic by Nature,* edited by David Steinberg and published by Shakti Books/Red Alder Books, 1988.

"Brother Balm" by Gerard Wozek originally appeared in *Gents, Bad Boys, and Barbarians,* edited by Rudy Kikel and published by Alyson Publications, 1995.

"Survival" by Karen Lee Osborne originally appeared in *Common Lives/Lesbian Lives* 44 (1992).

"Every Last Drop" by Allison J. Nichol originally appeared in *Hammers* 7 (1993).

"Scott McPherson, Danny Sotomayor, and Scout" by Genyphyr Novak originally appeared in *Outlines* 6, no. 1 (June 1992).

"An Interview with Scott McPherson" by Owen Keehnen originally appeared in *Outlines* 6, no. 1 (June 1992).

"Moving In" by Terri L. Jewell originally appeared in *The Lavender Letter* 5, no. 10 (1985).

"Frog Prince, Cape Cod" by Jim Elledge originally appeared in *Sandscript* 17 (1990).

"Rua de São Pedro, the Alfama: Market Day" by Jim Elledge originally appeared in *Zone 3* 5, no. 1 (1990).

Contributors

CLAUDIA ALLEN is the author of more than a dozen plays, two of which, *Still Waters* and *The Long Awaited*, have won Joseph Jefferson awards. *Hannah Free* is included with three other lesbian plays in her collection *She's Always Liked the Girls Best* (1993). Her plays have been produced in Chicago, New York, and many other cities. She recently completed the screen adaptation for *Don Juan in the Village*. She lives in Chicago, where she teaches playwriting at several institutions.

CAROL ANSHAW's novel *Aquamarine* (1992) won the Carl Sandburg Award and the Society of Midland Authors Award. She has also received the New York Book Critics' Circle Award for excellence in reviewing and a National Endowment for the Arts Creative Writing Fellowship. She lives in Chicago.

ANTLER's collections of poetry include *Factory* (1980), *Last Words* (1986), and *Ever-Expanding Wilderness*. He is a winner of the Walt Whitman Award, the Witter Bynner Prize, and the Pushcart Prize. He lives in Milwaukee, Wisconsin.

EDUARDO APARICIO is a Cuban artist and writer who currently lives in Miami. He resided in Chicago for several years, where he designed and produced the project "Colectivo Latinos Atrevidos/Provocative Latins Collective" in cooperation with several Latino organizations. A contingent of people of color carried these placards at the 1993 March on Washington for Lesbian, Gay, and Bisexual Equal Rights and Liberation.

NIKKI BAKER was born in 1962. SHE IS THE AUTHOR OF *Long Goodbyes* (1993), *The Lavender House Murder* (1992), and *In the Game* (1991). Her work has appeared in several anthologies, including *Out for Blood*

(1995). Although she recently relocated to the West Coast, she considers herself a consummate midwesterner.

MARY JO BANG is completing an M.F.A. in poetry at Columbia University after living and writing in Chicago for several years. She is the editor of *Whatever You Desire* (1990), an anthology of British lesbian poetry. Her poems have been published in journals such as *The Nation* and in the anthologies *Life on the Line* and *Word of Mouth.*

CHARLES DERRY is the author of *The Suspense Thriller: Films in the Shadow of Alfred Hitchcock* (1988) and *Dark Dreams: A Psychological History of the Modern Horror Film* (1977). His experimental film *Cerebral Accident* has been screened at many festivals, and his play *Joan Crawford Died for Your Sins* premiered at the Reality Theatre in 1993. He teaches cinema at Wright State University in Dayton, Ohio.

JIM ELLEDGE is the author of several collections of poetry, including *Nothing Nice* (1987), *Various Envies* (1988), *Earth As It Is* (1994), and *Into the Arms of the Universe* (1995). He has also authored the critical studies *Frank O'Hara: To Be True to a City* and *Weldon Kees: A Critical Introduction.* He edited *Sweet Nothings: An Anthology of Rock and Roll in American Poetry* (1994). Formerly an assistant editor of *Poetry*, he is now editor of *Illinois Review* and an associate professor of English at Illinois State University.

ROBERT KLEIN ENGLER's poems and stories have appeared in *Borderlands, Hyphen, Christopher Street, Kansas Quarterly*, and other journals. The recipient of an Illinois Arts Council Literary Award, he has published two books of poetry, *Adagio* (1994) and *Stations of the Heart* (1994). He lives in Chicago.

RICARDO GARZA lives on the South Side of Chicago. He received his B.F.A. from Columbia College and is employed at a commercial photographic studio. His work has been featured at Artikizm and in shows such as the multicultural queer exhibit, *The World of Difference.*

JEANNETTE GREEN is a founding member of the poetry/art collective Shiva. Her poetry takes on the multiethnic, multimedia personae of those around her. "Wire-Rims" is from a longer work that tells the love story of two young women and the histories of their families. She lives in Chicago.

RENÉE LYNN HANSEN is the author of the novel *Take Me to the Underground* (1990). Her fiction has also appeared in several anthologies and in journals such as *Christopher Street*. She teaches gay and lesbian literature at Columbia College of Chicago and lives in Michigan.

TERRI L. JEWELL was the author of *The Black Woman's Calendar/ Engagement Book* (1993) and *Succulent Heretic* (1994), a collection of poems. In addition, she was the editor of *The Black Woman's Gumbo Ya-Ya: Quotations by Black Women* (1993) and *DreadWoman/LockSister* (1995), a collection of writing and photographs of black women with dreadlocked hair. Her poetry and essays appeared in more than three hundred journals and anthologies. Jewell grew up in Kentucky and lived in Lansing, Michigan, until her death in 1995.

LINNEA JOHNSON is the author of *Chicago Home* (1986), a book of poems that won the Beatrice Hawley Award. Her poetry and fiction have appeared in *American Poetry Review, Prairie Schooner, Spoon River Quarterly, Women's Review of Books*, and other journals, as well as in the anthologies *Right in the Middle: Feminism and Mothering, Benchmark: An Anthology of Contemporary Poetry in Illinois*, and *My Mother's Daughter*. She has received grants from the Arts Councils of Illinois, Nebraska, and Pennsylvania. Born and raised in Chicago, she currently lives in Pennsylvania.

OWEN KEEHNEN is a longtime employee of Unabridged Bookstore in Chicago. He has published fiction and nonfiction in *Christopher Street, Ecce Queer, Thing, Stonewall News, Holy Titclamps*, and *Riot Gear*. His interviews appear regularly in *Outlines* and other newspapers, including the *San Francisco Sentinel, The Wisconsin Light*, and *Southern Exposure*.

KATHRYN KIRK's photographs have been featured in solo and group exhibitions throughout the United States and Canada and have been published in several books and magazines, including *Dolce Vita* and *New York Newsday Sunday Magazine*. "Three Dancers" is from her

solo exhibition "A Small Town in Ohio" at the County Courthouse in
New Phildaelphia, Ohio, 1985. A native of Ohio, she now lives in
Brooklyn.

DAVID KODESKI is a performance poet and writer who lives in Chicago. A member of the cast for *Too Much Light Makes the Baby Go Blind*,
a long-running late-night sensation in Chicago, he has also published
poetry in journals such as *Hammers* and *Stray Bullets*.

JOSEPH LIKE's poems have appeared in *Illinois Review*, *Pikestaff Forum*,
Rockford Review, *River Styx*, and others. Three of his poems are included in the anthology *Gents, Bad Boys, and Barbarians* (1995). He
earned his M.F.A. in creative writing from Indiana University and has
taught at Bradley University and Beloit College. He lives in Rockford,
Illinois.

DON MAGER's two books are *To Track the Wounded Ones* (1986) and
Glosses (1995). He was raised in New Mexico and Iowa and also lived
in Detroit, where he was the founder and first executive director of
the Michigan Organization for Human Rights. His poems have appeared in *Mouth of the Dragon*, *Christopher Street*, and other literary journals. He now lives and teaches in Charlotte, North Carolina.

CAROLE MASO's most recent novel is *Defiance* (1996). She is also the
author of the novels *The American Woman in the Chinese Hat* (1994),
Ava (1993), *The Art Lover* (1990), and *Ghost Dance* (1986). The recipi-
ent of numerous awards, including a Lannan Foundation Literary
Fellowship, she also directs the Graduate Writing Program at Brown
University in Providence, Rhode Island.

ALLISON J. NICHOL's poems have been published in such journals as
The Pegasus Review, *Queer Planet Review*, and *Thing*, as well as the anthologies *Off the Rocks* and *A Loving Testimony: Remembering Loved Ones
Lost to AIDS*, edited by Lesléa Newman. Formerly of Chicago, she now
lives in Washington, D.C.

GENYPHYR NOVAK's photographs have appeared in publications
such as *The Advocate*, *L.A. Weekly*, *On Our Backs*, *Metropolis*, *New City*,
and *P-Form*. She photographed the late Scott McPherson, author of

the acclaimed play *Marvin's Room*, with his partner, the late Danny Sotomayor, and their dog Scout in 1992. She lives in Chicago, where she earned her B.F.A. from the School of the Art Institute.

PAMELA OLANO is a doctoral candidate at the University of Minnesota in the Department of English and the Center for Advanced Feminist Studies. She is the author of a forthcoming book, *The Lavender Menace: Lesbians and the Women's Movement.*

KAREN LEE OSBORNE (coeditor) is the author of the novels *Carlyle Simpson* (winner of the Friends of American Writers Award in 1987) and *Hawkwings* (1991). She edited *The Country of Herself: Short Fiction by Chicago Women* (1993). Her work has appeared in many journals and anthologies. The film *A Common Flower* (1992), directed by Doreen Bartoni, was based on one of her stories. She has taught at Illinois Wesleyan University and now teaches at Columbia College of Chicago.

MICHELLE PALADINO grew up in Michigan and recently completed her B.A. at Columbia College of Chicago. Her photographs have appeared in several exhibitions.

GARY POOL was born in Indianapolis and now lives in Bloomington, Indiana. A graduate of Indiana University, he earned a Master of Music degree from Florida State University and an advanced business degree from New York University. He sang with the New York Lyric Opera, the Metropolitan Opera Studio, the Lake George Opera Festival, and the New York City Opera. He has published fiction in *Christopher Street* and is a feature writer for *The Word*, a gay and lesbian newspaper.

LEV RAPHAEL is the author of a novel, *Winter Eyes* (1992), and a collection, *Dancing on Tisha B'av*, which won a 1990 Lambda Literary Award. A frequent contributor to journals and anthologies, he is also the author of *Edith Wharton's Prisoners of Shame* (1991). He lives in Michigan.

WILLIAM REICHARD is a widely published poet and an editor of the *James White Review*. He is the recipient of a Loft/Mentor Award and a creative writing fellowship from Stanford. Currently he is a Ph.D. candidate at the University of Minnesota.

ROBERT RODI's most recent novel is *Drag Queen* (1995). His other novels are *What They Did to Princess Paragon* (1994), *Closet Case* (1993), and *Fag Hag* (1992). He lives in Chicago.

D. TRAVERS SCOTT studied writing and performance at the School of the Art Institute in Chicago. His work has appeared in *Art Papers, New Art Examiner, Harper's, High Performance,* and *Steam.* Currently he lives in Portland, Oregon.

MAUREEN SEATON's first book, *The Sea among the Cupboards,* won the Capricorn Award in 1992. Her second book, *Fear of Subways* (1991), won the Eighth Mountain Poetry Prize. Her third collection, *Furious Cooking,* was published by Iowa University Press (1996). Seaton's poems have appeared in *The Atlantic, Paris Review, Kenyon Review, Ploughshares, New England Review,* and other journals. Formerly a resident of New York, she has lived in Chicago for several years and has received an Illinois Arts Council Fellowship.

GREGG SHAPIRO's story collection, *Indiscretions,* was published on computer disk by Spectrum Press in 1994. His poetry and fiction have appeared in journals such as *Modern Words, The Evergreen Chronicles, Amethyst,* and *The Quarterly,* as well as in the anthologies *Mondo Barbie, Unsettling America,* and *Mondo Marilyn.* He lives in Chicago, where he has been a frequent contributor to *Gay Chicago Magazine* and *Nightlines.*

VIRGINIA SMILEY is the coauthor of *Girl Party* (1994), a long-running lesbian comedy in Chicago. Many of her plays have been produced around the country, and her plays for children have toured schools throughout Illinois. Her fiction and nonfiction have been published in *Redbook, Essence,* and *New Woman.* She is a native Chicagoan.

WILLIAM J. SPURLIN (coeditor) is a cultural critic and the author of numerous essays in such journals as *College English.* He coedited and contributed to *The New Criticism and Contemporary Literary Theory: Connections and Continuities* (1995). His work in lesbian and gay studies has appeared in several scholarly collections both in the United States and abroad, including *Literature and Psychology* (1994) and *Lesbian and Gay Studies: Coming out of Feminism?* (forthcoming 1997). He has taught at Illinois State University and is currently Visiting Scholar at Columbia University.

EDWARD THOMAS-HERRERA received his bachelor's degree in musicology from Rice University in Houston and has been living, working, writing, and performing in Chicago since 1989. He wrote the adaptation of Letitia Baldridge's *Diamonds and Diplomats* for a production at Live Bait Theater in 1995.

KITTY TSUI is the author of *The Words of a Woman Who Breathes Fire* (1983), a collection of poetry, and has contributed work to more than twenty-five anthologies, including *Chloe Plus Olivia* and *The Variant Side*. She recently completed a historical novel, *Bai Sze, White Snake*. Formerly of San Francisco and Chicago, she now lives in Indiana.

JESS WELLS is the author of the novel *AfterShocks* (1992) and two collections of short fiction, *Two Willow Chairs* (1987) and *The Dress and The Sharda Stories* (1986). Her work has also appeared in numerous anthologies. She grew up in Michigan and lives in San Francisco.

DIANE WILLIAMS, a recipient of the Pat Parker Memorial Poetry Award, has published poetry and fiction in *New American Writing, Common Lives/Lesbian Lives, The Country of Herself, West Side Stories,* and *Resist: Essays against a Homophobic Culture.* Her chapbook of poems is *The Color of Enlightenment* (1991). A cofounder of *Kaleidoscope*, a journal devoted to works by women of color, she grew up and lived until recently on Chicago's West Side. She teaches at the College of Lake County in Gurnee, Illinois.

GERARD WOZEK currently teaches English and the humanities at Robert Morris College in Chicago. He has published poetry in several journals and anthologies, including *Prairie Street Companion, Off the Rocks, Gents, Bad Boys, and Barbarians* (1995), and *Eros in Boystown* (1996). His first book, *The Changeling's Exile,* was published in 1995.